BATTLE OF BRITAIN

July to October 1940

COVER PHOTO: *Spitfire Mk IAs of 610 Squadron on patrol from RAF Biggin Hill, July 1940.*

First published in September 2015
Reprinted in 2016

A catalogue record for this book is available from the British Library.

ISBN 978 0 85733 508 1

Library of Congress control No. 2014953497

Published by Haynes Publishing,
Sparkford, Yeovil,
Somerset BA22 7JJ, UK.
Tel: 01963 440635
Int. tel: +44 1963 440635
Website: www.haynes.co.uk

Haynes North America Inc.,
861 Lawrence Drive, Newbury Park,
California 91320, USA.

Printed in Malaysia.

BATTLE OF BRITAIN

July to October 1940

RAF Operations Manual

Insights into how science, technology and defence
systems helped the RAF win the Battle of Britain

Andy Saunders

Contents

OPPOSITE Sgt Pilot John McAdam sits astride the engine cowling of his 41 Squadron Spitfire Mk I. He survived the Battle of Britain only to be shot down and killed over Dover on 20 February 1941.

BELOW Group Operations Room, General Situation Map raid marker showing 'Hostile raid No 3, 50+ aircraft'.

Introduction

'This is the BBC Midnight News read by Alvar Lidell. Up to ten o'clock one hundred and seventy five German aircraft had been destroyed in today's raids over this country. Today was the most costly for the German air force for nearly a month. In daylight raids between three hundred and fifty and four hundred enemy aircraft were launched in two attacks against London and south-east England. About half of them were shot down.'

(BBC Home Service, Sunday 15 September 1940)

On 18 June 1940, before a packed House of Commons, Prime Minister Winston Churchill delivered one of his most famous pieces of oratory. He said: 'What General Weygand has called the Battle of France is over . . . the Battle of Britain is about to begin. Upon this battle depends the survival of Christian civilisation. Upon it depends our own British way of life, and the long continuity of our institutions and our Empire.' What he said was perhaps the very first time that the term 'Battle of Britain' was used. Ultimately, it would refer to a battle that stands very much in the British nation's consciousness as an epic and unequal struggle for survival, as well as being a worldwide landmark in the fight against tyranny and oppression.

Following the fall of France and the Low Countries, and the evacuation from Dunkirk, it was inevitable that the Germans would seek to invade and occupy the British Isles from its newly conquered territories. Ultimately, the German forces drew up plans for Operation *Seelöwe* (Sealion), which would comprise a seaborne and airborne invasion of Britain. It was, necessarily, a hastily put together plan and one that would have carried enormous military risks, particularly in view of the lack of specialised maritime assault and landing craft

and the enormous threat posed by the Royal Navy who, as a significant maritime power, were in a position to wreak havoc upon any invasion fleet in the Dover Strait and English Channel. However, the Luftwaffe remained confident that its bomber force (and especially the Junkers 87 Stuka) would be able to deal with the concentration of British naval vessels interfering with the invasion. Indeed, the Stuka in particular had already shown what it could do against shipping involved in Operation *Dynamo*, the evacuation from Dunkirk, and more recently in attacks on Channel convoys and shipping. However, the Luftwaffe's confidence perhaps presupposed one thing – that it had already wrested air superiority from the RAF. Thus, as soon as Luftwaffe forces were established and organised at their new bases across northern France, Belgium and in the Netherlands, so the air assault against the British Isles commenced and what Churchill had already referred to as the Battle of Britain got under way.

Officially, the Battle of Britain commenced on 10 July and ceased on 31 October 1940. However, these are entirely artificial dates that were set, post-war, by the British. In reality there was clearly no defined beginning or end to the battle. Initially, and in its 1941 publication

OPPOSITE Prime Minister Winston Churchill: 'This was their finest hour.'

ABOVE The Thin Blue Line: Hurricane pilots of 501 Squadron wait for the call to scramble in August 1940.

on the Battle of Britain, the Air Ministry had stated the commencement date to have been 8 August 1940. Whilst there was some merit to the allocation of this date due to the first massed air assaults against British targets taking place (in this instance, coastal convoys) it was also the case, for example, that huge air attacks had also taken place on 4 July against Portland Royal Navy base and English Channel shipping. It was the former Commander-in-Chief (C-in-C) of RAF Fighter Command, Air Chief Marshal (ACM) Sir Hugh Dowding, who would later, and somewhat hesitantly, set the official and definitive battle dates in his 'Despatch on

the Battle of Britain' to the *London Gazette* on 10 September 1946:

'It is difficult to fix the exact date on which the Battle of Britain can be said to have begun. Operations of various kinds merged into one another almost insensibly, and there are grounds for choosing the date of the 8 August, on which was made the first attack in force against laid objectives in this country, as the beginning of the Battle. On the other hand, the heavy attacks made against our Channel convoys probably constituted, in fact, the beginning of the German offensive; because the weight and scale of the attack indicates that the primary object was rather to bring our fighters to battle than to destroy the hulls and cargoes of the small ships engaged in the coastal trade. While we were fighting in Belgium and France, we suffered the disadvantage that even the temporary stoppage of an engine involved the loss of pilot and aircraft, whereas, in similar circumstances, the German pilot might be fighting again the same day, and his aircraft airborne in a matter of hours.

'In fighting over England these considerations were reversed, and the moral and material disadvantages of fighting over enemy country may well have determined the Germans to open the attack with a phase of fighting in which the advantages were more evenly balanced. I have, therefore, somewhat arbitrarily, chosen the events of 10 July as the opening of the battle. Although many attacks had previously been made on convoys, and even land objectives such as Portland, the 10 July saw the employment by the Germans of the first really big formation (70 aircraft) intended primarily to bring our fighter defence to battle on a large scale.'

However, the relative merits of commencement and end dates to this epic battle are somewhat academic. But, in setting the scene for this book it is important to understand that this was not a battle that began suddenly and came to dramatic halt on the achievement of a clear victory. In that respect, this was a battle perhaps quite unlike any other fought during the Second World War. It was also different, from Britain's perspective, because for the first time in the history of this nation it saw a battle fought out in full view of its population and with significant numbers of that population in the front line. Of course, the history of that battle, and the Blitz that followed, have been covered in detail in countless works on the subject and it is not the purpose of this book to cover any of that ground. Instead, the aim of this book is to set out the planning, organisational and operational detail of how the RAF, and specifically Fighter Command, fought that battle.

Unlike the evacuation from Dunkirk, which was very much made up and on-the-hoof, RAF Fighter Command already operated within a fully integrated air defence system that had a comprehensive command and control organisation, comprising not only the fighter squadrons themselves but also radar, the Observer Corps, Balloon Command and Anti-Aircraft Command. To a certain extent, defeat in France had been brought about through the lack of any such centralised and coordinated command and control structure in the French air defence system. It would be a different story during the defence of the British Isles during the Battle of Britain, though.

This book, then, looks in detail at how that system worked and how all of the parts of the system meshed together in order to allow RAF Fighter Command, hard-pressed and outnumbered, to fight the Luftwaffe in an organised and effective fashion. Not always, however, did the system work exactly as planned but it has often been said that a battle plan rarely survives first contact with the enemy. Without that 'battle plan', though, the air defence of Britain in 1940 could not have had a successful outcome and this detailed examination also looks at the nuts and bolts and minutiae of the system – the weapons, tactics, operational procedures, equipment, terminology, individual units and organisations, casualties, the commanders and other participants.

BELOW The aggressors: Reichsmarschal Hermann Göring inspects Luftwaffe bomber crews of *Kampfgeschwader* 76 at Beauvais in northern France during the Battle of Britain.

Chapter One

The air defence of Great Britain

Protecting Britain's skies

The air defence of Great Britain in the Battle of Britain was based around the 'Dowding System', providing an organised plan of defences in the air and from the ground, and with a centralised command and control structure. This had largely been developed since Fighter Command's creation, with Dowding in charge.

OPPOSITE Although pictured here in 1941 when the organisation had become the Royal Observer Corps, this photograph of an Observer Post in the Watford Group is typical of the Battle of Britain period.

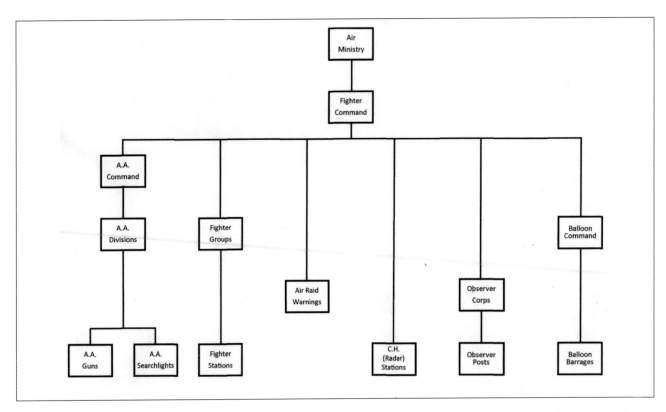

ABOVE Organisational chart showing the air defence of Great Britain in 1940 with RAF Fighter Command at the 'sharp end'. (All photographs and illustrations are from the author's collection unless credited otherwise)

In considering the overall picture of the air defence of Great Britain during 1940 and the Battle of Britain, RAF Fighter Command may be regarded to have been at the sharp end of that defence. However, elements other than direct fighter protection were very much part of the integrated air defence system, although overall control of the entire system rested with Fighter Command. In order to better understand how each part of the air defence plan worked, the organisational chart and command structure shown above gives a simplified over-view of the system.

Radar

The radar-based system of early warning, interception and control

'All the ascendancy of the Hurricanes and Spitfires would have been fruitless but for this system which had been devised and built before the war. It had been shaped and refined in constant action, and all was now fused together into a most elaborate instrument of war, the like of which existed nowhere in the world.'

(Winston S. Churchill)

Britain's system of early warning, interception and control has widely been called the 'Dowding System' after the C-in-C of RAF Fighter Command who instigated its planning and implementation in the years immediately before the war. This system, the first of its kind in the world, comprised a network that stretched from the northernmost parts of Scotland down to the south coast of England. Although the inner workings of Fighter Command's system of command and control remained a closely guarded secret throughout the war, a surprising public glimpse of the system was given in 1941 when the illustrated HMSO booklet, *The Battle of Britain: August– October 1940*, was published with its outline of the system. However, the schematic diagram was somewhat economical with its detail and, importantly, it left out one particular element from the explanation of how the organisation worked – radar.

Although the Germans were far from being unaware of radar, and were indeed developing and using systems of their own, their failure to understand its role within the command and control structure of Fighter Command placed them at a most serious disadvantage during the Battle of Britain. However, they were more than aware of the chain of radar stations which had sprung up around Britain's coast during the late 1930s sporting huge arrays of aerials and concrete bunkers, and although they acknowledged these sites to be significant they did not fully appreciate to what extent. For this reason, perhaps, their concentration of attacks on them was somewhat piecemeal and rather lacklustre in effort. That said, the relatively few attacks mounted by the Luftwaffe on these sites did have some results with stations being knocked off the air, albeit temporarily. Had sustained efforts been made to attack them then Fighter Command could have effectively been 'blinded' and the outcome of the battle would have certainly been different. As it was, the Luftwaffe could not 'see' their efforts and only appreciated that the towers were hard if not impossible to topple and the hardened structures difficult to hit or make much impression on. This, however, overlooked the fact that the infrastructure (in particular power supplies and communications) was being hit and the stations disabled as a result, even if no outwardly visible post-strike signs of damage or destruction were in evidence.

In summary there follows a description of the various elements that made up RAF Fighter Command's early warning, interception and control system during the Battle of Britain – Radio Direction Finding (RDF), Observer Corps, Filter Room, Group Operations Room and Sector Operations Room.

Radio Direction Finding (RDF or radar)

The keystone of the air defences was the network of RDF (radar) stations and in the summer of 1940 the radar chain consisted of 22 Chain Home (CH) stations, supplemented by 30 Chain Home Low (CHL) stations for the detection of low-flying aircraft. These stations (not all of them ready for use when the battle began) were positioned to ensure that, at least in theory, every aircraft approaching the British Isles from the east, the south, or the south-west would be detected by at least two RDF stations.

The existence of the CH stations with their impossible to hide 350ft lattice masts became known before the war to the Germans, who sent the airship *Graf Zeppelin* to reconnoitre

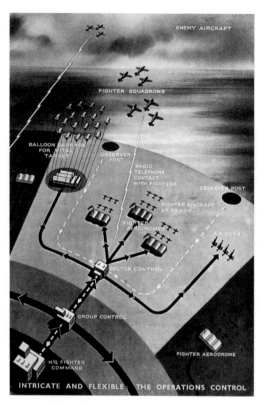

INTRICATE AND FLEXIBLE: THE OPERATIONS CONTROL

some of them in the late 1930s. But Göring's advisers believed that the men who worked the equipment would be unable, at times of stress, to distinguish between large and small formations, and that the system would break down if large numbers of aircraft approached the country simultaneously. Thus the effectiveness of the early warning system remained a well-kept secret.

The CH stations were capable, in theory, of

LEFT How the 'Dowding System' of RAF Fighter Command was portrayed in the 1941 HMSO booklet about the Battle of Britain. However, this depiction of the system omitted one important element of the air defence of Great Britain – radar.

BELOW A typical east coast Chain Home (CH) radar station of the Battle of Britain period showing the metal girder construction transmitter masts and the four smaller wooden lattice-work receiver masts.

detecting aircraft at ranges of the order of 100 to 200 miles, but in practice their performance was limited by such factors as atmospheric conditions, the skill of the individual operators, the height at which the enemy aircraft flew and the presence or absence of distracting echoes from friendly aircraft or natural features. Accurate location of approaching raids at distances of 60 to 80 miles or more from the coast was not uncommon and estimates of strength, although often vague, became more reliable as the range shortened.

All of the radar stations, except those in 10 Group's area (which reported to the Western Filter Room at Group Headquarters), passed

their information by direct landline to the underground Filter Room at RAF Bentley Priory. Here the information was sorted out by filterers and filter officers, displayed on a gridded map and passed by tellers through closed speech circuits both to the adjacent Command Operations Room and to the operations rooms of appropriate Groups and Sectors. Usually, about four minutes divided the first observation by a radar operator from the appearance of the corresponding plot in operations rooms.

Officially, the RDF (or radar) establishments around Britain's coast were known as Air Ministry Experimental Stations, this euphemistic name further obscuring the true purpose of these highly secret sites. Considerable speculation surrounded the building of these stations, with the most popular rumour being that the tall aerial masts emitted a 'death ray' to stop the engines of enemy aircraft. Had they known the truth, then those same curious members of the public would perhaps have been equally amazed to learn that the tall masts could detect, at very long range, any approaching aircraft.

During 1940 there were two types of Air Ministry Experimental Stations: AMES Type 1 CH (Chain Home) and Type 2 CHL (Chain Home Low). The network of these was still being expanded and developed during 1940, and by July there were a total of 21 Chain Home and 29 Chain Home Low stations, either in existence or under construction, situated along Britain's east, south and south-west coasts. These stretched from the Shetland Isles to the Pembrokeshire coastline but did not come under the direct operational control of RAF Fighter Command. Instead, they were part of the establishment of the RAF's 60 (Signals) Group.

Chain Home RDF station

The AMES Type 1 CH station was described as being of the 'floodlit' variety and was the first type of RDF station to be erected, with those along the south and east coasts having 360ft-high self-supporting steel masts (being the transmitting towers) and shorter wooden lattice-work masts which held the receiving arrays. These establishments could only 'look' seawards along their line of shoot and were unable to 'see' aircraft that

THE RADAR CHAIN AND OBSERVER CORPS NETWORK, JULY 1940.

LEGEND
C.H. Stations
C.H.L. Stations
Observer centres
Western limit of observed area
Unobserved tracks within observed area

SHETLAND ISLANDS.

A close-up of the entrance to the RAF Poling CH site in West Sussex with the receiver masts in the foreground and the transmitters in the far distance. In order to hide the true nature of what went on at these vital locations they were all rather euphemistically called 'Air Ministry Experimental Stations', or AMES for short.

had passed behind them. At each of these stations massive concrete structures were built to house the primary equipment: the transmitter block, the receiver block and the generator block. Protected by huge blast walls, and with tons of blast-absorbing shingle several feet thick held within retaining walls on the roof, the essential equipment was well protected. Each site had an establishment of 123 permanent personnel, although almost all of them were billeted away from the stations. With the stations maintaining a 24-hour and 365-day monitoring of all approaches to Britain's shores, the personnel were generally organised into three 'watches'. The typical CH site establishment was as follows:

AMES Type 1 Chain Home (CH) – typical personnel establishment

	Establishment	
	RAF	WAAF
Operational		
Supervisors	1 F/O	2 S/Os
RDF operators (G)	1 Sgt 1 Cpl 5 ACs	2 Sgts 3 Cpls 12 ACWs
Technical		
Signals RDF	1 F/O	
RDF mechanics	1 F/Sgt 1 Sgt 4 Cpls 6 ACs	
Administration and GD		
Officers	1 F/Lt	1 S/O
Clerks GD	1 Cpl	2 ACWs
ACHs/GD	1 Cpl 4 ACs	1 Sgt 1 Cpl 6 ACWs
Equipment assistants	–	1 Cpl 1 ACW
Motor transport	–	1 Cpl 3 ACWs
MT mechanics	1 AC	–
Cooks and butchers	1 Cpl 2 ACs	3 Cpls 6 ACWs
Stewards	–	9 ACWs
Telephonists	–	1 Cpl 3 ACWs
Nursing orderlies	1 Cpl 4 ACs	2 ACWs
Service police	1 Sgt 2 Cpls 6 ACs	–
Gunners	1 Sgt 2 Cpls 16 ACs	–
Totals	**63**	**60**

ABOVE A general view of the remaining receiver block at Pevensey in East Sussex showing the extensive protective blast walls. The station was heavily dive-bombed on 12 August 1940 by Messerschmitt 110s of *Erprobungsgruppe* 210. The attack resulted in the station being temporarily put out of action when a main power cable was severed, although the raid demonstrated the difficulty of actually hitting or toppling the masts, despite their size. *(Peter Hibbs)*

ABOVE The concrete bases of one of the receiver masts at Pevensey CH radar station. *(Peter Hibbs)*

ABOVE A typical CHL (Type 2) radar mast with its transmitter/receiver aerial located on top of the Caledon Mk II rotation gear.

BELOW Inside the main receiver room at a CH station with the operations console at the right and the RF8 receiver to the left. Noteworthy are the number of WAAF operatives on duty. Roughly half of the entire operating staff at both CH and CHL stations were formed by WAAF personnel.

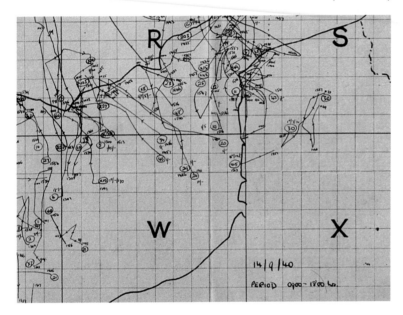

ABOVE A typical raid map translated from plots received from CH and CHL stations along Britain's south-east coastline. The map is dated 14 September 1940.

Calibrator Circuit

Radio Frequency Amplifier
Mixer and Buffer
Amplifier
Interference Rejection
Units

Band Width Switch

Wave Range Switch

Goniometer Control

CRT Compartment

Timing Circuit & Time Base
Power Unit

Calibrator Timing Circuit
& Black-out Control
Power Unit

Spongy Lock & Multivibrator

Phase Shifter

CRT Control Panel

The transmitters at the CH stations used water-cooled de-mountable valves and transmitted to the order of 1,000 kilowatts (kW), operating on two wavebands: namely, 10.10 to 13.27 (long wave) and 5.9 to 7.1 (short wave), although the majority were operating on the longer wave.

Chain Home Low RDF station

The AMES Type 2 CHL stations were 'beam' stations designed to detect and report low-flying aircraft and were also situated near the coastline. The aerial equipment consisted of five-bay four-stacked arrays, power-turned by means of Caledon turning gear, which rotated at speeds between 1.0 and 3.3rpm. The equipment permitted a continuous rotation of the array, which functioned as both a transmitting and receiving aerial and mounted on either a 20ft or 185ft tower according to the

LEFT Seventy-five years on and this is the view inside the Receiver Room at Pevensey CH station in East Sussex. This photograph makes an interesting comparison with the view opposite of the same room in use during 1940.
(Peter Hibbs)

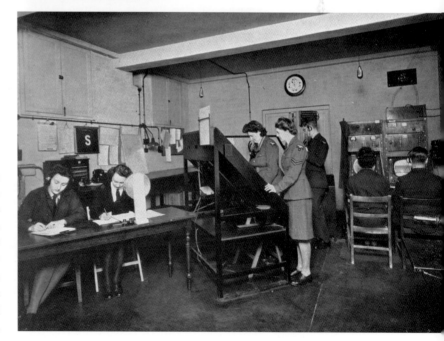

RIGHT A view inside the Receiver Room at a CHL station. The operatives seated far right with their backs to the camera are working at the R3101 receiver, whilst other personnel plot the readings and relay information directly to RAF Fighter Command's HQ Filter Room. Again, WAAF personnel make up a significant proportion of the duty staff. Note also the colour-change clock on the back wall (see page 78), which used colour-coded segments to define the timings of received plots.

nature and height of the site above sea level. The stations operated on a wavelength of 1.5m and the transmitter radiated a peak power of around 150kW.

The typical personnel establishment at a CHL station was around 74 persons, both RAF and Women's Auxiliary Air Force (WAAF). Unlike the CH stations, the CHL aerial array was designed for all-round looking and was only limited in this respect by the nature of the site and the surrounding terrain. To all intents and purposes, though, the stations were only of value in detecting and tracking aircraft or formations approaching from the sea during the 1940 period.

The Observer Corps

Commandant, Observer Corps
Air Commodore Alfred Drummond Warrington-Morris CB, CMG, OBE, AFC

Born in 1883 and formerly a Royal Navy officer, Warrington-Morris had transferred to the Royal Naval Air Service (RNAS) in 1916 and then to the Royal Flying Corps, subsequently becoming an officer in the newly formed Royal Air Force in April 1918. As a wing commander he became Deputy Director of Flying (Instrumentation), continuing the signalling, information and technology-based speciality he had followed since transferring to the RNAS. Between 1928

and 1934 he was appointed Commandant RAF Signals Branch before leaving the service. In 1934 he became Deputy Commandant of the Observer Corps, then Commandant (Southern Area) Observer Corps in 1935. In April 1936 Warrington-Morris took control of the Observer Corps and oversaw the move of HQ Observer Corps to RAF Bentley Priory and the Corps' adoption by RAF Fighter Command. He controlled the Corps during the Battle of Britain and was still Commandant when the Observer Corps became a uniformed branch of the RAF as the Royal Observer Corps. He was Mentioned in Despatches in July 1940 and died in 1962.

The Corps in operation
'German fighters can now reach this country and [observer] post crews will be expected to report the types of German aircraft when seen.'
(Air Commodore A.D. Warrington-Morris, 29 May 1940)

Although operationally the Chain Home radar stations had failings and weaknesses in their operation during 1940, and in the interpretation of results, it was also the case that they had one major flaw: a fixed line of sight. In other words, they could only 'see' in the direction that the radar was directed, and this, of course, was away from the coast and towards the anticipated approach of any threat. That is to say, once the threat had passed over the radar sites and was inland and behind them, then these plots became invisible to radar. From this moment on, then, the approaching threats were monitored visually (or audibly if at night or in conditions of poor visibility) by a network of ground-based observers – the Observer Corps.

The Corps was by no means new in 1940. In fact, its history went back to the First World War when it was the RNAS that was responsible for Britain's home defence. It was the duty of the local police to act as observers and to report to the Admiralty any sightings of enemy aircraft. It was not until 1921 that a civilian group of 'observers' was given the title 'Observer Corps'. It was a title that was to stay with them when Dowding took over RAF Fighter Command in 1936.

Dowding saw the importance of the Observer Corps and immediately took steps that they should work within the air defence

BELOW Once enemy aircraft had passed behind the coastal CH and CHL stations they became invisible to radar and therefore the raid's progress had to be plotted by the Observer Corps. Here, men of the Observer Corps on duty in one of the numerous and often very remote posts monitor the progress of an incoming raid using the Post Instrument.

system in conjunction with the Radio Direction Finding (RDF or radar) stations. It would be the task of RDF to detect hostile aircraft while still out to sea, then it would be the job of the Observer Corps to track them once they were over land. However, the men of the Observer Corps were much more highly trained whilst operating under the general aegis of Fighter Command than were those observers of the First World War. Lectures in aircraft recognition became mandatory, as did lessons in judging aircraft height. Although they were not equipped with any elaborate instruments, it was mainly their enthusiasm, an aircraft recognition booklet, a pair of binoculars and a simple yet effective sighting instrument that were the only tools with which this dedicated band of men tackled their all-important duty.

Once radar had picked up an enemy sighting and the information passed on to the Filter Room at Fighter Command HQ, Group Operations Room contacted the Observer Corps centres in the Group's operating area who in turn notified the small Observer posts scattered at between 6 and 10 miles apart along the coastline, where it would be apparent that the detected enemy formation would possibly be sighted. As soon as the call was received, the post, normally manned by three to five men would scan the skies with their binoculars and keep a keen ear out for the sound of aircraft engines. During inclement weather, and on days with low cloud, visual sighting was almost impossible and detection could only be made by sound.

Once a sighting had been made the observers had to detect which type of aircraft

were in the formation, how many, the heading they were taking and their height. All these factors were of vital importance because it was the picture this information presented that gave the Sector Stations an overall view of the unfolding situation. Unlike radar stations, which gave Fighter Command HQ their plots first, the Observer Corps gave details of their first sighting to the Fighter Sector Station in their area. This was in order that when fighters were 'scrambled' the Sector Controller had the most up-to-date information available to him. The observers would, where possible, give the type of aircraft detected (following Warrington-

ABOVE Apart from the height and course of enemy aircraft it was important that observers could identify the aircraft types involved and the estimated numbers. This formation of 24 bombers would be reported as: 'Dornier 17s. 20 plus.'

RIGHT High-altitude dogfights (such as this one over Portchester near Portsmouth on 6 November 1940) or aircraft movements at height produced tell-tale vapour trails. Even if the aircraft types involved could not be positively identified they were still plotted by the Observer Corps and if neither they nor Fighter Command could identify the plot concerned then it would be marked down as an 'X' raid until it was either identified as 'friendly' or else confirmed as hostile, in which case it would be allocated an 'H' prefix on the plotting tables.

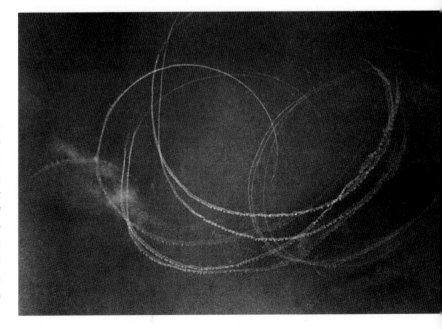

Morris's directive of 29 May 1940) – eg, Heinkel 111, Junkers 88 etc. They did not have to count every single aircraft as this would take up valuable time but, instead, they had been trained to observe a formation and accurately estimate its strength. The strength would be reported as '20 plus', '50 plus', '100 plus' etc. If any fighter escort could be visually seen it would be reported but, generally, fighter escorts flew higher than the bomber formations they were protecting and were harder to detect.

The importance of information gleaned by the Observer Corps and its value to Fighter Controllers during the Battle of Britain cannot be overestimated. Its volunteer observers worked around the clock, 7 days a week, 365 days a year, to keep this vital flow of crucial information feeding into the command and control system.

The motto of the Corps, bestowed after the battle, succinctly summarised its absolutely vital importance to RAF Fighter Command: 'Forewarned is Forearmed'.

(Note: *In recognition of its service to the RAF during and prior to the Battle of Britain the Observer Corps was granted the title 'Royal', thus becoming the Royal Observer Corps from April 1941. From that date it was also granted its badge along with the organisation's highly appropriate motto.*)

The Observer Post Instrument

To assist in the identification and location of enemy aircraft, Observer Posts were equipped with a mechanical sighting instrument mounted over a gridded map. The gridded map was a circular representation of the reporting area for that particular post. The instrument had been designed in 1934 by R.B. Pullin and replaced an earlier pantograph-type device. By 1940 the instrument was improved with the addition of a height corrector known as a 'Micklethwait' after the observer who developed and patented it in order to enable heights to be calculated more easily and accurately. (This instrument is often called, incorrectly, the 'Micklethwait', although this only refers to the height corrector. The equipment was, simply, the Observer Post Instrument.) It worked on the basis that if the height of an aircraft was known then it was possible, from its horizontal bearing and vertical angle, to calculate a locational position.

After setting the instrument with an estimate of the aircraft's height, the observer would align a sighting bar with the aircraft. This bar was mechanically connected to a vertical pointer, which would indicate the position of the aircraft on the map. Observers then reported the map coordinates, height and number of aircraft for each sighting to their Observer Centre. The initial estimates of heights were corrected during the plotting process through communication between the Observer Centre and other Observer Posts in the area by using triangulation between other posts' sightings, or else the direct report of an aircraft's position directly above a post.

This relatively simple piece of equipment became crucial in the plotting and reporting of enemy aircraft as they moved inland from the coast. Without it, accurate information for RAF Fighter Command from behind the radar station's line of shoot would have been impossible.

RAF Fighter Command

The principal defensive 'instrument' of the overall air defence system was, of course, the RAF's air arm dedicated to the provision of home defence fighters – Fighter Command.

At the time of the huge RAF Expansion Plan of 1935, five new Home Commands were established to fulfil the home-based functions of the air force, namely: Bomber, Coastal, Training, Maintenance and Fighter Commands. The latter came into being on 14 July 1936 with

BELOW The Observer Corps Post Instrument, which became an absolutely vital piece of equipment during the Battle of Britain.

Air Marshal Sir Hugh Dowding as Air Officer Commanding-in-Chief. Under the pre-war leadership of Dowding modern fighter aircraft (the Spitfire, Hurricane and Defiant) came into service and new fighter squadrons were either formed or re-formed. As a result of the foresight and leadership of Dowding a system was in place by 1940, which was organised into operational Groups (10, 11, 12 and 13 Groups) with squadrons strategically placed around Britain to offer the most effective defence of potential military and industrial targets as well as centres of population. By the commencement of the Battle of Britain RAF Fighter Command maintained a strength of approximately 350 Hurricanes and 200 Spitfires, along with about 70 Blenheims and 25 Defiants.

(Note: *between November 1943 and October 1944 RAF Fighter Command became RAF Air Defence Great Britain (RAF ADGB) but reverted to RAF Fighter Command on 15 October 1944. In 1968 it was subsumed into the RAF's new structure as part of RAF Strike Command.*)

Senior command structure
Air Officer Commanding-in-Chief, RAF Fighter Command
Air Chief Marshal Sir Hugh C.T. DOWDING GCVO, KCB, CMG

Hugh Caswall Tremenheere Dowding was born in Moffat on 24 April 1882 and educated at St Ninian's School and Winchester College. He was commissioned as a second lieutenant in the Royal Garrison Artillery in 1900. In August 1914 he joined the Royal Flying Corps (RFC) as a pilot on 7 Squadron, thereafter enjoying regular promotions.

Dowding was given a permanent commission in the RAF on 1 August 1919 with the rank of group captain. After a series of senior roles he was appointed in July 1936 as the first chief of the newly created RAF Fighter Command in which he conceived and oversaw development of the Dowding System of integrated air defence. He also introduced modern aircraft into service, including the eight-gun Spitfire and Hurricane. Due to retire in June 1939, Dowding was asked to stay on until March 1940 because of the tense international situation. He would continue until November 1940.

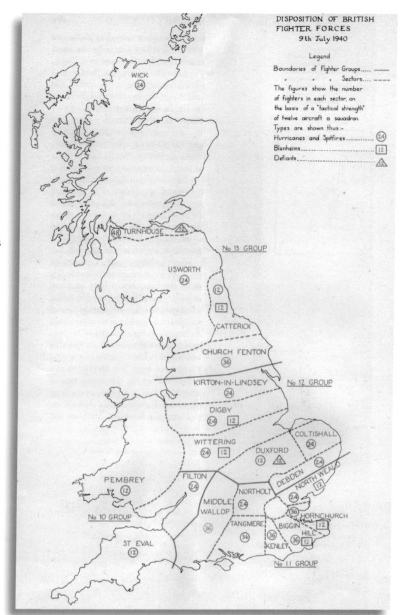

DISPOSITION OF BRITISH FIGHTER FORCES 9th July 1940

Legend
Boundaries of Fighter Groups _____
Sectors _____
The figures show the number of fighters in each sector, on the basis of a "tactical strength" of twelve aircraft a squadron. Types are shown thus:-
Hurricanes and Spitfires _____ 24
Blenheims _____ 12
Defiants _____ 12

Nicknamed 'Stuffy' by his men, Dowding proved unwilling to sacrifice aircraft and pilots in the attempt to aid Allied troops during the Battle of France. He resisted repeated requests to weaken home defence by sending precious squadrons overseas.

His other vital contribution was to marshal resources behind the scenes (including replacement aircraft and aircrew) and to maintain a significant fighter reserve while leaving his subordinate commanders' hands largely free to run the battle in detail.

Known for his humility and great sincerity, Fighter Command pilots came to characterise him as one who cared for his men and had their best interests at heart. He often referred to his

ABOVE The disposition of RAF fighter forces as at July 1940 showing the boundaries between 10, 11, 12 and 13 Groups of RAF Fighter Command and the various Sectors within each of those Groups.

RIGHT Air Chief Marshal Sir Hugh C.T. Dowding GCVO, KCB, CMG, the C-in-C of RAF Fighter Command during the Battle of Britain.

RIGHT Air Vice-Marshal Sir C.J. Quintin Brand KBE, DSO, MC, DFC, AOC 10 Group.

BELOW Air Vice-Marshal Sir Keith R. Park GCB, KBE, MC and Bar, DFC, AOC 11 Group.

'dear fighter boys', who included his son Derek, as his 'chicks'.

Dowding died at his home in Royal Tunbridge Wells, Kent, on 15 February 1970. His ashes were laid to rest at Westminster Abbey.

Air Officer Commanding 10 Group (HQ: Box, Wiltshire)
Air Vice-Marshal Sir C.J.Q. BRAND KBE, DSO, MC, DFC

Christopher Joseph Quintin Brand was born in Beaconsfield, South Africa, on 25 May 1893. In 1915 he travelled to England and joined the RFC in which he served with distinction, ultimately becoming the highest scoring RAF night-fighter pilot of the First World War. During the Second World War, Brand was Air Officer Commanding 10 Group responsible for the defence of south-west England and South Wales. He actively supported Air Vice-Marshal Keith Park in advocating the use of small, rapidly deployed groups of fighters to intercept Luftwaffe raiders. Under Brand's command, 10 Group played a vital role in the Battle of Britain by defending south-west England and providing support to adjacent 11 Group as required. Brand later became the Air Officer Commanding 20 (Training) Group and retired from the RAF on 6 November 1943. Quintin Brand died in Southern Rhodesia on 7 March 1968.

Air Officer Commanding 11 Group (HQ: Uxbridge, Middlesex)
Air Vice-Marshal Sir K.R. PARK GCB, KBE, MC and Bar, DFC

Keith Rodney Park was born in Thames, New Zealand, on 15 June 1892. As an NCO in an artillery battalion he saw action at both Gallipoli and on the Western Front before joining the RFC in December 1916, serving with success and claiming a final tally of five aircraft destroyed and fourteen 'out of control'. In the interwar years Park commanded RAF stations, including RAF Tangmere, and was an instructor before promotion to air commodore and an appointment as Senior Air Staff Officer at Fighter Command under Dowding in 1938. In April 1940, Park took command of 11 Group, responsible for the fighter defence of London and south-east England. It was coordinated by fighter controllers in the

FAR LEFT Air Vice-Marshal Sir Trafford Leigh-Mallory KCB, DSO, AOC 12 Group.

LEFT Air Vice-Marshal Richard E. Saul CB, DFC, AOC 13 Group.

11 Group Operations Room in the underground bunker (now known as the Battle of Britain Bunker) at RAF Uxbridge. Park himself was not based in the bunker but did visit at key points. He personally commanded RAF forces on three important dates: 13 August, 18 August and 15 September. After further appointments in the Middle East and Far East, Park retired and was promoted to air chief marshal on 20 December 1946. He returned to New Zealand where he died on 6 February 1975.

Air Officer Commanding 12 Group (HQ: Watnall, Nottinghamshire)
Air Vice-Marshal Sir T. LEIGH-MALLORY KCB, DSO

Trafford Leigh-Mallory was born in Mobberley, Cheshire, on 11 July 1892. He was educated at Haileybury and at Magdalene College, Cambridge, where he knew Arthur Tedder, the future Marshal of the Royal Air Force. Intending to become a barrister, he volunteered for the Army on the outbreak of the First World War. After recovering from wounds sustained at Ypres, Leigh-Mallory joined the RFC in January 1916. Post-war, with little prospect of a law career, he stayed in the recently created RAF with promotion to squadron leader on 1 August 1919. He rose through the ranks and was appointed to lead 12 Group Fighter Command in December 1937. His controversial 'Big Wing' concept of massed fighter formations to combat German bombers led to serious disagreements with AVM Park of 11 Group.

Shortly after the end of the Battle of Britain he took over command of 11 Group. In 1942 he became the Commander-in-Chief (C-in-C) of Fighter Command before being selected in 1943 to be the C-in-C of the Allied Expeditionary Air Force, which made him the Supreme Air Commander for the Allied invasion of Normandy. On 14 November 1944 when en route to Ceylon to take up a new post, his aircraft crashed in the French Alps and Leigh-Mallory, his wife and eight others were killed. He was the most senior RAF officer to be killed in the Second World War.

Air Officer Commanding 13 Group (HQ: Kenton, Tyne and Wear)
Air Vice-Marshal R.E. SAUL CB, DFC

Richard Ernest Saul CB, DFC, RAF, was born in Dublin, Ireland, on 16 April 1891. At the start of the First World War he was a second lieutenant in the Army Service Corps but by 1916 he was a flying officer (observer) with 16 Squadron of the RFC. He rose to command several squadrons. During the Second World War Saul was AOC 13 Group from 1939. He headed 12 Group from late 1940 and was then AOC Air Defences Eastern Mediterranean from 1943. Saul retired from the RAF on 29 June 1944 and after stints with the UN in the Balkans and the International Transport Commission in Rome, he took up employment in 1951 as the manager of the University of Toronto bookshop until finally retiring in 1959. He died on 30 November 1965.

RAF Fighter Command order of battle – 1 September 1940

Because the Battle of Britain was a fast-moving and ever-fluid battle, so the organisation of the defending forces changed, too. Squadrons and other units were rested and rotated, and thus the following Order of Battle merely provides a snapshot of the situation at a fixed date, roughly in the middle of the battle:

Sector	Squadron	Aircraft	Combat ready (unserviceable)	Base airfield	Pilots on state	Commanding officer(s)
10 Group, HQ Rudloe Manor, Box, Wiltshire						
Pembrey	92 Sqn	Spitfires	12 (4)	Pembrey	19	Sqn Ldr F.J. Sanders
Filton	87 Sqn	Hurricanes	9 (6)	Exeter	18	Sqn Ldr R.S. Mills
	213 Sqn	Hurricanes	8 (7)	Exeter	19	Sqn Ldr H.D. McGregor
St Eval	236 Sqn	Blenheims	12 (5)	St Eval	22	Sqn Ldr G.W. Montagu
	238 Sqn	Hurricanes	11 (4)	St Eval	20	Sqn Ldr H.A. Fenton (absent wounded)
Middle Wallop	152 Sqn	Spitfires	12 (4)	Warmwell	19	Sqn Ldr P.K. Devitt
	234 Sqn	Spitfires	12 (5)	Middle Wallop	19	Sqn Ldr J.S. O'Brien
	249 Sqn	Hurricanes	15 (1)	Boscombe Down	18	Sqn Ldr J. Grandy
	604 Sqn	Blenheims	11 (3)	Middle Wallop	20	Sqn Ldr M.F. Anderson
	609 Sqn	Spitfires	11 (5)	Middle Wallop	20	Sqn Ldr H.S. Darley
11 Group, HQ Uxbridge, Middlesex						
Biggin Hill	79 Sqn	Hurricanes	10 (5)	Biggin Hill	17	Sqn Ldr J.H. Heyworth
	501 Sqn	Hurricanes	12 (5)	Gravesend	22	Sqn Ldr H.A.V. Hogan
North Weald	25 Sqn	Blenheims	14 (2)	Martlesham	24	Sqn Ldr W.W. Loxton (acting)
	56 Sqn	Hurricanes	9 (5)	North Weald	18	Temporarily unfilled
	151 Sqn	Hurricanes	9 (4)	Stapleford	17	Temporarily unfilled
Kenley	72 Sqn	Spitfires	15 (3)	Croydon	20	Sqn Ldr A.R. Collins
	85 Sqn	Hurricanes	13 (3)	Croydon	17	Sqn Ldr P.W. Townsend
	253 Sqn	Hurricanes	10 (4)	Kenley	17	Temporarily unfilled
	616 Sqn	Spitfires	12 (4)	Kenley	20	Sqn Ldr M. Robinson
Northolt	1 Sqn	Hurricanes	10 (3)	Northolt	14	Sqn Ldr D.A. Pemberton
	1 (Can.) Sqn	Hurricanes	13 (4)	Northolt	24	Sqn Ldr E.A. McNab
	303 Sqn	Hurricanes	13 (5)	Northolt	24	Sqn Ldr R.G. Kellett Sqn Ldr Z. Krasnodebski
Hornchurch	54 Sqn	Spitfires	11 (5)	Hornchurch	14	Temporarily unfilled
	222 Sqn	Spitfires	12 (3)	Hornchurch	18	Sqn Ldr J.H. Hill
	600 Sqn	Blenheims	9 (5)	Hornchurch	23	Sqn Ldr D. de B. Clark
	603 Sqn	Spitfires	13 (3)	Hornchurch	18	Temporarily unfilled
Tangmere	17 Sqn	Hurricanes	12 (5)	Tangmere	19	Sqn Ldr A.G. Miller
	43 Sqn	Hurricanes	10 (4)	Tangmere	19	Sqn Ldr C.B. Hull
	602 Sqn	Spitfires	12 (4)	Westhampnett	19	Sqn Ldr A.V.R. Johnstone
Debden	111 Sqn	Hurricanes	11 (5)	Debden	19	Sqn Ldr J.M. Thompson
	257 Sqn	Hurricanes	12 (5)	Debden	20	Sqn Ldr H. Harkness
	601 Sqn	Hurricanes	12 (5)	Debden	22	Sqn Ldr Sir Archibald Hope, Bt
12 Group, HQ Watnall, Nottingham						
Duxford	19 Sqn	Spitfires	11 (4)	Fowlmere	22	Sqn Ldr P.C. Pinkham
	310 Sqn	Hurricanes	10 (4)	Duxford	24	Sqn Ldr G.D.M. Blackwood
Coltishall	66 Sqn	Spitfires	10 (6)	Coltishall	19	Sqn Ldr R.H.A. Leigh
	242 Sqn	Hurricanes	11 (4)	Coltishall	21	Sqn Ldr D.R.S. Bader
Kirton-in-Lindsey	264 Sqn	Defiants	8 (7)	Kirton-in-Lindsey	18	Sqn Ldr G.D. Garvin
Digby	29 Sqn	Blenheims	10 (4)	Wellingore	23	Sqn Ldr S.C. Widdows
	46 Sqn	Hurricanes	15 (2)	Digby	20	Flt Lt A.D. Murray
	611 Sqn	Spitfires	12 (6)	Digby	23	Sqn Ldr J.E. McComb
Wittering	23 Sqn	Blenheims	11 (6)	Wittering	26	Sqn Ldr G.F.W. Heycock
	74 Sqn	Spitfires	11 (5)	Wittering	20	Sqn Ldr A.G. Malan
	229 Sqn	Hurricanes	12 (4)	Bircham Newton	18	Sqn Ldr H.J. Maguire
	266 Sqn	Spitfires	8 (4)	Wittering	17	Temporarily unfilled

Sector	Squadron	Aircraft	Combat ready (unserviceable)	Base airfield	Pilots on state	Commanding officer(s)
13 Group, HQ Newcastle, Northumberland						
Church Fenton	64 Sqn 73 Sqn 302 Sqn	Spitfires Hurricanes Hurricanes	12 (6) 11 (4) 12 (4)	Leconfield Church Fenton Leconfield	22 19 26	Sqn Ldr A.R.D. MacDonald Sqn Ldr M.W.S. Robinson Sqn Ldr W.A.J. Satchell Sqn Ldr M. Mumler
Catterick	32 Sqn 41 Sqn 219 Sqn 607 Sqn 610 Sqn	Hurricanes Spitfires Blenheims Hurricanes Spitfires	8 (6) 14 (3) 8 (5) 16 9 (2)	Acklington Catterick Leeming Usworth Acklington	15 20 18 22 18	Sqn Ldr M.N. Crossley Sqn Ldr H. West Sqn Ldr J.H. Little Sqn Ldr J.A. Vick Sqn Ldr J. Ellis
Turnhouse	141 Sqn 605 Sqn	Defiants Hurricanes	9 (7) 12 (5)	Turnhouse Drem	22 19	Sqn Ldr W.A. Richardson Sqn Ldr W.M. Churchill
Dyce	145 Sqn 263 Sqn	Hurricanes Hurricanes	9 (5) 5 (3)	Montrose Dyce Grangemouth	18 10	Sqn Ldr J.R.A. Peel Flt Lt T.P. Pugh
Wick	3 Sqn 504 Sqn	Hurricanes Hurricanes	15 (2) 14 (2)		22 21	Sqn Ldr S.F. Godden Sqn Ldr J. Sample

The typical RAF fighter station of 1940

Station commander

Generally, the officers commanding RAF fighter stations were either group captains or wing commanders from the General Duties (Flying) branch of the service. For the most part, these were older officers who perhaps no longer held an active flying authorisation but had usually been operational flyers, either pilots or observers. In many cases they had been operational during the First World War in the RFC and RAF and were deemed to thus have an empathy and understanding with the operations of active fighter squadrons. However, at least some of these station commanders flew operationally on occasion with the squadrons based on the stations they commanded. These included Gp Capt Stanley Vincent (RAF Northolt) who became the only fighter pilot credited with destroying enemy aircraft in both wars, Wg Cdr John Dewar (RAF Exeter) who was killed over the English Channel in unexplained circumstances on 12 September 1940 and Wg Cdr Victor Beamish (RAF North

BELOW By the outbreak of war the largely unpainted buildings of the permanent RAF stations in Britain had been hastily painted with brown and green camouflage. Here, the buildings at RAF Kenley (in this case the accommodation barrack blocks) can be seen in their warpaint (the station was heavily bombed on 18 August 1940).

RIGHT An aerial view of a typical pre-war permanent home station of RAF Fighter Command, in this instance RAF Tangmere in Sussex. Typically, such stations would have no hard runways until much later in their histories. This allowed fighters to simply take off into wind, directly from their dispersal points, rather than have to taxi to runways and line up for take-off. The brick-built accommodation blocks, messes, administration and engineering buildings, etc, were clustered around the main hangars. In this instance the hangars were the large Belfast trussed-type structures.

BELOW The layout of a typical RAF fighter station of the period, in this case RAF Debden in Essex.

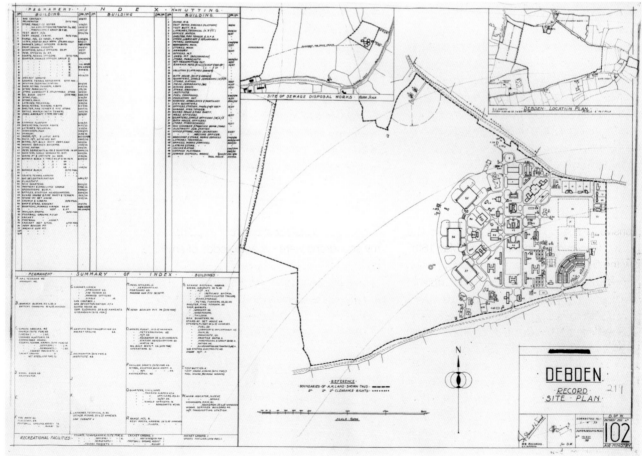

Weald) who flew frequently with the squadrons on his station but was ultimately killed when flying operationally on 28 March 1942.

Inevitably, and in line with typically irreverent service humour, the station commander was generally known as the 'Station Master'.

A station commander's story – Gp Capt Cecil 'Boy' Bouchier, Station Commander, RAF Hornchurch, 1940

(Note: *this is a contemporary account told in Bouchier's own words from a BBC broadcast of January 1941. During that broadcast neither the identity of Bouchier nor his fighter station was revealed.*)

'I have been asked to tell you something of what goes on at a fighter station. I'll try to do this insofar as my station was concerned. We all knew, of course, it was going to be an air war, and you can imagine, therefore, our intense excitement when war was actually declared. But how different those first seven or eight months turned out to be. There was no immediate "Blitz" and my pilots spent their time incessantly chasing the odd elusive Hun far out over the North Sea, with only here and there a success. I remember in those early days the shrieks of almost childish joy with which the very sight of an enemy aeroplane was hailed by our boys in the air, and the tears of anguish when one got away by diving into clouds after a long chase, far out over the North Sea.

'Little did we know then that the Hun was progressively to switch the whole weight of his Air Force on to a single objective. And our turn was not yet. Little did we know then of the intensive air fighting that was so soon to come.

'And then came a red-letter day. May 16th saw the first Spitfire squadron leave my station to make an offensive sweep over the Continent. Two hours later the squadron returned, having patrolled as far north as Ostend. The enemy had not been engaged, but throughout the whole station there was a feeling of satisfaction and anticipation – that at last things were beginning to move; and a few days later, on a similar patrol, a Junkers 88 was shot down in a smother of sand near Flushing. ... I remember the high, excited voice, the breathless excitement of the youngster as he "hared"

home to report in person. His little dance of joy on the aerodrome as I met him – bright-eyed – indescribably happy.

'Less than a week later was to see the great Battle of Dunkirk, and the evacuation of our Army in the face of the whole might of the German Air Force, but with the 4th June, the Dunkirk days were over. What a difference the complete collapse of France which followed meant to us. Now we were faced with the enemy a few miles across the water, and rapidly occupying aerodromes all along the French and Belgian coasts. From these bases – from June to the beginning of August – he concentrated his attacks on our shipping. Often my squadrons were engaging odds of anything up to 10 to 1, and rarely less than 5 to 1, but in 6 weeks fighters from my station added a further 135 enemy aircraft destroyed, together with another 60 "probables" to their score.

'And then, suddenly in mid-August, the Hun switched his offensive from our shipping and then for about a month launched a bitter and relentless attack against our fighter aerodromes, admitting by this change of tactics that our fighters were getting the upper hand of him and that his only hope was to smash them and break their morale.

'By sheer weight of numbers he hoped to do this, and to blot out the hornets' nests which alone stood between him and the daylight annihilation of London. Hundreds of bombers, supported by high-flying fighters, came over day after day – but more and more of the all-important bombers fell to my squadrons, and still we stayed on top. Steadily we took our toll, until in the end even the Hun couldn't take any more. During this short period we added another 125 destroyed and from the air the Thames Estuary and Kent could be seen strewn with his wreckage.

'I hope I'm not giving you the impression that all this was "just too easy" – it wasn't. Here and there, we had to "take a bit" ourselves. I well remember the days when his bombers got through . . . and fairly blew blazes out of my station – on one occasion twice in one day, until the whole place was rocking. I remember thinking after each attack how incredible it was that so many bombs could fall all together – produce such an infernal noise – blot out the station and aerodrome with their black and yellow smoke, in so short a space of time . . . and yet, when the smoke cleared, do so little real damage. But then, we were always a lucky station. I remember every man and woman turning to and filling in the hundreds of craters, rushing round in circles organizing the labour – rounding up steam-rollers from near and far. I remember also the fabulous bills that came in to me afterwards for the free beer which I had promised . . . but it was well worth it – we were never out of action for a single day.

'I like to remember with a grateful heart what a privilege it has been to serve and live amongst the people of my station. Of the happy spirit that permeates my station – and all those unsung airmen and airwomen who have worked so unceasingly – so uncomplainingly, day and night to keep the airscrews turning. Their loyalty and confidence in me, has made my work such a joy.

'Of my pilots, I like to remember their simple modesty and the way they could always raise a laugh, as, over their beer at the end of each interminable day's fighting that summer, they swopped experiences; tired to death, but unconquerable of spirit.'

Squadron organisation

A single-seat fighter squadron at the time of the Battle of Britain would typically have had an establishment of around 20 to 22 pilots and, perhaps, 15 or 16 aircraft. Generally, though, a squadron would be considered to be flying 'at squadron strength' with 12 aircraft although, more often than not, the numbers would be significantly less than that due to losses and serviceability issues. The complement of 20 pilots would allow for anticipated shortfalls due to sickness, injuries or leave.

The typical fighter squadron would then be divided into 'A' and 'B' Flights, generally led by a flight lieutenant who would be designated flight commander. The two Flights would further be broken down into Red, Yellow, Green, and Blue Sections. In the air, the Sections would be organised into three aircraft formations known as a 'Vic', although how the Sections were organised and the formation the squadron adopted in the air varied from squadron to squadron. This could depend upon the latest perceived wisdom or on the personal preference of the squadron commander.

With the squadron's commanding officer (CO) generally being of squadron leader rank, the rest of the squadron would typically be made up of several pilots at pilot officer and flying officer rank and a complement of sergeant or flight sergeant pilots. It is often considered that the NCO contingent formed the very backbone of some squadrons, with many of the pilots in that grouping often having vastly more flying and combat experience than those of senior rank. Indeed, at times an NCO pilot would lead the squadron into action, taking precedence over senior commissioned officers by virtue of his experience. An example of this was the

BELOW RAF Fighter Command squadron organisation.

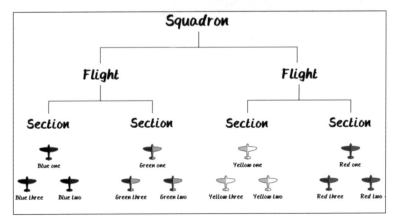

leadership into battle of 46 Squadron by Flt Sgt Eric Williams on some sorties during the early autumn of 1940.

On occasion, supernumerary officers were posted to squadrons to gain operational flying experience before being sent to their own squadron.

During 1940, a total of 71 squadrons and other units officially took part in the Battle of Britain. These were:

1, 1 (RCAF), 3, 17, 19, 23, 25, 29, 32, 41, 43, 46, 54, 56, 64, 65, 66, 72, 73, 74, 79, 85, 87, 92, 111, 141, 145, 151, 152, 213, 219, 222, 229, 232, 234, 235, 236, 238, 242, 245, 247, 248, 249, 253, 257, 263, 264, 266, 302, 303, 310, 312, 501, 504, 600, 601, 602, 603, 604, 605, 607, 609, 610, 611, 615, 616, 804 (FAA), 808 (FAA), plus 421 Flight, 422 Flight and the Fighter Interception Unit.

Three of the above squadrons (235, 236 and 248) were attached to Fighter Command from Coastal Command.

Of the above squadrons and units, the majority were day-fighter squadrons and units. However, on occasion day fighters were called upon for operational flying at night, either for interceptions or patrols. Specifically, though, 23, 25, 29, 219, 600 and 605 Squadrons were dedicated night-fighter units, together with the specialised Fighter Interception Unit (FIU).

(Note: *night-fighting was very much in its infancy during the Battle of Britain, although the earliest installations of Airborne Interception (AI) radar were already being trialled. However, single-seat fighters were frequently detailed to carry out night patrols. This was often a terrifying experience for pilots unskilled in night flying. The glare from the exhaust was such that a special shield had to be fitted between the exhaust ports and the cockpit for night-flying purposes.*)

Aside from the flying personnel, each squadron would have its own ground-based establishment comprising, among others, an engineering officer, an adjutant and an intelligence officer (IO), along with a complement of groundcrew fitters, riggers and armourers. The latter three groups would be mostly made up of other ranks (aircraftmen, aircraftmen I and II and leading aircraftmen) led by NCOs (corporals, sergeants and flight sergeants).

NIGHT FIGHTING

The object in night fighting is to 'stalk' the enemy and to reach a firing position without being observed. The following points should be noted.

a) Under normal conditions of darkness aircraft which are not illuminated by searchlights can best be spotted when they are between 40° and 60° above you.

b) Cockpit and instrument lighting should be reduced to the barest minimum to assist you in searching for the enemy, and to prevent your own presence being revealed.

c) The illuminated ring sight should be dimmed so that it is only just visible.

d) Before opening fire the aircraft must be positively identified as an enemy. This is best achieved from a position below him.

e) The following method of attack is recommended by Fighter Command: having reached a position below the enemy and regulated your speed to his, slightly raise the throttle opening; you will thus rise behind the enemy. Keep below his slipstream – if you have difficulty in holding your aircraft out of the slipstream it is usually an indication that you have reached too great a range.

f) The range at which the enemy is engaged should be as short as possible; in no circumstances should it be greater than 150 yards

BELOW The crew of a 29 Squadron Blenheim Mk IF night fighter clamber aboard their aircraft for a night interception sortie during the Battle of Britain.

However, the home station would provide, for example, catering and messing facilities, transport, arrangements for local airfield defence, general administration, medical services, discipline, accountancy, stores etc.

Only the squadrons and units listed above were officially accredited as having taken part in the Battle of Britain.

The fighter pilot's day – 1940

Life for a fighter pilot or aircrew member during the Battle of Britain was a taxing and gruelling one, whether engaging the enemy or just waiting for the call to battle. Physical and mental exhaustion constantly wore down the airmen of RAF Fighter Command in 1940 in day after day of flying, fighting and waiting. They were days that often began around 4.00am when officer pilots or aircrew were roused by their airmen batmen with a cup of tea. Sergeants, on the other hand, had to get themselves up and make their own tea before a truck would collect all flying personnel and drive them out to the squadron dispersal points. Generally, this would be at around dawn and far too early for the men to have made use of the station's mess facilities for breakfast. In any event, the nervous tension did not usually enhance any appetite for food and if the fliers wanted to eat then often some of the airmen ground personnel at dispersal would often cook bacon and eggs. Tea and cocoa, however, was always in plentiful supply although eating and drinking was normally the last thing on the mind of a Battle of Britain airman during operational periods.

At dispersal, the squadron commander (or flight commander) would be making sure his pilots had been allocated their aircraft and would update them with any specific orders, information and instructions of the day. Meanwhile, the fitters, riggers and armourers would be busy getting 'their' aircraft ready for the day and checking fuel, oil, oxygen and ammunition and carrying out the routine Daily Inspection (DI). With everything ready and signed off for flight, the accumulator starter trolley would be plugged in and the aircraft started up by the fitter. With the engine run up and warmed, the aircraft now stood ready for instant action and the pilot would check final cockpit details: gun-sight working and illuminated, seat and rudder pedals adjusted for his height, parachute and flying helmet stowed and ready. By now, the CO (or flight commander) would have rung through to the Sector Operations Room to declare his squadron were now ready for business and would therefore be declared 'Available'. Now, the waiting would begin.

If they were lucky, pilots might be released from dispersal, one section at a time, for breakfast, lunch or dinner. Otherwise, it was a case of impromptu meals whilst at dispersal. Here, the waiting time would be taken up with reading or else playing chess, cards or darts. Anything to ease the nervous tension and boredom, and mostly lounging on the grass or in wicker Lloyd-Loom chairs. If it was chilly, then maybe the pilots would assemble in the dispersal hut with a pot-bellied stove providing some comfort during the cold mornings and evenings of the latter stages of the battle. Here, at dispersal, there was not the rigid segregation between officer and NCO pilots found elsewhere in service life.

Sometimes, the waiting at dispersal could become seemingly interminable but when it was shattered it was, inevitably, by the telephone. The tight nervous knot in the stomach of every waiting pilot was something that never went away, and even the most seasoned fighter pilots would privately admit they were often afraid and would say of those who claimed that they were not afraid that they were either liars or foolish. However, the strident jangling of the telephone could mean several things, of course. Sometimes, to intense relief, it could send a message to merely 'Stand Down'. Other times it could call

BELOW Waiting at dispersal for the call to scramble.

pilots to Readiness, and from that state to the heart-pounding order 'Scramble!'

On that order there would be a mad helter-skelter rush by the pilots to their allocated aircraft where the fitter and rigger would be ready and waiting – the rigger on the wing ready to help in his pilot, the fitter standing by with the trolley accumulator plugged in on the starboard side of the engine. Heaving himself into the cockpit, the pilot would be going through a number of tasks – helmet pulled on, oxygen plugged in, radio jack-plug in its socket, magneto switches 'on', Ki-gas cylinder priming pump given a couple of brief strokes and thumb ready on the starter. Meanwhile, the fitter leaning into the cockpit had been helping the

pilot with his parachute harness straps, then his Sutton seat harness. By this time, though, the starter button had been pushed after a thumbs-up from the fitter who had then unplugged the starter trolley and ensured it was clear of fouling the aircraft. Unable to communicate over the roar of the Merlin engine the pilot and rigger would exchange a 'thumbs up', the rigger would invariably slap his pilot on the shoulder in a message of good luck and leap from the trailing edge of the wing. As he did so, the aircraft would already be rolling and the rigger would dodge and duck out of the way of the tailplane as he was buffeted by the slipstream, kicking up dust and grass and assailed by a blast of hot exhaust gases. Now, the aircraft

ABOVE Spitfires of 222 Squadron (ZD) and 603 Squadron (XT) at RAF Hornchurch in Essex during the battle.

LEFT One of the most famous photographs of the battle shows these Hurricane pilots of 32 Squadron relaxing on the grass between sorties at RAF Hawkinge in Kent during the high summer of 1940.

was gathering speed ahead, into wind, as it
bounced and rocked across the grass airfield
with others around it in the organised chaos of
a squadron scramble.

As they got airborne the pilots would be
concentrating on keeping station, selecting
'Gear Up', closing the cockpit canopy and
listening out intently for instructions from the
CO or flight commander who would already
be talking to the Sector Operations Room and
garnering instructions as to heading, altitude
and what it was they were intercepting. So, it
may well have been an instruction along the
lines of 'Mitor squadron, Angels 18, vector
two-three-zero. Fifty plus. Buster.' Listening
in, the other pilots would be able to interpret
the instructions thus: '41 Squadron to climb to
18,000ft on a heading of 230 degrees. Fifty plus
enemy aircraft. Maximum cruising speed.'

Settling into the climb, the pilots would
automatically slide into their correct section
order and the preferred squadron formation.
Meanwhile, the CO or flight commander would
be concentrating on setting course as the
other pilots began to concentrate on what was
going on in the cockpit – oil temperatures and
pressures, fuel state, oxygen state and 'On',
microphone not on 'Transmit', straps tight,
gun-sight 'On' and illuminated. The workload
had been high, and still they must concentrate
on formation keeping whilst, all the time,
maintaining a wary eye open for the enemy and
quartering the sky in a relentless search. The

squadron 'Weaver', though, winding from side
to side, was especially vigilant as the squadron
got closer by the second to their suspected
quarry.

Brief instructions might crackle through the
headphones: 'Close up Red 2' or, on receipt of
further instructions from the fighter controller,
following the leader's instruction: 'Turning to
port, go!' Meanwhile, pilots would be fiddling
with the radio tuner as they struggled to tune
and re-tune their wireless sets in a constant
battle to receive and properly understand the
messages being sent. Sometimes, a squawk of
static would drown out anything intelligible and,
occasionally, this would result in one section
haring off suddenly, upwards or downwards, as
the rest of the squadron watched on, puzzled,
because either they received no transmission or
could not understand it.

There was also a constant juggling of the
throttle setting with the left hand and judicious
adjustment of position through the control
column and rudder pedals in order to keep
station. It was hard and exhausting work,
mentally and physically draining. By now, the
squadron was 'on oxygen' and the masks were
clamped securely to the pilots' faces as the
cold began to permeate the cockpit. And now,
with all the hard work of take-off, formation
flying and getting to altitude came the realisation
that the enemy must be near. Then, once more,
the tight knot of fear returned as the gun-sight
was checked and the 'SAFE' and 'FIRE' ring

on the gun button turned, ready, to the 'FIRE' position. Goggles were pulled down. And then came the shout!

'Bandits! Ten o'clock, above. Coming down now! Break, break, break. . . .'

Suddenly, to avoid the 'bounce' of fighters coming out of the sun the squadron had dispersed in a pre-ordered plan, and now the enemy fighters were in among them. This time, there was no chance of a well-ordered textbook 'Number One Attack'. Instead, it was pretty much everyone for himself, although with 'wing men' desperately trying to maintain station and protect their section leader. Perhaps, now, the pilots were climbing and hanging on their props, the sun glaring and blinding as they turned, all the while listening out and looking out.

Now, there were shouts: 'Behind you Blue 3!' and the chatter of gunfire. A cacophony of yells and static made communications unintelligible but one pilot may be drawing a bead on a Me 109 who had overshot, although his three-second burst had missed by a mile, hosing the air well ahead of his quarry who dived away. Meanwhile, a distinct cry of panic from an unidentified pilot was followed by a brief glimpse of a Spitfire falling away, vertically, trailing a red streak of flame and an ugly banner of black smoke. But no time to watch, however awfully mesmerising the sight and however much the desire to know who it was and if they had got out safely.

In just a few minutes the pilot had pulled

'G', almost greyed out, been shot at, briefly shot at something himself, rolled, dived, bunted and looped in his efforts to avoid hostile fire and to get on the tail of an enemy. The artificial horizon and compass spun wildly, and nausea overcame the sweating, aching and frightened young pilot. Sometimes he was sick; a combination of airsickness and of fear. Now though, he was alone and not an aircraft was in sight. He could hear nothing anymore in his headphones, and his wireless was now completely off-tune, anyway. In a short span of time he had lost 10,000ft of altitude but his fuel

LEFT Successful sortie. Plt Off Eric Lock DSO, DFC and Bar, 41 Squadron, gives the thumbs up. He was killed in action on 3 August 1941.

CATERPILLAR CLUB AND GQ PARACHUTE CLUB

When the lives of pilots or aircrew were saved by parachute, the manufacturers of the parachutes that saved them (mostly Irvin, but GQ in the case of Defiant crews, for example) presented the survivor with lapel badges or brooches.

In the case of Irvin, the recipient would get a tiny gold 'caterpillar', although in reality this represented a silk worm. These tiny brooches, with a pin fixing to the rear, also had the recipient's name and date when their life was saved by parachute engraved on to the reverse. Made from solid gold with eyes of semi-precious stones, they were prized badges of honour. It has long been suggested that the colour of the eyes represented something of the circumstances in which the parachute had been used, with red, for example, being said to signify escape from a burning aircraft. However, the colour of the eyes held no significance and was randomly dependent upon manufacturer and what colour stones were available. When awarded, some pilots and aircrew unofficially wore them on their tunics or, sometimes, hidden under a lapel.

In the case of GQ, a small lapel pin in the form of the company logo was presented to the recipient. Although it was again engraved on the reverse it was rather less grand in a base metal alloy rather than gold.

ABOVE AND BELOW The GQ Parachute Company parachutist badge issued to those who had successfully used the GQ parachute or 'Parasuit'. In this instance, Badge No 2 of the entire badge run has been awarded to Plt Off Eric Farnes, a Boulton Paul Defiant air-gunner with 141 Squadron who was shot down over the English Channel on 19 July 1940.

state and low ammunition meant he couldn't loiter. It was a case of setting course, alone, back to his home airfield – checking all the while on his aircraft for damage and functionality. Was everything still OK? Pressures and temperatures? Fuel state? Meanwhile, he knew he was a sitting duck, alone, and constant head swivelling was essential to make sure no unseen Messerschmitt should sneak up, or dive out of the sun.

Moments later he is on finals to his home airfield and on a wide curving approach. Canopy back, and locked. Air speed, checked. Gear down, three greens. Flaps, set. Over the hedge. One bounce, and down. A careful taxy back to dispersal, fish-tailing for visibility, and already checking to see who was back. A quick blip of the throttle as the aircraft was swung around, already pointing back into wind and ready. Then, switch off. The propeller staggered to a stop and the sound of metal contracting, tinking and pinging, as the engine cooled. Meanwhile, exhausted, sweating and shaking the pilot pulled off his helmet and mask. The rigger, on the wing, asked an enthusiastic 'Any luck, Sir?' before noticing the vomit-stained Mae West and the pilot's grey pallor. Exhausted, the pilot hauls himself from the cockpit and faces a barrage of questions.

Crowding round, the armourer, rigger and fitter need to know of any snags as they ready the aircraft for immediate action once again. 'No. All fine' might be all he could mumble before the intelligence officer is badgering him for details of the engagement. His halting account, though, might be interrupted by a shout from his rigger: 'Sir! Take a look at this!' Three neat bullet holes in the fuselage are pointed out. 'Nothing important hit though, sir!' The information might be cheerily shrugged aside, the pilot hiding his feelings as he did so. However, those holes were but 18 inches from where he sat. He hadn't even been aware, and yet death had come so perilously close. As if to reinforce things, word came through that the new sergeant pilot in Blue Section was the man going down in flames. Blue Two had watched as he had baled out, but then he fell, faster and faster, like a flaming comet as his burning parachute trailed uselessly behind him. Bullet holes in his own aircraft and one man down and dead in the most horrible of circumstances. But, now, he must be ready to go again. Perhaps in 20 minutes. And perhaps twice more that day. And again tomorrow. If he lived.

For now, it is back to the awful waiting. Exhaustion has taken over, and perhaps the pilot will fall fast asleep, but perhaps nerves and nagging fear will beat the fatigue and yearned for sleep just won't come easily. Either way, it isn't even midday yet and there are still a good six hours or so before the squadron will be stood down for the day. Then, those with enough energy might make it to the local pub. Most won't have the energy or the inclination, but will simply collapse into bed in the mess. In just a few short hours it will start all over again.

Summing it all up

Summing it all up, Wg Cdr 'Paddy' Barthropp told how it was to be a fighter pilot during the Battle of Britain:

'In 1940 he had total control of a 350mph fighter and eight machine guns – with no radar, auto-pilot and electronics.

'At the touch of a button he could unleash 13 pounds of shot in 3 seconds. He had a total of 14 seconds of ammunition. He needed to be less than 250 yards away from the enemy to be effective.

'He and his foe could manoeuvre in three dimensions at varying speeds and with an infinite number of angles relative to each other. His job was to solve the sighting equation without becoming a target himself.

'His aircraft carried 90 gallons of fuel between his chest and his engine.

'He often flew at over 20,000ft without cockpit heating or pressurisation. He endured up to six times the force of gravity but with no "G" suit.

'He had no crash helmet or protective clothing other than ineffective flying boots and gloves.

'He had about three seconds in which to identify his foe and slightly longer to abandon his aircraft if hit. He had no ejector seat.

'Often, as in my case, he was only 19 years old. He was considered too young and irresponsible to vote, but not too young to die.

'His pay was the modern equivalent of around 60 pence per day in 1940.

'Should he have been stupid enough to be shot down and taken prisoner, a third of that sum was deducted at source by a grateful country and never returned.

'However, every hour of every day was an unforgettable and marvellous experience spent in the company of the finest characters who ever lived.'

LEFT Although this photograph was taken just after the Battle of Britain, this group of Spitfire pilots are typical of the period and mostly include pilots who had taken part in the battle, including Flg Off Patrick 'Paddy' Barthropp, seated on the tail and wearing his uniform tunic.

Chapter Two

Equipping The Few

The tools to do the job

RAF Fighter Command's two principal fighter aircraft in 1940 were the state-of-the-art single-seaters, the Rolls-Royce Merlin-powered Spitfire and Hurricane, but it also operated the Defiant, Blenheim, Beaufighter and the biplane Gladiator. These aircraft provided gun platforms for the main gun armaments of the day – the Browning .303 machine gun, 20mm Hispano cannon and Vickers 'K' gun.

OPPOSITE Spitfire Mk Is of 19 Squadron at RAF Fowlmere near Duxford, Cambridgeshire, in the summer of 1940. *(IWM CH1452)*

RIGHT The Boulton Paul Defiant Mk I was intended as a bomber-destroyer and in this role it would likely have excelled were it not for the fact that the Air Ministry planners of the mid-1930s had not envisaged a scenario whereby bomber aircraft would be heavily escorted by single-seat fighters. During 1940 the Defiant proved to be no match for the Messerschmitt 109s pitched against them and the type was ultimately withdrawn from front-line daytime use and employed instead as a night fighter, where it had a better measure of success. (WW2 Images)

The details of RAF Fighter Command's fighter aircraft participating in the Battle of Britain are well known and widely published, but it would be impossible in any work of this nature not at least to give these main aircraft types, along with their opposition, some brief coverage together with appropriate leading particulars.

The defenders – Royal Air Force

Boulton Paul Defiant Mk I

The Defiant was of relatively conventional construction but its all-important gun turret singled it out as unusual for a single-engine fighter. It had been conceived very much as a bomber formation destroyer at a time when the concept of fighter-escorted bombers attacking Britain had not been foreseen. Whilst conventional wisdom might have us believe that this was a hopelessly outmoded design concept for modern air fighting, it was certainly not as ill-conceived as has subsequently been suggested. Such suggestions inevitably arise from its poor performance during the daylight fighting of the Battle of Britain where it proved to be no match against enemy fighters and the tactics then being employed by both sides. Certainly, it lacked forward-firing guns and had to be manoeuvred into a fighting position by its pilot in order for its gunner to get a bead on his quarry. However, it was never designed for fighter-on-fighter combat. Consequently, its daylight participation in the Battle of Britain had to be curtailed in light of its poor performance against single-seat fighters, but there is no truth in the story that German fighter pilots, having first mistaken them for Hurricanes, learned how to deal with the turreted fighters as a consequence.

BELOW With its Boulton Paul power-operated gun turret the Defiant could pack a formidable punch, but it very quickly became obsolete when faced with the speed and tactics of Luftwaffe fighter aircraft in the Battle of Britain. (WW2 Images)

Technical data	
Dimensions	Span 39ft 4in, length 35ft 4in.
Power plant	Rolls-Royce Merlin III delivering 1,030hp at 16,250ft.
Maximum speed	304mph.
Initial rate of climb	2,120ft/min.
Service ceiling	30,200ft.
Armament	Four .303 Browning machine guns in a power-operated turret.

Bristol Blenheim Mk IF

Between 1934 and the spring of 1935 the Bristol Aeroplane Company built a fast civil transport aircraft of advanced design to the order of Lord Rothermere, a private customer. When this proved faster than most contemporary military aircraft, Lord Rothermere presented the aircraft to the nation.

From Rothermere's aircraft the manufacturers developed the Blenheim Mk I bomber, of which the prototype first flew in June 1936. At the request of the Air Ministry, the Bristol Aeroplane Company also developed a fighter version, the Blenheim Mk IF. During the Battle of Britain the Blenheim Mk IF was used as both a day and night fighter. As a day fighter it had limited value unless used against unescorted bombers although, by 1940, it was unable to catch the German bombers then in use if engaged in a tail chase. The Blenheim could not be pitched against escorted raids of the nature being experienced, for example, in the 11 Group area at the height of the battle and was clearly no match for either the Me 109 or Me 110.

ABOVE The Bristol Blenheim Mk IF was generally not employed as a front-line fighter that would routinely have been scrambled to deal with daylight raids during the Battle of Britain as its size, speed and armament did not best suit it for combat with German fighters. It also had difficulty catching German bombers in a tail chase. Nevertheless, it was one of RAF Fighter Command's fighters of the battle, albeit employed by only six squadrons. It was often used in either the night-fighting role or else in carrying out Sector or convoy patrols. (Shown here is the sole restored and airworthy example now operated by the Aircraft Restoration Company at Duxford.) (Samantha Lou Photography)

Technical data

Dimensions	Span 56ft 4in, length 39ft 9in.
Power plants	Two Bristol Mercury VIII engines, each delivering 840hp.
Maximum speed	260mph.
Initial rate of climb	1,540ft/min.
Service ceiling	27,280ft.
Armament	Four .303 Browning machine guns in ventral pack plus one in port wing. One Vickers K gun in dorsal turret.

Bristol Beaufighter Mk IF

Like the Blenheim, the Beaufighter started out as a private-venture design but as a twin-engine, cannon-armed fighter, although by July 1938 the Air Ministry had decided to adopt the type and it immediately went into production. By the end of 1940 only 110 had been built. The aircraft entered service in August 1940 and although originally intended as a day fighter it quickly became apparent

BELOW The Bristol Beaufighter Mk IF was only just coming into service towards the end of the Battle of Britain, with just over a hundred having been built and delivered to the RAF by the end of 1940. Primarily, its success with Fighter Command would come as a night fighter when the Battle of Britain evolved into the Blitz. Here, a Beaufighter is seen under construction in the Bristol Aeroplane Company's factory at Filton, north of Bristol.

it was more suited to the night-fighter role, largely because of ample space in which to fit Airborne Interception (AI) radar. Like other cannon-equipped RAF aircraft that were put in service around this time, the weapon proved troublesome, with feed mechanism issues and also vibration in the mountings causing inaccurate firing. Once these problems were ironed out the Beaufighter became an impressive night fighter. It was only just coming on stream with a few Fighter Command squadrons and units as the Battle of Britain drew towards its zenith, with the first (day) sortie being carried out by 29 Squadron on 18 September. Successful engagements had taken place by the end of September, although by this time it was being employed exclusively in the night-fighting role.

Technical data	
Dimensions	Span 57ft 10in, length 41ft 8in.
Power plants	Two Bristol Hercules IIIs each delivering 1,375hp.
Maximum speed	320mph.
Initial rate of climb	1,600ft/min.
Armament	Four 20mm Hispano cannon.

BELOW The Gloster Gladiator Mk II was already outdated by the start of the Battle of Britain, but a few gave valuable service in providing fighter cover for the naval dockyards at Plymouth, operating from a grass strip that was unsuitable for Spitfires and Hurricanes. This far west there was no likelihood of encountering the Messerschmitt 109 fighter. *(Andy Thomas)*

Gloster Gladiator Mk II

The Gladiator biplane single-seat fighter was developed by the Gloster Aircraft Company as a private venture, but was found to conform to Air Ministry Specification F7/30 of 1930, which was a requirement for a new RAF fighter. The prototype first flew in September 1934. Production models were built to an amended specification drawn up in 1935 and the type entered service as a front-line fighter with the RAF.

During the Battle of Britain the Gladiator, although obsolescent, continued to be used by one flight of 247 Squadron operating from a rudimentary airstrip at Roborough, near Plymouth, which was unsuitable for Spitfires or Hurricanes. From here, fighter protection could be provided for the Royal Navy Dockyard and on 28 October, for example, Flg Off R.A. Winter intercepted a He 111 over Plymouth.

In general terms the Gladiator was not suited for modern air combat against fighters like the Me 109, but it had already given a good account of itself in the Norwegian Campaign against He 111, Ju 88 and Me 110 types. The aircraft was the last of the RAF's biplane fighters.

Technical data	
Dimensions	Span 32ft 3in, length 27ft 5in.
Power plant	Bristol Mercury IX delivering 840hp.
Maximum speed	253mph.
Initial rate of climb	2,300ft/min.
Service ceiling	33,000ft.
Armament	Four .303 Browning machine guns.

Hawker Hurricane Mk I

The Hurricane low-wing monoplane single-seat fighter was designed by Sydney Camm and developed by Hawker Aircraft as a private venture. At one time Hawkers proposed to modify the aircraft in order to conform to Air Ministry Specification F5/34 of 1934. Eventually the Air Ministry drew up an amended specification, which preserved the salient features of the original design. The prototype first flew on 6 November 1935 and became the most numerous fighter in RAF service during the Battle of Britain. The airframe was rugged and could take considerable punishment and also afforded an excellent gun platform for its battery of eight .303 machine guns.

Technical data

Technical data	
Dimensions	Span 40ft, length 31ft 5in.
Power plant	Rolls-Royce Merlin III delivering 1,030hp at 16,250ft.
Maximum Speed	325mph.
Initial rate of climb	2,420ft/min.
Service ceiling	34,000ft.
Armament	Eight .303 Browning machine guns.

Supermarine Spitfire Mk I

The Spitfire, a low-wing monoplane single-seat fighter, manufactured by the Supermarine division of Vickers-Armstrong, was developed from the record-breaking seaplanes built by Supermarine for the international Schneider Trophy contest. The designer was R.J. Mitchell and his first design for a high-performance fighter with retractable undercarriage and enclosed cockpit met Air Ministry Specification F5/34, but a new specification was drawn up after Mitchell decided he wanted to adopt a more advanced power unit. The prototype first flew on 5 March 1936 and after the Spitfire went into production it first entered service with the RAF in 1938. Together with the Hurricane, the Spitfire formed the backbone of RAF Fighter Command's defensive force during the Battle of Britain.

Technical data

Technical data	
Dimensions	Span 36ft 10in, length 29ft 11in.
Power plant	Rolls-Royce Merlin III delivering 1,030hp at 16,250ft.
Maximum speed	355mph.
Initial rate of climb	2,530ft/min.
Armament	Eight .303 Browning machine guns (the Mk IB was equipped with two 20mm Hispano cannon).

ABOVE The Hawker Hurricane Mk I proved itself a robust and reliable fighter workhorse during the Battle of Britain. It could take considerable punishment, was a stable gun platform and its wide-track landing gear made it easier to land than its contemporary the Spitfire. It could out-turn the Messerschmitt 109 and also accounted for the greatest share of victories over enemy aircraft when compared against the RAF's other fighters of the day.

BELOW The Supermarine Spitfire Mk I was arguably the darling of both RAF Fighter Command and the British public during the period of the Battle of Britain. Such was its reputation among the Luftwaffe, for example, that the German fighter ace Oberst Adolf Galland is said to have asked of Reichsmarschall Herman Göring 'Give me a squadron of Spitfires', while German aircrews shot down during the Battle of Britain adopted a certain 'Spitfire snobbery' in wanting to believe they had been shot down by Spitfires rather than any 'lesser' types.

ABOVE The Dornier 17-Z was one of the principal bomber types operated by the Luftwaffe during the Battle of Britain, although it was a medium rather than heavy bomber. It could carry a bomb load of either twenty 50kg bombs or four 250kg bombs stowed in internal racks. (In 2013 the RAF Museum salvaged the only known example of the Dornier 17-Z from near the Goodwin Sands in the English Channel.)

The opposition – Luftwaffe

The main types used by the Luftwaffe during air operations against Britain in 1940 were the Dornier 17-Z, Heinkel 111, Junkers 88 (bombers); and the Messerschmitt 109 and Messerschmitt 110 (fighters). Although there were a number of sub-variants of each type, leading particulars of the principal versions are shown below. Although it is difficult to make objective comparisons between the aircraft types of the opposing air forces, it was certainly the case that in different circumstances and in the hands of skilful pilots and crew, even the poorest performers could sometimes have unexpected successes against more capable or superior aircraft. A case in point, perhaps, is the performance of the Gloster Gladiator in Norway earlier in 1940, or the shooting down of a Hurricane by a cumbersome He 59 seaplane

in August. Certainly, RAF fighter pilots could not afford to be complacent when tackling even the lightest armed or least agile of aircraft.

Dornier 17-Z

The Dornier 17 high-wing monoplane was intended by Dornier-Werke GmbH as a commercial aircraft, but a demonstration of the prototype in the autumn of 1934 brought no orders from Lufthansa. A bomber version first flew in 1935 and was developed for the Luftwaffe, achieving some success in the Spanish Civil War. Eight variants of the Dornier 17 (in addition to two variants of a type known as the Dornier 215) were used in 1940 as bombers or reconnaissance aircraft. The bomber versions of the Dornier 17 were types in the 'Z' series, with the reconnaissance version being the 'P'. The slim fuselage of the Dornier 17 earned it the nickname 'Flying Pencil'. The type, as a bomber, served on through the Blitz into 1941 although by then it had been pretty much phased out. It carried a crew of four.

Technical data (Dornier 17-Z2)	
Dimensions	Span 59ft, length 53ft 5.5in.
Power plants	Two Bramo-Fafnir 323 P radial engines, each delivering 1,000hp.
Maximum speed	265mph with normal load.
Service ceiling	26,740ft.
Range	Normal, 745 miles (with overload tank 1,860 miles).
Bomb load	Normal, 2,200lb (with maximum fuel, 1,100lb).

LEFT Another Dornier 17 variant was the Dornier 17-P, which operated as a photo-reconnaissance type. The slim lines clearly visible in the 'P' model reveal exactly why it became known as the 'Flying Pencil'. (The Luftwaffe also operated a small number of the Dornier 215 aircraft. Outwardly, the type was broadly similar to the Dornier 17-Z but was equipped with in-line Daimler-Benz DB 601-A engines and intended as an export model.) (Chris Goss)

RIGHT Both the 'P' and 'H' variants of the Heinkel 111, one of the most widely used of the Luftwaffe's bombers, were flown during the Battle of Britain. The He 111-P models were fitted with the Daimler-Benz DB 601-A engines, the improved He 111-H version with the Junkers Jumo 211 engines. Shown here is an He 111-P aircraft. *(Chris Goss)*

Heinkel 111

The He 111 was a low-wing twin-engine monoplane long-range bomber with a crew of four. It was developed by Ernst Heinkel Flugzeugwerke GmbH and first flew in 1935 before entering service with the expanding Luftwaffe in 1937. Early models of the type took part in the Spanish Civil War and it became one of the mainstay bombers across all Luftwaffe air fleets during 1940. Nine different variants were used during 1940, including a version that operated with the Daimler-Benz DB601 engine. The aircraft proved too slow and too lightly armed to escape heavy losses during daylight action, although it became a successful night bomber. For simplicity, the technical data (below) selects just one of the models commonly in use, the He 111H-3.

Technical data	
Dimensions	Span 74ft 3in, length 54ft 6in.
Power plants	Two Junkers Jumo 211 D-1 engines, each delivering 1,200hp.
Maximum speed	255mph with normal load.
Service ceiling	25,500ft.
Range	Normal, 1,540 miles; with additional fuel, 2,640 miles.
Bomb load	Maximum 4,400lb (with increased fuel load 2,134lb).

Junkers 88

The Junkers 88 low-wing monoplane first flew in December 1936 with the manufacturers, Junkers Flugzeug und Motorenwerke AG, intending it as a high performance bomber with a turn of speed that would enable it to dispense with any fighter escort. Hopes of outdistancing

any pursuing fighters were dashed, though, with the advent of the Spitfire and Hurricane. Yet, it remained a fast and agile aircraft and was considered the hardest of the German bombers to catch and shoot down. Two variants, the A-1 and A-5, were used in 1940. They carried a crew of four.

BELOW Of all Luftwaffe medium-bomber types in service during the Battle of Britain the Junkers 88 was the fastest and sleekest, and was capable of a relatively high performance when compared against other German bombers. Like the He 111, the Ju 88 remained in service throughout the war – albeit in the form of updated models and types. *(Chris Goss)*

Technical data (Junkers 88A-1)	
Dimensions	Span, 59ft 10.75in (increased in the A-5 to 65ft 10.5in) length, 47ft 1in.
Power plants	Two Junkers Jumo 211B-1 engines, each delivering 1,200hp.
Maximum speed	286mph.
Service ceiling	26,500ft.
Range	Normal, 1,553 miles.
Bomb load	Normal, 3,968lb; maximum 5,510lb.

(Note: *all German bomber types in use during the Battle of Britain carried 7.92mm MG 15 defensive machine guns, flexibly mounted. Generally, four or five weapons were carried as standard but a desire for greater defence led to field modifications resulting in individual peculiarities. Some examples of the Dornier 17-Z during the Battle of Britain carried a fixed 20mm MG FF cannon in the nose for ground attack purposes.*)

Junkers 87

The crank-winged and angular Junkers 87 Stuka dive-bomber was the most recognisable Luftwaffe type used in the Battle of Britain and was deployed in its role as dive-bomber against Channel shipping and south coast targets. It first flew in 1935 and was introduced into service in 1937. In Poland, France and the Low Countries it was used to devastating effect but its successes in the Battle of Britain were limited and offset by heavy losses. It was little used after 18 August 1940. As a pinpoint weapon, though, it was extremely accurate and effective. It carried a

crew of two; three variants were in use during the Battle of Britain – the B-1, B-2 and the R.

Technical data	
Dimensions	Span 45ft 4in, length 36ft 5in.
Power plant	Junkers Jumo 211-D, delivering 1,150hp.
Maximum speed	232mph.
Service ceiling	24,500ft.
Range	Junkers 87B-1 and B-2, 370 miles with normal bomb load; Junkers 87R, 875 miles with reduced bomb load and additional fuel in supplementary tanks.
Bomb load	Normal, 990 to 1,100lb, maximum at short ranges, 2,200lb; Junkers 87R at extreme range, 550lb.
Armament	One rearward-firing flexible 7.92mm MG 15 machine gun, two fixed forward-firing 7.92mm MG 17 machine guns.

Messerschmitt 109E

This was the principal Luftwaffe fighter of the Battle of Britain and was first flown in 1935 before entering service and seeing action in the Spanish Civil War in the B and C types. A number of variants of the E model were used in 1940, including the E-1, E-3 etc.

One of the chief assets of the type was its fuel injection system, which could give an advantage by being able to go into a steep dive without loss of power. However, the aircraft was less robust and more difficult to handle than the Spitfire or Hurricane and prone to landing mishaps. As an escort fighter the Me 109 had a theoretical radius of just over 200 miles at a cruising speed of 298mph, but this was greatly reduced by the distance covered in making rendezvous with the bombers and in taking evasive action etc. Its fighting time over Britain was thus very limited and a considerable number of Me 109s were lost in the Channel or just managed to make France running short of fuel. Contrary to popular belief the Me 109E did not have a cannon firing through the centre of the propeller boss. The aircraft was also modified for use as a fighter-bomber later in 1940 with a centrally mounted single 250kg bomb.

Technical data (Me 109E-3)	
Dimemsions	Span 32ft 4in, length 26ft 8in.
Power plant	Daimler-Benz DB601A engine delivering 1,150hp (direct fuel injection).
Maximum speed	354mph.
Initial rate of climb	3,100ft/min.
Service ceiling	36,000ft.
Armament	(Variable through different models) Two x 7.92mm MG 17 machine guns above the engine and one in each wing, or two 7.92mm MG 17 machine guns above the engine and one 20mm MG FF cannon in each wing.

ABOVE The Messerschmitt 109-E model was operated in the form of several sub-variants during the Battle of Britain and was the Luftwaffe's principal fighter. In the hands of a capable and experienced pilot it was a formidable opponent for RAF Fighter Command and was responsible for most RAF losses during the battle. However, it was hampered through lack of range and thus only able to loiter over mainland Britain for a very short period before being forced to return across the English Channel. A number of Me 109s only just made it to the French coast before finally running out of fuel and an even greater number were lost in the Channel itself. *(Chris Goss)*

Messerschmitt 110

The Me 110 low-wing two-seat monoplane was intended as a long-range escort fighter and built by Messerschmitt AG. During the Battle of Britain it was outmanoeuvred with ease by the Spitfire and Hurricane and its value was thus limited. However, it had a powerful punch in the nose with two closely spaced 20mm cannon and four 7.92mm machine guns. Two types, the C and D, were used during the Battle of Britain with the D variant being deployed as a fast fighter-bomber where it achieved some successes. It was also used in the photo-reconnaissance role. It carried one rearward-firing 7.92mm machine gun operated by a wireless operator/air gunner.

BELOW The Messerschmitt 110 was employed in both the C and D variants during the Battle of Britain, with the type known as the *'Zerstorer'* (Destroyer). Certainly, the closely grouped nose armament of two 20mm cannon and four 7.92mm machine guns packed a powerful punch, but it proved no match against the more manoeuvrable Spitfire and Hurricane and was not a combat success, suffering a high level of operational losses. *(Chris Goss)*

Technical data	
Dimensions	Span 53ft 5in, length 40ft 4in.
Power plants	Two Daimler Benz DB601-A or 601-N engines, each delivering around 1,100hp.
Maximum speed	340mph.
Initial rate of climb	2,120ft per minute.
Service ceiling	32,000ft.
Armament	Four 7.92mm MG 17 machine guns and two 20mm MG FF cannon firing forward and one 7.92mm MG 15 flexible machine gun in dorsal position.

Driven more by a patriotic desire to help the war effort than having any realistic effect on the pace of Spitfire production, the Spitfire Fund of 1940 was nonetheless a significant feature of the Battle of Britain. Of course, the real shortages for RAF Fighter Command during the Battle of Britain rested with pilots and aircrew rather than with the production and supply of fighters, or in paying for them. Nevertheless, the Spitfire had caught the imagination of the British public (as well as Commonwealth and ex-patriate communities overseas) and the government encouraged the implementation of community-based 'Spitfire Funds'. These comprised locally organised funds, based on cities, towns and villages, as well as those set up by companies and organisations. Fund-raising efforts became common and the Ministry of Aircraft Production (MAP) helpfully provided a price list of some of the Spitfire's major components, along with a brief summation:

'Here is an early costing of a Spitfire, which those who take the trouble to add up will find amounts to a sum considerably in excess of £5,000. But then it has been agreed that that sum should be the share of the voluntary contributor, and enable him to name the machine.

Engine:	£2,000 – 0 – 0
Fuselage:	£2,500 – 0 – 0
Wings:	£1,800 – 0 – 0
Undercarriage:	£800 – 0 – 0
Guns:	£800 – 0 – 0
Airscrew:	£350 – 0 – 0
Tail:	£500 – 0 – 0
Petrol tank (top):	£40 – 0 – 0
Petrol tank (bottom):	£25 – 0 – 0
Oil tank:	£25 – 0 – 0
Compass:	£5 – 0 – 0
Clock:	£2 – 10 – 0
Thermometer:	£1 – 1 – 0
Sparking plug:	£0 – 8 – 0
Rivet:	£0 – 0 – 6d

(Note: *it is sobering to note that at the time of going to press a 1940 Spitfire Mk I was on the open market for auction with an estimated price tag of £2.5 million.*)

Whilst there were a few generous individual donors, the majority of what became known as Presentation Spitfires came from towns and cities (and sometimes villages) around Britain. A case in point was the four Spitfires given by the people of Hendon following on from that municipal borough's 'Four Fighter Fund'. By

BELOW The public were encouraged during 1940 to donate to their local 'Spitfire Fund' with the residents of Hendon in north-west London having a rather more ambitious four-fighter fund. Savings cards were introduced with 'savers' able to add stamps to their cards. On filling the entire card the owner was awarded a colourful Stamp of Honour.

BELOW Lapel brooches of the Spitfire were also sold to raise funds.

and large, however, the finished and delivered Presentation Spitfires tended to be coming on stream with the RAF very much towards the end of 1940 and into 1941, notwithstanding the fact that the funds were being set up during the period of the Battle of Britain. Many of those fund-raising efforts revolved around the public display of shot-down enemy aircraft that were taken around the country for exhibition. Those coming to view these spoils of war were either required to pay to see them, or else collecting tins were rattled. In some cases it was possible to sit in the cockpit. The going rate for such a 'Messerschmitt experience' was usually 6d, although it would have needed an awful lot of sixpences to get to the required £5,000!

The dummy Hurricane

Rather less glamorous than the Presentation Spitfire was the dummy Hurricane. These were full-size wood and fabric mock-ups of Hurricanes that were designed for realism and to place on what were decoy airfields situated near to established RAF fighter stations.

In November 1939 Messrs Green Brothers of Hailsham in East Sussex were given an order by the Air Ministry to build over 100 dummy Hurricanes. Green Brothers were specialist garden furniture manufacturers and this was just one of the war-work tasks that factories hitherto engaged on non-essential production were detailed to undertake. These 'Hurricanes' were built in kit form and transported from the Hailsham factory to various locations and placed on decoy airfields. For example, in March 1940 a number were taken to a site at Gumber, near Slindon in West Sussex, which was intended as a decoy airfield for the nearby RAF stations at Tangmere and Ford.

Whilst the effectiveness or otherwise of these dummy fighters remains open to some doubt, they would almost certainly have passed for the real thing from the air. Quite apart from the contract to manufacture and supply a large number of these dummies, Green Brothers were also kept busy repairing damaged examples. However, it is probable that such damage was more likely occasioned by high winds or general wear and tear than to any attention from the enemy.

ABOVE Additionally, shot-down German aircraft were displayed in towns and cities around the country. Here, the good folk of Hendon have paid their 6d to view a Messerschmitt 110 that had been brought down in Kent on 15 August 1940 after a raid on RAF Croydon, Surrey. The sum raised by those seen in this picture would have amounted to 12 shillings – still a long way to go to achieve the requisite £5,000 to purchase a Presentation Spitfire! However, Hendon ultimately achieved their goal and presented four Spitfires to the RAF.

BELOW Perhaps the most unusual 'participant' in the Battle of Britain, the dummy or decoy Hurricane, was a full-sized model of the aircraft that quite closely resembled the original. It was intended that these pretend aircraft be placed at decoy airfields with the purpose of luring away the Luftwaffe from attacking nearby real aerodromes. Their success was probably limited, although their construction and repair by a garden furniture manufacturer was among the most unusual war work allocated to a factory whose peacetime business had fallen off.

Armour

An important and life-saving feature on the
Spitfire and Hurricane during the Battle of
Britain was the addition of armour protection.

Weight considerations obviously prevented
an aircraft being completely armoured and what
armour could be allowed had to be put where
it was the most effective. In the British fighters
it was mainly designed to shield the pilots
themselves as they were the most valuable item
as well as the most difficult to replace. In the
Hurricane the fuel header tank was protected
from the front but not from the stern and there
was armour for the wing tanks. The pilot was

protected against stern attacks by armour
plating behind the seat and directly behind his
head. He also had a thick laminated glass bullet-
proof windscreen in front of him. The Spitfire
pilot had similar personal security, but there was
protection for the fuel tank in front of his feet.

When the Germans fitted armour it was
not always easy to make the best use of it in
an aircraft not designed to take it. In the case
of the Me 109 the pilot sat on a seat-shaped
fuel tank and the armour had to be placed
well back behind the pilot. This left the pilot
and tank vulnerable to deflection shots when
bullets could bypass the armour and ignite
the tank or hit the pilot. Fuel tank armour was
more important to the Germans than to the
British because of the RAF's more effective
incendiary ammunition.

Camouflage and markings

Whilst the subject of camouflage
and markings (and in particular its
application to specific aircraft and squadrons)
is dealt with in countless specialist publications
it is relevant, here, to look at the generality
of the standard camouflage schemes and
patterns applied to the fighters of the Battle
of Britain period along with the application of
national markings, code letters and
serial numbers.

The question of camouflage and markings
on RAF aircraft of the period is a vastly
complex one, with a myriad variations on a
theme. These variations were often subject to
interpretation at factory, maintenance unit or
squadron level, thus providing for particular
oddities within what were supposedly rigidly
laid down schemes. However, and whilst the
camouflage patterns applied to RAF aircraft
might at first sight appear quite random,
they were certainly very far from being so.
All conformed to strict rules. For the most
part these owed their origins to research
programmes carried out under the supervision
of the Chemistry Department of the Royal
Aircraft Establishment from 1933 onwards,
and in what were ever developing and evolving
camouflage patterns.

Broadly speaking, the upper camouflage

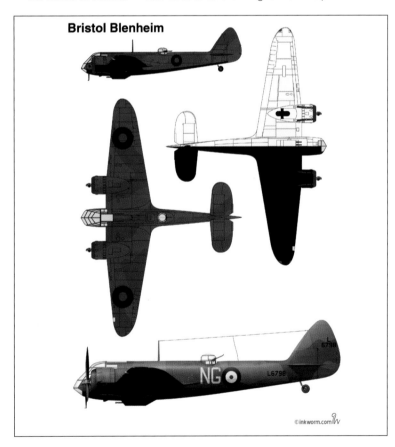

Bristol Blenheim

©inkworm.com

Boulton Paul Defiant

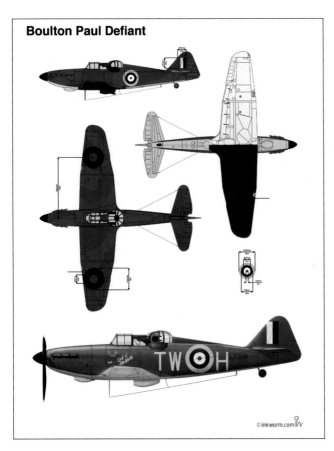

Gloster Gladiator

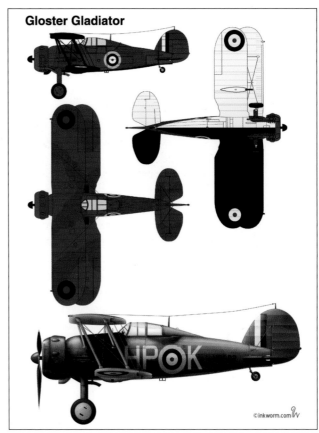

Hawker Hurricane

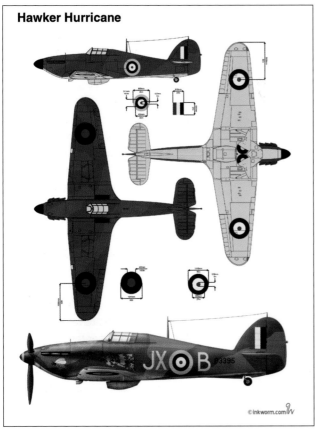

Supermarine Spitfire

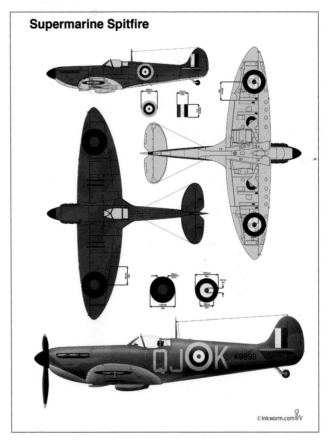

©inkworm.com

colours on RAF fighter aircraft in 1940 were in Dark Earth and Dark Green, applied in two distinct patterns – 'A' Scheme and 'B' Scheme. The 'B' Scheme was simply a mirror pattern of the 'A' Scheme, and of these two schemes there is evidence that they were applied alternately on airframes coming from the production line and depending upon whether the RAF serial ended in an odd or an even number. For the Hurricane it was generally accepted that the 'A' Scheme would be applied to aircraft with even serials and 'B' to odd ones. With the Spitfire, however, this seems to have been reversed.

The system for camouflaging and marking aircraft was affirmed by the Air Ministry Order No 154/39 with a supplement, No A.298/39, issued on 27 April 1939. A number of Air Ministry Orders (AMOs) followed throughout the 1940 period giving a variety of instructions and orders as to changes, for example, in national markings, code letters etc.

The principle of camouflage was that it should break up the outline of the aircraft on the ground and render them less visible. For this reason, the varying 'A' and 'B' Schemes were important in that this potentially made a group of aircraft together on the ground less obvious due to the non-uniformity of the camouflage schemes.

Underside markings of the period were in variations of what was called Sky Type 'S' and Duck Egg Blue. Variations included a Duck Egg Green and Eau-de-Nil, with differences again caused by lack of stocks of the correct shades, and interpretation. Again, these colours had been developed to render the aircraft less visible from beneath, and against what might have been considered an average sky. Earlier underside markings in 1940 had included a half black/half white scheme, developed largely to aid instant recognition from the ground of RAF fighters by anti-aircraft gunners and Observer Corps personnel. This scheme had been phased out by the start of the official period of the Battle of Britain, but had been partly reintroduced again in the winter of 1940.

The paint colours applied to RAF aircraft at this time had all been laid down by the Air Ministry Directorate of Technical Development (DTD) and, as such, were each given specific DTD reference numbers.

As previously alluded to, the subject of camouflage and markings on RAF fighters during the Battle of Britain is a complex one. It is best addressed here by the illustration of representative schemes on RAF fighters of the period.

Rolls-Royce Merlin engine

It has often been said that the Merlin engine was the engine that won the Second World War, and while that might be open to some question there can be no such debate when it comes to the Battle of Britain. Without a doubt the Merlin was the engine that won that battle – powering as it did the Spitfire, Hurricane and Defiant. Of course, there were two other engine types used on RAF Fighter Command aircraft during 1940, the Bristol Mercury (Blenheim and Gladiator) and the Bristol Hercules (Beaufighter). However, the overall significance of these types, and of these engines, is relatively insignificant when compared to the Rolls-Royce Merlin III, which powered all three of the RAF's primary fighters in 1940.

The Merlin was a liquid-cooled V-12 piston aero engine, of 27-litre (1,650cu in) capacity. Rolls-Royce at first designed and built an engine that was initially known as the PV-12, although this would later evolve and develop into the classic aero engine which today is as world-famous as the aircraft it would later equip. The first operational aircraft to enter

BELOW The Rolls-Royce Merlin III was the main engine in use by RAF Fighter Command aircraft during 1940, powering the Hurricane, Spitfire and Defiant. Here, a Merlin III is seen installed in a Spitfire Mk I at Duxford in 2013. In this photograph the HT leads have been disconnected from the sparking plugs.

service using the engine were the Fairey Battle, Hawker Hurricane and Supermarine Spitfire, and the Boulton Paul Defiant.

In the early 1930s Rolls-Royce had started to plan its future aero engine development programme and realised that there was a need for an engine larger than their 21-litre (1,296cu in) Kestrel that had been used with great success in a number of 1930s aircraft. Consequently, work was started on a new 1,100hp aero engine designated the PV-12, with PV standing for 'private venture' because the company received no government funding for work on the project. The PV-12 was first run on 15 October 1933 and first flew in a Hawker Hart biplane (K3036) on 21 February 1935. The engine originally used the evaporative cooling system then in vogue, but this proved unreliable and when supplies of ethylene glycol from the United States became available the engine was adapted to use a conventional liquid cooling system.

In 1935 the Air Ministry issued specification F10/35 for new fighter aircraft with a minimum airspeed of 310mph (500km/h). Fortunately, two designs had been developed: the Supermarine Spitfire and the Hawker Hurricane, although the latter was designed in response to another specification, F36/34. Both were designed around the PV-12 instead of the Kestrel, and were the only contemporary British fighters to have been so developed. Production contracts for both aircraft were placed in 1936 and further development of the PV-12 was given top priority as well as essential government funding. Following the company convention of naming its piston aero engines after birds of prey, Rolls-Royce named this engine the Merlin.

Initially the new engine was plagued with problems, such as failure of the accessory gear trains and the coolant jackets. Several different construction methods were tried before the basic design of the Merlin was set. Early production Merlins were also unreliable and common problems were cylinder heads cracking, coolant leaks, and excessive wear to the camshafts and crankshaft main bearings. These were problems that still beset operational engines in 1940. However, it was in-service experience and operational demands and requirements that would lead to ongoing developments of the Merlin engine to the extent

that later variants were a far different, more reliable and much improved animal than were the early models such as the Merlin III as used in the Battle of Britain.

This engine replaced 'ramp' cylinder heads with parallel pattern heads (valves parallel to the cylinder) scaled up from the Kestrel engine, with its 400hr flight endurance tests carried out at the Royal Aircraft Establishment in July 1937 and the acceptance test completed on 22 September 1937. The engine was first widely delivered as the 1,030hp (770kW) Merlin II in 1938, and production was quickly stepped up as war clouds loomed.

The Merlin II and III series were the first main production versions of the engine type, but the Merlin III was manufactured with a 'universal' propeller shaft, allowing either de Havilland or Rotol manufactured propellers to be used, with

ABOVE A top view of the same Merlin III showing to advantage both banks of the mighty 'V' block 12-cylinder engine.

the first Merlin III being delivered to the RAF on 1 July 1938.

Mention of the Merlin engine would be incomplete without a description of the fuel used to power these engines. From late 1939, 100-octane fuel became available from the United States, the West Indies, Persia and also domestically, and the Merlin IIs and IIIs were adapted to run on this new fuel using an increased boost pressure of +12lb/sq in (183 kPa; 1.85 atm). Small modifications were made to the engines, which were now capable of generating 1,310hp (977kW) at 9,000ft (2,700m) whilst running at 3,000rpm. This increased boost was available for a maximum of 5 minutes, and if the pilot resorted to emergency boost he had to report this on landing and have it noted in the engine log book. Using +12lb/sq in (183 kPa; 1.85 atm) of boost was considered a 'definite overload condition on the engine' and the engineering officer was subsequently required to examine the engine and reset the throttle gate.

In terms of day-to-day maintenance and overhaul of engines, the airman fitter assigned to each aircraft had effective charge of 'his' engine. However, Rolls-Royce technical staff and engineers were on hand to resolve issues in the field, as it were, although any more major work and engineering that was required would result in them being returned to Rolls-Royce at Derby for attention.

Incredibly, perhaps, Merlin engines remain in RAF service today with the Battle of Britain Memorial Flight (BBMF) and are thus the longest-serving engine in the air force, having been fully in continuous use for well over 75 years. As an engine, however, it is true to say that the Rolls-Royce Merlin III was significantly, and quite naturally, far less reliable than the later marks of Merlin, and it is later marks that power the RAF's BBMF aircraft. However, as the Spitfire Mk IIa came on stream later in the Battle of Britain, these were already being fitted with the improved Rolls-Royce Merlin XII engine.

The airscrew problem

When the first Spitfires and Hurricanes were delivered to the RAF in 1938 they were factory fitted with two-blade fixed-pitch Watts wooden propellers, but the later production Hurricane and Spitfire Mk Is were fitted with three-blade de Havilland propellers. This was a vast improvement over the fixed-pitch two-bladers.

By January 1939 all Hurricane aircraft coming off the production line had the three-blade metal de Havilland two-pitch metal propeller, the Spitfires also being similarly equipped. The de Havilland unit had two settings – fine for take-off and coarse for top performance. It worked well until a pilot forgot to select fine pitch for take-off, which was a cardinal error, particularly for many nascent Spitfire pilots of the period – notably Douglas Bader who had just such an incident at RAF Duxford in early 1940. In Paul Brickhill's biography of Bader, *Reach for the Sky,* the story is told:

'Quickly he strapped his straps and pressed the starter button; the still hot engine fired instantly and he was still winding his trimming wheel as the plane went booming across the grass. The other two Spitfires were shooting past him, pulling away, and he sensed vaguely at first, and then with sudden certainty, that his aircraft was lagging. A quick glance at the boost gauge; the needle was quivering on 6½lb maximum power. She must be alright; but she was still bumping over the grass, curiously sluggish, running at a low stone wall on the far side of the field. The fence was rushing nearer, but she still stuck to the ground. He hauled desperately on the stick and the nose pulled

BELOW When it first entered service the Hurricane Mk I was fitted with a Rolls-Royce Merlin II engine and a fixed-pitch two-blade Watts wooden propeller. Speed, efficiency and altitude were added once these two-blade propellers began to be replaced with three-blade two-pitch metal blade propellers made by de Havilland. This photograph also shows useful detail of the Hurricane being refuelled using a process and a vehicle bowser type that remained unchanged during the Battle of Britain.

up as she lurched off at an unnatural angle, not climbing. His right hand snapped down to the undercart lever but almost in the same moment the wheels hit the stone wall and ripped away. At nearly 80mph the little fighter slewed and dipped a wing-tip into a ploughed field beyond; the nose smacked down, the tail kicked up as she nearly cartwheeled, the tail slapped down again and she slithered and bumped on her belly with a rending noise across the soft earth.

'The brain started working again and began wondering what had happened as he sat there. With everything so suddenly quiet he could hear the silence and the hot metal of the engine tinking as it cooled. Automatically his hand went out and cut the switches and then he was motionless again apart from the eyes wandering round the cockpit looking for the answer. It stared back at him – the black knob of the propeller lever on the throttle quadrant poking accusingly at him, still in the coarse position.

'His stomach turned. Oh, hell no, not that classic boob! He couldn't have. But he had. Angrily he banged the knob in.'

Quite apart from the cockpit workload issues, and setting aside its improvement over the fixed-pitch two-blade propellers, it was soon clear that the de Havilland two-pitch manually operated unit needed yet further improvement. Consequently, on 5 April the

Air Ministry asked de Havilland if it would be possible to convert the propellers to constant-speed units of the type that were already fitted to many multi-engine aircraft then in service. De Havilland were not overly impressed with the suggestion, and although they offered alternative solutions nothing further happened until 9 June 1940 when an RAF engineer officer contacted de Havilland again to ask if a propeller on one of his Spitfires could be converted to constant speeding 'without a lot of paperwork and fuss'. It could, they said, and the process of converting all of the existing units was set in motion, as well as the implementation of the constant speed unit in future production Spitfire Mk Is. However, and because of the somewhat 'irregular' manner in which this process had been put in place,

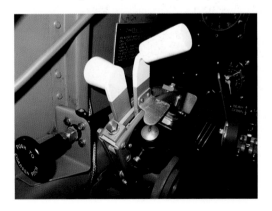

LEFT The simple in–out control knob for the two-position bracket propeller – coarse pitch pushed in and fine pitch pulled out. In this instance the control knob is seen fitted in the cockpit of a Spitfire Mk I.

ABOVE AND RIGHT Hurricane L1574 fitted with the first of the de Havilland variable-pitch two-position bracket-type propellers for trials at Brooklands, Surrey, during 1938. Here, test pilot Flt Lt George Bulman explains the finer points of the new propeller to Lord Balfour the Air Minister, as test pilots Philip G. Lucas and Flt Lt R.C. Reynell look on. (Reynell was later a Hurricane pilot in RAF Fighter Command who was killed in action on 7 September 1940.)

DE HAVILLAND HYDROMATIC PROPELLERS

NOTES FOR PILOTS AND GROUND STAFF

FOURTH EDITION

there were apparently protracted problems between the MAP and de Havilland. It is said that the company were never properly paid for the work, and legend has it that a clerk who worked for de Havilland commented: 'We shall probably never get paid for this work' to which his colleague is said to have responded 'Well, if it doesn't get done we may never live to be paid for anything.'

In-service Spitfires were all to have been converted to constant speed by 20 July by teams of de Havilland engineers working with RAF squadron fitters, and it was reported on 16 August 1940 that all Spitfires and Hurricanes in squadron service or held in storage had been converted to constant-speed units. It is recorded that the constant-speed conversions resulted in a much improved rate of climb in the Spitfire Mk I, for example, and gave that fighter a surprising extra 7,000ft of altitude. Additionally, it was noted that the new constant-speed units gave an improved manoeuvrability at altitude, a reduced take-off run and, overall, were noted to have an efficiency of 91%. It can be considered as just one of the timely factors that helped achieve RAF Fighter Command's success during the Battle of Britain.

Weaponry

Browning .303 machine gun

Throughout the First World War and into the 1920s, the mainstays of early British air service machine guns were the .303 Lewis and .303 Vickers machine guns, both of which, whilst primarily developed to be used on land, were adapted for air service.

Of course, reliability was important for both of these guns, but when fitted to early aircraft they were largely accessible to the operator who could reload them and clear any stoppages or correct any problems that might occur. As a result, with the first aircraft this combination worked. In the early to mid-1930s, however, there were huge advances in aircraft design. With this new generation of fighter aircraft, which were built to have guns that would be located in the wings, and therefore remote from the pilot, came the requirement for a new machine gun.

Not only would these guns have to be extremely reliable, as manual intervention would be impossible in the event of a problem, they would also be required to operate at a very high rate of fire, be able to cope with the conditions imposed by high altitudes, and, lastly, the difficulties created by high-speed combat manoeuvres.

The Air Ministry was aware of the recoil-operated Colt machine gun, designed by John Browning during the First World War. Indeed, they had even trialled it in 1918 whilst fitted to a Bristol Fighter. In 1924, the British firm Armstrong-Whitworth acquired the rights to manufacture it.

After the end of the First World War, however, the Air Ministry decided to investigate larger-calibre machine guns. Interestingly these tests soon established that the larger experimental .50in ammunition had little advantage over the smaller .303 ammunition then in service. With the subsequent loss of interest in the bigger-calibre weapons, attention once again returned to rifle-calibre machine guns.

In 1926 the Air Ministry ordered six guns in .303-inch calibre from Armstrong-Whitworth for tests. Delivered in 1927 and tested between 1927 and 1928, the guns performed well, although some modifications were required. Further trials were held in 1931 where two guns were fitted to an Armstrong-Whitworth Siskin aircraft. These were extremely successful with the guns firing 20,000 rounds between them with only three stoppages (two of which were caused by ammunition problems).

ABOVE The standard-fit machine gun for the Spitfire, Hurricane and Defiant was the Browning .303, which is seen here complete with belted ammunition. As the bullets fed into the gun they were separated from the individual Prideaux metal belt links and the fired cases and links were ejected from the gun.

CENTRE Belted .303in ammunition.

FAR LEFT AND LEFT Close-up of one of the gun bays in a Spitfire wing showing the installed weapon and its mounting. The top and bottom wing panels were removable for access to each gun.

ABOVE Two armourers of 312 (Czech) Squadron prepare to replenish the ammunition tanks of Hurricane L1926 with belted .303 incendiary rounds.

BELOW Chart showing .303 ball and tracer rounds, and images of packaged ammunition.

In 1928 Armstrong-Whitworth amalgamated with Vickers to become Vickers-Armstrong. With a strong pedigree of machine-gun design and manufacture through the Vickers line, the new company relinquished the manufacturing rights to the Browning design in 1932. The manufacturing rights for the gun in Great Britain and the Empire, now available after being relinquished by Vickers-Armstrong, were purchased by the Air Ministry and it was decided that the guns would be manufactured by the Birmingham Small Arms Company (BSA).

The story of British armament design and adoption is laced with unsung heroes. The eventual, successful, design and adoption of the .303in Browning machine gun can be attributed to three men: Maj H.S.V. Thompson, Capt E.S.R. Adams and a civilian, Mr P. Higson.

Thompson and Adams worked for the Ministry of Munitions; Higson for Vickers-Armstrong. Largely as a result of the work carried out by these men in 1934 it was decided to adopt the Browning (classified as the Colt MG40) as the new gun for aircraft use.

The Colt MG40 was similar in appearance to its original First World War predecessor, but had been heavily modified for British service. A further series of trials were now carried out, but this time problems were encountered. When fitted to a Gloster Gauntlet, during a sustained 100-round burst trial one gun exploded. The Browning was designed to operate with a closed bolt. This means that while ammunition remains in the gun a round is always retained in the chamber ready for firing. It was ascertained that the problem was due to the gun heating up and the chamber getting so hot that it had caused the round in the chamber to 'cook-off'. (Cooking-off, as it is called, is different to a round deliberately being fired in the chamber as the propellant reacts in a different way. During normal firing the propellant burns very quickly through its layers. When a round 'cooks off', this layered burning is replaced by a spontaneous combustion of all the propellant, thus causing an explosion with pressures far greater than the chamber is designed for, often wrecking the gun.)

For the Browning this problem was found to be peculiar to the British ammunition. The propellant used in British .303 ammunition was cordite, but the original US-manufactured guns were designed to be used with nitro-cellulose propellant, which is less prone to 'cook-off' – and when it does, with less violence. There could be no change in the choice of .303 ammunition, as its manufacture was designed around use in the Army where cordite survives better in hot and humid climates – and therefore it was better suited for use around the Empire.

A solution was badly needed. Enter another one of our unsung heroes – Maj Reginald Shepherd. Working as the Engineering Director for BSA, Shepherd cured the problem and also introduced other modifications to improve the gun.

The Browning entered service during the crucial rearmament phase of the mid-thirties. It was fitted to both of the new eight-gun fighters of the RAF, the Hurricane and Spitfire. It was also employed as defensive armament

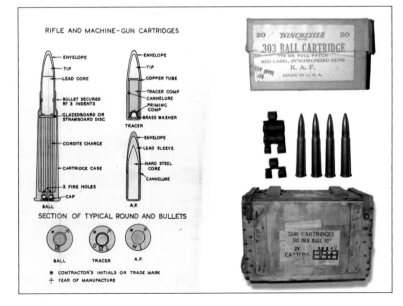

RIGHT The 'A' type turret equipped with a battery of four .303 Browning machine guns as fitted to the Boulton Paul Defiant aircraft during the Battle of Britain. Each gun had 600 rounds in individual tanks beneath each gun. The turret was hydraulically operated via its own electrically powered pump. It had two speeds of movement, the higher speed being controlled by pressing a button. The total weight of the turret, guns and ammunition (but without the gunner) stood at 590lb.

BELOW The business end. This unusual view is looking down the blast tube of a Spitfire's wing-mounted .303 machine gun (one of eight) and straight into the muzzle. *(Col Pope)*

LEFT The starboard top wing of a Spitfire Mk I showing all the upper gun access doors removed. *(Col Pope)*

BELOW To prevent drag and to stop dirt, insects and debris fouling the guns, each gun port was covered over before flight with red-doped fabric. Here the process is under way. *(Col Pope)*

BROWNING .303IN MACHINE GUN	
Operation	Gas-operated.
Cooling	Air-cooled.
Rate of fire	1,100 rounds/min.
Type of fire	Automatic.
Weight	24lb.
Manufacturer	Birmingham Small Arms Co. Colt Patent Firearms Manufacturing Co.
Muzzle velocity	2,440ft/sec.
Muzzle energy	2,300ft/lb.
Ammunition	.303 British.

on bombers and other aircraft types. The last major modification to the Browning was carried out in 1939.

No individual British, or indeed Allied, weapon can be singled out as responsible for winning the war. The overall importance of a particular weapon can, however, be measured more clearly and, to this end, the contribution made by the Browning machine gun can be recognised as significant.

As the standard wing-mounted gun in the Spitfire and Hurricane during the Battle of Britain, the Browning .303in was carried in batteries of four guns in each wing. In the case of the Defiant, a battery of four guns was carried in a power-operated turret.

Vickers Gas Operated (GO) Mk 1 or Vickers 'K' gun

The Vickers Gas Operated (GO) machine gun was designed as a replacement for the recoil-operated Vickers machine gun and the Lewis gun fitted in open positions on RAF aircraft as defensive armament. The original design of the Vickers GO was based on a French machine gun designed by a French general named Berthier. Rights for the Berthier gun had been acquired after the First World War by Vickers, who after further development and redesign marketed the new gun as the Vickers Berthier light infantry machine gun. This gun was offered as a replacement for the Lewis gun to the British Army in the 1930s, but lost out to a Czechoslovak design that after modification eventually became adopted as the Bren gun. A replacement was still required, however, for the existing Vickers and Lewis guns for air service. The Vickers Berthier had been adopted by the Indian Army, who had found the gun extremely robust and reliable.

The Air Ministry therefore decided to carry out trials with the Vickers Berthier gun during 1931. The results were promising. The gun was found to be light and easily handled. Various modifications to improve performance were proposed and resulted in a new gun known by Vickers as the 'Class K' gun. The new design produced a heavier, more robust gun with an increased rate of fire. During 1935 competitive trials were carried out. The new Vickers gun competed against four other designs. However, only two were considered suitable for further trials – the drum magazine-fed Vickers design and the French belt-fed Darne gun. As a result of the trial the RAF favoured the Vickers design as the drum-magazine was handier to manipulate, but the Air Ministry technical officers favoured the Darne gun. Due to this disagreement it was decided to stage a demonstration of both guns, which would be attended by senior officers.

The demonstration was carried out by none other than Air Marshal Hugh Dowding, who was then member of the Air Council responsible for Supply and Research. Dowding insisted on operating both guns during the trial, flying in the rear cockpit as air gunner. The trial resulted in Dowding siding with the RAF. With further modifications (including an increase in magazine capacity from 60 to 100 rounds) the new gun was adopted in service with the RAF in 1937 as the Vickers GO Gun No 1 Mk 1. During its service, the gun was also known by unofficial titles as the 'Class K'; 'Vickers K' and as the 'VGO'.

In service the gun performed well, although initial problems were encountered with the magazine and breakages of some components. Modifications were made and an endurance trial in June 1939 found the changes made to be very successful. It was noted that the minimum life of any component was 10,000 rounds with the recoil piston lasting for 14,000 rounds. The outbreak of war in September 1939 found the gun fully developed and ready for action. So well did the Vickers GO perform that only one further modification was needed during its service and this was not as a result of performance issues, but due to problems with the supply of steel. The tensioning spring in the magazine was originally made of high-quality Swedish steel. When supplies of this were cut off it was found that there was British-manufactured steel available of comparable standard. As a result the magazine was slightly modified and capacity was simply dropped from 100 rounds to 96 rounds, which then allowed the gun to function without difficulty.

The Vickers GO was eventually replaced in RAF service by the .303in Browning machine gun but was in use as a turret-operated weapon in the Bristol Blenheim during the Battle of Britain. It was also used in a number of other non-Fighter Command types during 1940 such as the Short Sunderland and Avro Anson, as well as sometimes being used for light anti-aircraft defence at some RAF stations. Many of the surplus RAF guns were re-employed with

Army units such as the Long Range Desert Group (LRDG) and the SAS where, mounted on vehicles, they continued to give sterling service.

.303IN VICKERS GAS-OPERATED (GO) GUN	
Calibre	0.303in.
Weight	20.5lb.
Muzzle velocity	2,400ft/sec.
Cyclic rate	950-1,100 rounds/min.
Maximum range	1,000yd.
Action	Gas-operated.
Ammunition feed	100-round drum magazine.
Cooling	Air.
Length	40in.
Rifling	Five-groove, left-hand twist.

Hispano 20mm cannon Mk I

The Hispano 20mm cannon was one of the most important guns used by the RAF. It was first introduced during the Battle of Britain when the Duxford-based 19 Squadron were rather unsuccessfully equipped with a number of cannon-armed Spitfires. Additionally, one or two Hurricanes of 151 Squadron were fitted experimentally with the guns. Once teething problems were ironed out, however, the gun became the standard RAF fighter armament by the end of the war.

During the 1930s designers of aircraft gun armament started to develop a new generation of larger-calibre guns. It was thought that rifle-calibre weapons did little structural damage and depended, chiefly, on killing the pilot, stopping the engine or setting fire to the fuel. Obviously, the effect would be much greater if an explosive shell could be used and it was thought that the smallest calibre that would cause sufficient damage was a gun that could fire a 20mm projectile. Based on this theory, European companies such as Oerlikon, Madsen, Hotchkiss and Solothurn produced 20mm guns for aircraft use. Another company, the French firm Hispano-Suiza, a producer of engines, had also designed a 20mm aircraft gun, specifically to be used with the Hispano-Suiza 12Y V-configured aero engine. This integral design combination incorporated the gun firing through the propeller, thus obviating the need for a gun mounted centrally on the fuselage of a single-engine aircraft to synchronise

BELOW A comparison photograph showing a single 20mm round beside a single .303 round, the latter with one of its belt linkages.

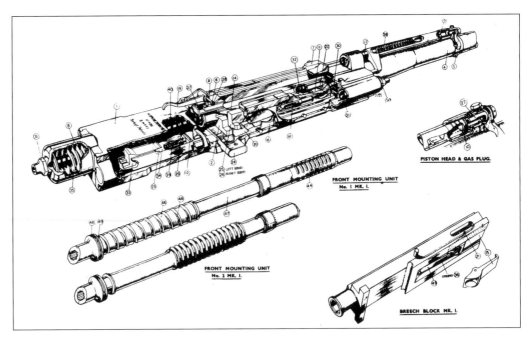

RIGHT Exploded diagram of the 20mm Hispano aircraft cannon.

RIGHT AND BELOW The tailplane of a Messerschmitt 109E, severed by the entry and explosion of a single 20mm shell, which resulted in the loss of the aircraft. Interestingly, this was actually caused by a German 20mm shell fired by another Me 109 in a 'friendly fire' episode on 30 September 1940 when Lt Herbert Schmidt of 6./JG27 was brought down and taken POW.

firing the gun through the propeller. At this time it was considered that a single gun firing a 20mm high-explosive projectile would be sufficient to destroy an aircraft – multiple wing-mounted guns were not a design consideration. British Air Ministry interest during 1935 resulted in the purchase of a French Dewoitine 510 single-engine fighter aircraft equipped with the Hispano-Suiza engine and gun combination.

As a consequence of trials with this aircraft it

BELOW An interesting comparison showing scores of .303 bullet strikes on the tail of a downed Heinkel 111, demonstrating the dramatic difference between a single 20mm hit in the right place and the (often) hundreds of hits from rifle-calibre .303in machine guns that might be required to bring down an aircraft.

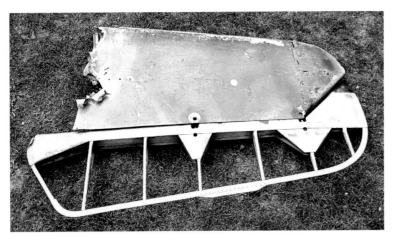

was decided to adopt the 20mm gun for British service. At this time government policy determined that weapons should not be dependent on a supply from a foreign country. As such, an arrangement was concluded with Hispano-Suiza where the guns would be manufactured by a subsidiary company in Britain. This company was named the British Manufacturing and Research Company (BMARC) and a new factory was built at Grantham, Lincolnshire. During 1938–39, and following further trials, a number of changes and improvements were incorporated into the gun design. During 1938 it had been decided to arm both Spitfire and Hurricane fighters with new the 20mm gun in multiple mountings fitted in the wings. A difficulty arose because of this requirement that would dog the early use of the Hispano in the Spitfire. The slim wings of the Spitfire required the gun to be mounted sideways, as the large 60-round drum magazine that was used to feed the ammunition to the gun was too bulky to be mounted upright. This resulted in problems with ammunition feed and spent case ejection. Difficulties were also experienced with the ammunition where some cartridge cases were prone to being 'crushed' as they were chambered, resulting in the gun's firing pin being unable to strike the cap on the base of the cartridge.

The Mk 1 version featured a pneumatic cocking mechanism that allowed the breechblock to be held in the open position, locked by a sear against the pressure of a return spring. When the firing control mechanism is operated, the spring drives the breechblock forward, which loads a round from the magazine into the chamber. The breech is then locked and the gun fired. After a round is fired, a portion of the propelling gases are vented from the barrel to a recoil piston, which then unlocks the breech block, drives the breechblock to the rear and ejects the empty case. The firing of the gun in operational use was via a pneumatically operated firing mechanism activated through a firing button on the pilot's control column. In armament terms the 20mm Hispano is classified as a cannon and fired at a rate of 650 rounds/min. The muzzle velocity was 2,880ft/sec. The overall length of the gun was 8ft 2½in and it weighed 109lb. The Mk 1 gun was fitted with a 60-round-capacity drum magazine that weighed 50lb when loaded.

OPERATIONAL FLYING WITH 20MM CANNON-EQUIPPED AIRCRAFT IN RAF FIGHTER COMMAND, 1940 – FLT LT R.L. SMITH

'Early in July 1940 I noticed a Hurricane in the hangar with tubes sticking out of each wing and I asked the Engineer Officer (Plt Off Ford) what they were. "20mm cannon" I was told. At this time cannons were dead secret, and normally would have been at the Experimental Establishments at Martlesham Heath or Boscombe Down, but this aircraft was L1750 and was marked up with the squadron code letters, DZ-Z. It had two cannon, which were cocked and fired by a very tricky procedure called "Eureka". As I had always been keen on guns, I asked why it was not being flown and was told that the other pilots considered it was a less-safe aircraft than the rest of the squadron's Hurricanes, which had eight Brownings, because it was much slower, less manoeuvrable and had guns which were highly unreliable and prone to stoppages. We were short of aircraft and the idea of flying an experimental system appealed to me. I was also now leading "B" Flight, and often the squadron, and having the leader with a slower aircraft helped the rest of the pilots keep up. I flew DZ-Z as a matter of routine and although the cannons were unreliable, due partly to their cocking systems, they improved by virtue of flying and firing them. In DZ-Z the cannon were upright in their mountings, as opposed to the Spitfires of 19 Squadron at this time who had been equipped with cannon-armed Spitfires. Their cannons were mounted on their sides and had to be withdrawn. However, by the time I had left 151 Squadron I had flown 133 sorties in a cannon Hurricane.'

Chapter Three

Fighter control

The 'Dowding System' in operation

The chain of command began with HQ RAF Fighter Command at Bentley Priory and trickled down to Group and then Sector level, with the Sector controllers guiding the RAF fighters on to the formations of enemy aircraft. Meanwhile, information was continually fed back into the integrated command and control system from both radar stations and the Observer Corps.

OPPOSITE The restored 11 Group underground Operations Room at RAF Uxbridge in Middlesex, set up exactly as the General Situation Map appeared at 11.30hrs on the morning of 15 September 1940. *(Steve Rickards)*

Essentially, there were three levels of Operations Rooms in RAF Fighter Command during 1940: Command, Group and Sector. Each had its clearly defined purpose and function within the Dowding System. This hierarchical system allowed information and orders to cascade down, but was also reliant upon information being relayed back up the system via its eyes and ears (RDF and Observer Corps) in order to allow it to function in the first place. Without that information no orders or instructions could be disseminated, and although the hierarchy of command should ordinarily dictate that the Fighter Command Operations Room should be at the top of the tree it would be more appropriate to look, first, at the point from which every direction from Command and Group Operations Rooms originated. This then fed down to Sector Operations Rooms in order that direct defensive fighter action could be ordered and controlled. The point of entry for this raw information from RDF and the Observer Corps was the Filter Room.

Filter Room

'The accuracy of filtering is of vital importance. At only one point in the whole vast network of the radar system does the information collected and forwarded by the radar chain assume a tangible form on which fighter action may be taken.'

(Air Ministry File S.47071, Minute 68)

The Filter Room at HQ Fighter Command, Bentley Priory, was arguably the most important link in the whole air defence command and control chain and this importance was succinctly set out by the Air Ministry in its minute (above), which established its vital significance. In broadly simplistic terms it was here that all incoming information was channelled (filtered) for assessment and action. (This was on a countrywide basis, except for 10 Group, which passed the information to the Western Filter Room in 10 Group's area.) The information was that which was being received from the Chain Home and Chain Home Low RDF stations, and from Observer Corps centres as well as RAF direction finding stations that were plotting the movements of friendly aircraft. The mass of incoming and ever-changing information was quickly assessed and interpreted by the Filter Room staff and passed, simultaneously, to the Command Operations Room and Group Operations Room for dissemination and appropriate orders. Upon the judgements and assessments made in the Filter Room rested decisions made by the fighter controllers for the deployment of defensive forces and its importance warrants an in-depth examination of the system.

From the beginning of the war until the end of 1939, aircraft of Fighter Command intercepted and engaged a total of 51 enemy aircraft, of which 31 were reported as destroyed. The destruction of 13 was confirmed. The comparatively light scale of hostile air activity continued in the New Year until the heavier raids began in the middle of 1940. These sporadic raids provided Fighter Command with much useful experience and gave an opportunity to improve the interception organisation. One source of constant concern was the time lag between detection of an aircraft at the radar station and the appearance of a corresponding plot on the Operations Room table. The increasing speeds of new types of aircraft made rapid plotting, filtering, identification and telling all the more important. One of the first steps taken was to move the liaison officers, who provided information on flights by Bomber, Coastal and French Air Force aircraft, from the Operations Room to the Filter Room. The work of identification could then be done simultaneously with the filtering, instead of afterwards. Responsibility for deciding the identification of raids fell on the operations controller of the Filter Room. The filtering process was still giving much trouble, and the radar officer who had previously been in charge of the Filter Room thenceforward gave his undivided attention to supervising filtering. His knowledge of the capabilities of radar stations was invaluable in sorting out erratic plots.

Complications in filtering

The number of stations reporting to the Filter Room increased steadily as the radar chain was extended along the south and east coasts. The number of plots to be dealt with multiplied as the Filter Room staff were collected and trained. Constant instruction was necessary by members of the Research Section who had moved from

Bawdsey to Headquarters Fighter Command for the purpose. Concentration of instructional effort shifted from position filtering, which was becoming better understood, to height filtering, which was even more complex. Height reports of aircraft received from two different stations sometimes conflicted widely. To strike an average between heights reported variously as 3,000ft and 17,000ft was clearly of value in interception. The filterer had to make up his mind which of the two readings was more likely to be correct. To come to some dependable conclusion he had to take into account both the range and the bearing at which the readings were taken on the aircraft by each individual station, and to assess which station had the better chance technically of being accurate. An important requirement, much stressed by the Air Staff, was the number of aircraft in a hostile formation. Skill in estimating numbers depended entirely on experience.

A further filtering complication appeared with the opening, on 1 November 1939, of the first of the low-looking CHL radar stations. The earlier stations, which were of the CH type, employed a transmission technique akin to flood-lighting. The transmission of the new CHL stations was in the shape of a searchlight beam, a property which enabled them to detect aircraft closer to the surface of the sea at longer range than could the CH. To the confusion of the filterers, positions of aircraft reported by the early CHL stations were accurate in bearing but less accurate in range, characteristics exactly opposed to those of the CH plots to which they had just accustomed themselves. It was no longer sufficient for filterers to think of plots as positions variable along the curve of a range-arc drawn from the respective radar stations. It was necessary to consider which type of station was reporting each separate plot, and to remember the possibility of inaccuracy along either a range-arc or a bearing-line drawn according to the position of the particular station. All of this had to be done at top speed.

Fortunately, the range reading of the CHLs was soon improved and the element of direct contradiction in the possibilities was removed. The CHL thus became fairly reliable in both range and bearing, but since its cover was restricted to low altitudes the CH station

remained the main source of information and the filterer's task was still confusing even to the most agile wits. The most trying factor was the ever-present need for lightning decisions and the knowledge of the grave consequences of a miscalculation. Varying probabilities of error had to be assessed in strictly limited time if filtering was to keep pace with the constant appearance of fresh plots in different tracks on the filter table.

No effort was spared to make as much information as possible clearly available. Specially shaped counters and arrows distinguished the CHL plots from the rest. Every item used was appropriately coloured, marked or shaped until the filter table was a display of bewildering variety to the uninitiated. Silent signalling devices reduced the distraction of noise and talking but could not altogether eliminate the atmosphere of feverish bustle during the busier periods. With all the supervision and aid that could be given, the clerks employed on filtering continued to struggle with their task. In January 1940 the late arrival of filtered tracks in the Operations Rooms was still a cause for concern. It had become the practice not to tell tracks to the Operations Room until they were fairly well developed. In the light of filtering difficulties this was understandable but it nevertheless reduced the chance of interception. The order was given that tracks were to be told immediately the first directional arrow had been placed on the filter table. This measure enabled fighters to be despatched some few minutes earlier but it made the importance of the filterer's first decision even more critical than before.

Scientific analysis of filtering

It was acknowledged early in 1940 that the results of the fighter control system were disappointing. The cause of the trouble was not clear. Most of the previous causes for complaint had been removed, the quality of radar and other equipment had become much better and there was no shortage of personnel; yet the results were worse than before. A scientific analysis was therefore made of the work of every class of individual employed in fighter interception. The analysis disclosed that the weakest link lay in the Filter

Room. Detailed examination of the process of filtering followed. Records of all plots made by the various radar stations during selected periods were collected together, and from the plots, tracks of raids were accurately reconstructed. The reconstructed tracks were compared with the tracings of tracks as plotted originally in Operations Rooms while the raids were in progress. The comparison proved beyond all possible doubt that some of the tracks produced during operations had been grossly incorrect. The air picture given had been so misleading as to preclude any chance of successful interception. Some radical improvement was clearly essential and, as an experiment, three technical assistants of science degree standard were given a short period of training in the principles of filtering. They then manned the filterer posts.

Despite their impatience, the tracks they produced under operational conditions were much nearer the accuracy required for interception, and a great improvement in reliability was observed. Only after this convincing demonstration was it generally accepted that men of special mental ability were required as filterers. A knowledge and appreciation of the capabilities and limitations of radar stations was also necessary. In his minute to the financial authorities, presenting the case for the establishment of commissioned filterer officers, the Wing Commander Operations, Air Ministry, summed up the situation and made perfectly clear what the result would be if the importance of the filtering process continued to be underestimated when he wrote:

'In the early days when radar was just beginning the whole system from radar station to Filter Room was in the hands of hand-picked enthusiasts, each selected for his particular suitability for the work. In the Air Exercises at 1938 it produced excellent results. Since those days there has been rapid expansion and consequent dilution of experience and technical aptitude amongst radar personnel. Today, the results obtained from the radar system are markedly inferior and Fighter Command have always had difficulty in finding filterers capable of replacing the original men. You will remember how NCOs at all trades were misemployed as filterers in the endeavour to get efficiency. Then,

how the best of the plotters were selected and regarded as filterers, then how Fighter Command suggested the taking in of the higher clerical grade of civil servants as direct entry NCOs for the purpose.

'The whole work of a filterer has been described by the officer entrusted with the investigation and analysis as "the assessing of a probability". The most accurate assessment of this probability depends on many factors, comprehension of which will never be found in the ordinary airman, nor indeed to the highest degree in the average officer. You know as well as I do the vital importance of accurate filtering.

'At the most critical point stands the filterer, and it is his responsibility and his alone that this tangible data is the most accurate which it is possible to obtain. Unless he has the peculiar knowledge and the ability to profit by the experience, which is ultimately the medium through which a filterer becomes an expert, we shall never get good filtering and the maximum number of interceptions. Without such filtering the whole of the fighter defence of this country will be most severely handicapped, and the ten and a half million pounds of capital sunk in the radar organisation itself will never give the results of which we know it should be capable.'

Not surprisingly, financial approval was subsequently granted for the appointment of pilot officers or flying officers to filterer posts in lieu of corporals on 19 February 1940. It thus became possible to select men for filtering duties from among those with the special mental qualifications for the task. Usually, they were university graduates in scientific or mathematical subjects. Whilst it cannot be said that all filtering troubles ceased with the appointment of the first fifteen trained officer filterers on 10 June 1940, there was undoubtedly thenceforward a much better chance that the accurate air information essential to fighter operations would be forthcoming. Officer filterer posts were later filled by members of the WAAF who had been, in fact, employed as plotters in the Filter Room since 20 September 1939. It should be mentioned that the majority of both Filter and Operations Room duties were ultimately carried out by women, and with conspicuous success.

The Operations Rooms

Command Operations Room

In 1925 the Air Ministry purchased the Bentley Priory estate at Stanmore in Middlesex and by May of the following year had established it as the RAF's Inland Area HQ. However, on the formation of Fighter Command in 1936 it was given over to the HQ of that organisation with the most important adaptation being the construction of two temporary Filter and Operations Rooms. They were to be the centre of the 'hub' that was the Dowding System. However, an enormous excavation just to the east of the main buildings was commenced in January 1939 for the construction of the underground command centre. The excavation reached 42ft and resulted in 58,000 tons of earth being removed whilst 17,000 tons of poured reinforced concrete encased the underground rooms with the whole complex having its own services, air filtration and gas-tight doors. It was completed in March 1940 and was thus operational just in time for the Battle of Britain.

Whilst the Fighter Command Operations Room at Bentley Priory might be considered the very nerve centre of the Battle of Britain it was, in reality, the Group and Sector Operations Rooms which more actively controlled the battle. That said, the Command Operations Room gave the C-in-C (or a nominated senior officer) an immediate overview of the whole situation across the country, Group by Group, Sector by Sector. From his gallery position the C-in-C could view the overall progress of battle at any given moment whilst looking down on the General Situation Map (GSM) marked out in the British Modified Grid (BMG) and with its constantly changing display of counters and markers being moved around by RAF and WAAF personnel using long magnetic rods. However, there were two important functions carried out by the Command Operations Rooms.

The first of these, from an overview of the situation, was to allocate specific incoming raids to the appropriate Group and depending upon which ground the raid was encroaching on to then designate the raid to that Group. Once handed on to the relevant Group then

ABOVE, LEFT AND BELOW General views of the organised chaos inside the original Bentley Priory HQ RAF Fighter Command Operations Room. Significant in the lower image is the National Air Raid Warning System map, with the British Isles divided up into some 130 'warning districts'.

that Group Operations Room would, in turn, delegate to the appropriate Sector or Sectors and their Operations Rooms.

Supplementary to this role, however, Command could order the deployment of squadrons from an adjoining Group to assist a hard-pressed neighbouring Group.

The other function carried out by the Command Operations Room was to operate the National Air Raid Warning System. This covered the whole of the country (with the exception of the Orkneys and Shetlands), which had been divided up into 130 individual 'Warning Districts'. These were determined by the regional layout of telephone networks and three Bentley Priory telephone operators were in constant contact with the trunk operators in London, Liverpool and Glasgow. With information coming in nationwide on an updated minute-by-minute basis it was only natural that this duty should fall, centrally, to the Command Operations Room of Fighter Command. The officer responsible for ordering that the warning should be issued could watch threats or potential raids unfolding on the General Situation Map and determine which districts were at risk. He would then issue the warnings; these were categorised as Yellow, Red or Green as below:

Also based at the Command Operations Room were liaison officers from Coastal and Bomber Commands who were on hand to assist in the identification of friendly formations from their commands that might otherwise be either regarded as potentially hostile and/or falsely trigger an air-raid warning.

However, Dowding realised that tactical control of the battle could not be centralised at Bentley Priory and also that Group commanders would be too busy making decisions to get involved with the minutiae of actual interceptions. Thus, cascading down from the Fighter Command HQ Operations Room there were two further tiers of operations room – Group Operations Rooms and Sector Operations Rooms.

Group Operations Room

Whilst the Command HQ Operations Room gave an overall picture of the defence of the British Isles, with its huge plotting table encompassing all three Groups in the command, the Group Operations Rooms map tables only reflected the area of responsibility for that Group, although with overlap into neighbouring Groups but only insofar as it covered the likely range of that Group controllers' fighters should they be needed to support those adjacent Groups.

Situation	Message	Text	To whom sent	Remarks
Raiding aircraft are approaching the UK.	PRELIMINARY CAUTION	'Air-raid message – yellow.'	Recipients on the district warning list of districts in which raiders appear to be heading.	This message was only a preliminary warning and was confidential. It was not to be passed on from one warning district to another nor to be conveyed to the public.
Raiding aircraft are heading towards certain districts, which may be attacked within from 5 to 10 minutes.	ACTION WARNING	'Air-raid warning – red.'	Recipients on the direct warning list of districts threatened.	Message passed by telephone to certain authorities on the warning list, who will sound the Air Raid Warning.
Raiding aircraft have left districts warned or no longer appear to threaten those districts.	RAIDERS PASSED	Air-raid message – green.'	All recipients of ACTION WARNING.	Message passed by telephone to certain authorities on the warning list, who will sound the RAIDERS PASSED.
The preliminary threat has passed.	CANCEL CAUTION	'Air-raid message – white.'	All recipients of the PRELIMINARY CAUTION (whether they had received the ACTION WARNING and RAIDERS PASSED or not).	This message was confidential. It was to be passed on only to those who received the PRELIMINARY CAUTION.

LEFT Battle of Britain period Fighter Command Operations Room at RAF Bentley Priory with WAAF plotters moving markers around the General Situation Map to allow the duty controller to allocate raids to the most appropriate Groups in the Command.

BELOW September 1940: HM King George VI and Queen Elizabeth visit RAF Bentley Priory escorted by Air Chief Marshal Sir Hugh Dowding.

The map grid system on the GSM in use at the Group Operations Room remained the same as that at the Command Operations Room. Generally, across all Operations Rooms, the GSM was updated with colour-coded tracks (see the Operations Room Clock, page 78) by mostly WAAF 'tellers' positioned standing around the map board and moving the markers using long rods, indicating the formation being tracked. Not surprisingly the WAAF operators became known as the 'croupier girls'.

Because the task of the Group Operations Room was the tactical control centre of the battle, the workings of the room were somewhat different to that at Command. Here, the senior controller and his assistants (rarely did the Group commander himself involve himself in the day-to-day control of the actual battle in his Group) were positioned in the central box overlooking the GSM and the tote board, the latter given an up-to-the-minute position of the situation regarding squadrons within his Group: how many squadrons were available, how many aircraft, how many pilots, wind direction, balloon heights etc, together with indicator boards which lit up to show which squadrons had left the ground, sighted the enemy, engaged the enemy or landed back. This gallery was soundproofed from all

ABOVE WAAF plotters and tellers at the General Situation Map working at moving the various raid markers and counters around the map board. Each is connected via headset to different sources of information coming in from the Filter Room. All of them wear chest-mounted microphones. The raid markers are three-tiered metal stands with removable number and letter plaques and, although different versions of the markers were used, those shown here are most likely those used just after the Battle of Britain.

LEFT Looking down on the map board from behind a glass screen was the Group controller and his assistants, who included liaison officers from the Army (Anti-Aircraft Command), from the Navy (to advise on convoy and shipping movements) and from other RAF Commands, including Balloon Command. From this gallery the Group controller could get an overview of activity as it unfolded on the map below him and could therefore direct his various Sector controllers accordingly, and order specific squadrons off to meet the various incoming threats.

LEFT The view looking up into the gallery to the duty controller's dais through its curved glass screen. The duty controller seated dead centre is Wing Commander Lord Willoughby de Broke.

RIGHT A contemporary view of the General Situation Map (GSM), marked out in its numbered and lettered grid squares and with the 'tote' visual display board behind, together with wind direction indicators to the left. At the back edge of the GSM board is the traffic light indicator box, which changed colour to red, yellow or blue to show the colour of the marker arrows indicating the track of raids that should currently be placed onto the map board.

BELOW A detail of the eastern edge of the map board showing Schiphol, Amsterdam and the Netherlands coastline. The marker indicates six friendly aircraft at 10,000ft and the arrows mark their track. A WAAF's headset and microphone rest on the edge of the map.

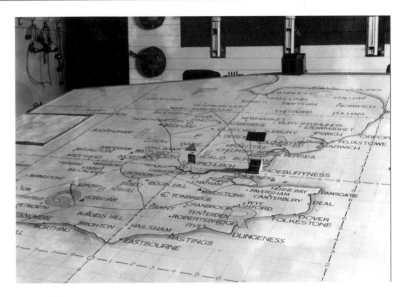

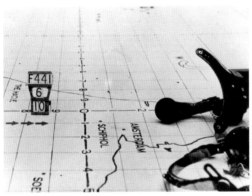

RIGHT The full tote board on the back wall of the Operations Room. From the allocation of various squadrons to their particular RAF stations it is possible to date this photograph as being taken between 20 and 23 May 1940, just before the Battle of Britain. It is therefore possible to say with a reasonable degree of confidence that the photographs of the map table and tote board would be very much as they appeared during the Battle of Britain. It will be noted that there are some subtle differences between how the restored map board and tote indicators now appear and how they most probably were during the Battle of Britain. The small indicator panels below each individual illuminated squadron panel show the cloud height and the extent of cover.

RIGHT Seated beneath the controller's dais were further monitoring staff receiving meteorological data, etc.

LEFT One of the types of markers used on the GSM board at 11 Group HQ, Uxbridge. This example indicates friendly aircraft of 65 Squadron (Spitfires) and is showing nine aircraft at 20,000ft. The squadron indicator is a removable metal flag and the aircraft numbers and heights were metal plaques that could be inserted or removed accordingly. The whole marker could be moved around the board by the WAAF plotters, along with the course and position arrows of the appropriate colour for that specific time that were associated with the incoming raid markers.

RIGHT Other indicator plaques used on the GSM included those to mark the position of convoys. RAF Fighter Command had a duty to provide standing patrols for convoys as they passed around the coastline, and the position of these groups of shipping also became important to the Group controller in assessing and countering any threat that might be heading towards them. During the early part of the Battle of Britain the Luftwaffe singled out convoys for attack. For instance, air attacks on a convoy in the English Channel on 8 August 1940 were particularly heavy and sustained. To the Royal Navy this was Convoy CW9 (Convoy Westbound No 9) but it was given the codename PEEWIT by RAF Fighter Command.

the noise and hubbub in the plotting room below by a glass screen and, on either side of this gallery, were two smaller boxes where Observer Corps, naval and anti-aircraft liaison officers sat. Alongside was a VIP viewing gallery. Within the room itself, supervisory personnel controlled the operations around the table giving directions and advice, and resolving any problems that arose.

Today, one intact Group Operations Room exists in a preserved state and this is, arguably, the most significant of all Battle of Britain Group Operations Rooms, that of 11 Group at Uxbridge. Sixty feet underground, the room was renovated by the RAF during the 1970s and is frozen in time, exactly as it was at 11.30hrs on the morning of 15 September 1940. By chance rather than design, Winston Churchill chose to visit this Operations Room on the day that was subsequently marked as the height of the Battle of Britain (although 18 August was the hardest-fought day) and watched the battle unfold. The map table is exactly as it was at that time, along with the tote board and all the associated maps, charts and equipment.

(Note: *this Operations Room is exactly replicated at the RAF Museum, Hendon, although it is possible to visit the Uxbridge Operations Room by special arrangement via the parent unit, RAF Northolt.*)

RIGHT No 11 Group Operations Room.

RIGHT Sector 'G' Operations Room at RAF Duxford. Note the squadron radio call signs for 242, 302 and 310 Squadrons on the wall.

CENTRE RAF Tangmere was Sector 'A' Station within Fighter Command, with each Sector being allocated its own unique letter. Although no photographs exist of the interior of the Sector 'A' Operations Room this artist's impression was drawn by one of the WAAF plotters who was stationed there. It shows the duty controller (seated centre) considering the deployment of squadrons under his control and issuing orders accordingly as he looks down on his own General Situation Map.

Sector Operations Room

Again, the Sector Operations Room was a further scale down from the Group Operations Room. The same principles of the overall operating methodology applied, although at this level the Sector controller was only interested in controlling his fighters on to the raids as directed from the Group Operations Rooms. Today, preserved examples of Sector Operations Rooms exist at the Imperial War Museum, Duxford (formerly RAF Duxford) and at the former RAF Digby. These two Operations Rooms are of the 'bungalow' type which had been built during the interwar period and were single-storey brick buildings with a pitched roof and protected only by the later addition of a blast wall, an earth bank and retaining wall just below eaves level.

The unsuitability of these almost unprotected Operations Rooms on Sector airfields soon became apparent and their vulnerability pointed up the need to move these Sector Operations Rooms to remote locations away from the airfields themselves. However, new 'L'-shaped Operations Rooms were built and ready for the battle at Tangmere, Hornchurch and North Weald, whilst that at Middle Wallop was completed during the battle itself. Meanwhile, Kenley, Duxford, Northolt and Biggin Hill all had to make do with the pre-war buildings although, as we will see, it was not long before the RAF relocated these vital centres away from the airfields. However, even the new reinforced concrete structures with heavy-duty blast walls were quickly recognised as vulnerable on airfields that were subject to attack. Indeed,

BELOW Photographed in the 1970s this was the Operations Room block at RAF Tangmere, a reinforced building protected by substantial blast walls. Despite its protection from blast, a heavy dive-bombing attack on Tangmere on 16 August 1940 (followed by others on the Sector stations of Kenley and Biggin Hill shortly after) prompted a decision to disperse the vital Sector Operations Rooms away from the actual stations themselves. In the case of Tangmere, the Operations Room was moved to St James's School in nearby Chichester.

INSTRUCTIONS TO CONTROLLERS

Although the instructions to controllers changed and evolved to meet changing German tactics and threats, and were to develop in light of operational experience, the following instructions for Sector controllers in 11 Group of 19 August very much sets the scene for the second phase of the Battle of Britain:

SECRET
No 11 GROUP INSTRUCTIONS TO CONTROLLERS. No 4

From: Air Officer Commanding, No 11 Group, Royal Air Force.
To: Group Controllers and Sector Commanders, for Sector Controllers.
Date: 19 August 1940.

The German Air Force has begun a new phase in air attacks, which have been switched from coastal shipping and ports on to inland objectives. The bombing attacks have for several days been concentrated against aerodromes, and especially fighter aerodromes, on the coast and inland. The following instructions are issued to meet the changed conditions:

a) Despatch fighters to engage large enemy formations over land or within gliding distance of the coast. During the next two or three weeks, we cannot afford to lose pilots through forced landings in the sea;

b) Avoid sending fighters out over the sea to chase reconnaissance aircraft or small formations of enemy fighters;

c) Despatch a pair of fighters to intercept single reconnaissance aircraft that come inland. If clouds are favourable, put a patrol of one or two fighters over an aerodrome which enemy aircraft are approaching in clouds;

d) Against mass attacks coming inland, despatch a minimum number of squadrons to engage enemy fighters. Our main object is to engage enemy bombers, particularly those approaching in cloud layer;

e) If all our Squadrons around London are off the ground engaging enemy mass attacks, ask 12 Group or Command Controller to provide squadrons to patrol aerodromes Debden, North Weald, Hornchurch;

f) If heavy attacks have crossed the coast and are proceeding towards aerodromes, put a Squadron, or even the Sector Training Flight, to patrol under clouds over each Sector aerodrome;

g) 303 (Polish) Squadron can provide two sections for patrol of inland aerodromes, especially while the older Squadrons are on the ground refuelling, when enemy formations are flying over land;

h) 1 (Canadian) Squadron can be used in the same manner by day as other fighter squadrons.

Note:
Protection of all convoys and shipping in the Thames Estuary are excluded from this instruction (paragraph (a)).

(Sgd) K.R. Park
Air Vice-Marshal,
Commanding, No 11 Group,
Royal Air Force.

after the heavy raid on Tangmere on 16 August 1940 the Operations Room was moved to a requisitioned school, St James's, in nearby Chichester. Quite simply, if these Sector Operations Rooms were disabled, or even the communications or power supplies to them interrupted, it would have been completely impossible for any fighter actions to be controlled from these centres.

How things worked from the Sector Operations Rooms are, perhaps, best explained through one of the many sets of instructions issued by 11 Group HQ and via the words of one of the hard-worked Sector controllers in that same group.

A Sector controller's account

Sqn Ldr Anthony Norman, who was one of the Kenley Sector fighter controllers, gave an account of his experience during the Battle of Britain:

'During the Phoney War we had done literally thousands of practice interceptions and these had involved the Observer Corps. By the summer of 1940 the system was well oiled and we were confident of its ability. Really, I believed that nobody could come over the coast without being seen by some element of our system and had absolute confidence in our ability to intercept anything that came over the coast. At our Sector Operations Room we could intercept anything if 11 Group gave the orders in time,

BELOW Sqn Ldr Anthony Norman was one of the Sector controllers at Kenley during the Battle of Britain.

but the task of a Group Controller was not an easy one and there was no way the Group Controller could have practised meeting large-scale attacks before the battle in the same way that we had practised simple ones.

'As soon as the first plots of a German build-up over Northern France or the Channel appeared on the Operations Room table I would bring the station defences to a state of Preliminary Air Raid Warning. At this, our "local" anti-aircraft airfield defence people manned their guns and the fighters held at "Available" were called to "Readiness". There wouldn't be any "Scramble" yet, and in any case it was the Group Controller's responsibility to decide which squadron he was going to use to intercept which raid. When that decision had been made, the order would be cascaded down to me in the Sector Operations Room, but already I had been watching the situation building on the map table below me. The first thing I'd see would be a raid counter appear on the situation map but this would only give me the estimated number of aircraft, and their height, but I would have no idea if they were fighters or bombers. Or both. So, when I was eventually ordered by 11 Group to scramble such-and-such squadron this would be the squadron that had been first called to readiness, and Group would be able to see from their state board which squadron that was. It is important, here, to emphasise that it was *never* the case that Hurricanes were dispatched to deal with the bombers and the Spitfires to engage the fighters, although it is often suggested that

ABOVE On 18 August 1940 a low-level attack by Dornier 17-Z aircraft of 9./KG76 was first spotted by the Observer Corps post on Beachy Head, Sussex. This photograph shows aircraft in the formation just approaching the coast off Eastbourne. The raid was plotted all the way inland by the Observer Corps and with its composition and track accurately relayed to the Kenley Operations Room this allowed Sqn Ldr Norman to assess the clear and present threat that was headed his way. Realising that Kenley must be the bombers' intended objective, the Sector controller didn't wait for orders from Group but, instead, took the initiative and scrambled all of his aircraft that were still on the ground in order to get them out of harm's way. Moments later, the airfield came under heavy attack.

BELOW Unlike Tangmere, the RAF Kenley 'B' Sector Operations Room was of the interwar bungalow type. This was a single-storey building with a pitched roof and was only protected by a blast wall that extended to below eaves level. Either a direct or a near hit could have been potentially catastrophic and would have resulted in the RAF fighters under the room's direct control being rendered impotent. Although it survived undamaged on 18 August 1940, the operations centre was immediately dispersed to a safe location outside the airfield. Again, this historic building has since been demolished.

this is what happened. Actually, that notion is complete rubbish because it was impossible, tactically, as we just didn't know, anyway, how the raid being intercepted was made up. So, at Kenley we could end up sending 615 Squadron's Hurricanes against fighters and then 64 Squadron's Spitfires off after a bunch of bombers. It had to be that way.

'Once I had ordered a squadron off on a scramble it was my job to direct the squadron commander not only to the interception but to try to get him up-sun if it was possible. I would not aim to go straight at the German formation, but would instead try to climb at a slight angle away from the raiders and position the fighters so that they could then turn round and attack out of the sun. As a constant reminder, the position of the sun at any time was marked up on what was called the Individual Interception Board (IIB). This was a blackboard facing me and with the raid details repeated there, along with the positions of our fighters. Sometimes, we would control our fighters into another Sector but if aircraft came into our Sector from, say, 12 Group then we couldn't control them because they were operating on another frequency.

After we had successfully controlled them onto the engagement, our job was pretty much all but done, although it would often be the case that there would be another raid

to immediately control other fighters in the Sector on to. The policy of 11 Group was to have the first squadrons back on the ground re-fuelling and re-arming as the last squadrons were taking off. In theory, this made it possible to meet all raids and very seldom were there absolutely no fighters available although there was the now famous occasion when Winston Churchill visited the 11 Group Operations room, I think it was on 15 September, and asked Park the question "Reserves?" only to be told "There are none, Sir."

'Sometimes we were able to use intercepted radio traffic information picked up by the "Y" Listening Service who could listen in on German wireless traffic and hear fighters going into the attack. On occasions, although not often, we could warn our fighters of an impending "Bounce". In fact, one of our listening staff was a Czech Jewish girl who got to know the pilots by their nicknames. She once said: "Sir, I know it sounds silly, but when I no longer hear them on the air, which means they have been shot down, then I really quite miss them!" As to ULTRA signals, these did come into 11 Group, but only after the Battle of Britain and so we could not make any use of such information in 1940. Again, it has sometimes been suggested this information helped us in the Control Rooms in 1940. It didn't. Even when this information did come in, we had no idea at our level where it had come from but were given the impression it was an extremely well-placed spy whose existence had to be safeguarded at all costs.

'After an interception we had no way of knowing, in the Operations Room, how the fighter squadrons had done with their combat success. Yes, we would have followed some of the R/T "chatter" but were only interested in the important job of controlling and giving instructions and then only getting relevant detail back. Again, the idea that we followed exactly what was happening in the battles is an erroneous one. We couldn't, and we didn't know how they had done until we asked the officers in the Mess afterwards. Of course, after an engagement we'd start getting information in from Observer Corps Posts and searchlight units; aircraft down in such a position, a parachute seen coming down in a particular grid reference etc. Then, after the battle, we'd also have to start ringing around to other airfields to try to discover anything about the fighters which had not landed back, although other pilots who had landed at other airfields, or who had made forced-landings or baled-out, would begin calling in to report their whereabouts and status.

'On one notable occasion at RAF Kenley, on 18 August 1940, we were bombed quite heavily but were not put out of action. We only lost a few of our telephone lines and in our Operations Room we had around 500 telephone lines; one from each Observer Post in the Sector, plus direct lines to all forward airfields and R/T relay stations, direct lines to all fixer stations, several direct lines to HQ Fighter Command and HQ 11 Group plus direct lines to the dispersal points at our own airfield and all other main airfields in the Sector. However, by and large the Operations Room kept going and the plotting and controlling continued throughout the raid – which only lasted about 20 seconds, anyway. People think it must have been much longer, although I admit that it did seem like it! Afterwards, we moved our Operations Room out to a requisitioned butcher's shop in Caterham High Street. The butcher's shop was extremely primitive, but it was chosen simply because of its proximity to where the main GPO telephone cables ran. We stayed there until the end of the Battle of Britain and never went

back to Kenley and afterwards we moved to a specially converted private house about two miles from the aerodrome. Again, there is a misconception as to why it was that we moved out of RAF Kenley to the butcher's shop and the common belief is that it was because the Operations Room there had been put out of action. It hadn't. As I said, only a couple of lines were down and our move was simply because of the concern that the Operations Room could easily be knocked out. It was only a kind of bungalow-type building, and hardly protected at all, so one bomb could have removed our ability to control any fighters in the Sector. The raid on 18 August 1940 highlighted that as a very real possibility. Hence the move.

'In total, we had four controllers at Kenley and so we ran four six-hour shifts, around the clock. Another of the controllers there was Flt Lt Cyril Raymond, later a very well-known actor. On each shift we had another officer on duty with us who was called "Ops B". He was the controller's right-hand man, their PA, getting information when it was needed and generally making sure that everything was working as it should. A good "Ops B" would foresee what was wanted and get it before even being asked.

'Overall, it was a really good command and control system. Along the way we tweaked and tinkered with the arrangements but the basic control arrangements in place at the start of 1940 worked efficiently throughout the Battle of Britain.'

Notwithstanding Sqn Ldr Norman's account of his time as Sector controller at RAF Kenley, it is necessary to look at his remarks relating to the use of Spitfires to engage the fighters and Hurricanes to engage the bombers against the context of an instruction to Sector controllers of 11 September 1940 by Air Vice-Marshal Park in which, inter alia, he stated:

'READINESS SQUADRONS: Despatch in pairs to engage the first wave of enemy. Spitfires against fighter screen, and Hurricanes against bombers and close escort.'

However, this does not address the issue raised by Sqn Ldr Norman which was simply that the controller had no means of knowing how the formations being intercepted were made up until the squadrons established visual contact. At that stage, it may have been possible for squadrons to engage more appropriately by fighter type but, very often, it was too late for Spitfires and Hurricanes to engage as Park had directed.

As regards to Sqn Ldr Norman's comments about the damage to the Kenley Operations Room, the report into the raid stated:

Operational Control:
The cables to the transmitter were cut during the raid and the R/T and electric supply failed.
Ground stripes were put out instructing aircraft to land at satellites.
R/T communication was broken at 13.23 hours but the reserve transmitter brought into action at 13.37 hours.
The Operations Room itself was undamaged but communications were cut and transmitter and power were off during the above period.
All dispersal tie lines and outward lines were cut, with the exception of Ops lines to 11 Group, Bromley (ROC Group HQ), Biggin Hill and S/L lines.

Recommendations:
The Operations Room, which is unprotected against overhead attack, should be scrapped and a new operations room fitted up away from the station in a concealed position. It is highly probable that in the next large scale raid the Operations Room and crew of 35–40 may be put out of action.

It was certainly the case that experience at Kenley led to re-appraisal of the housing of Sector Operations Rooms on airfields and the desirability of dispersing them away from the site and this matter was underlined with the destruction of the Biggin Hill Sector Operations Room just over two weeks later.

RAF Operations Room clock
Central, and indeed essential, to the proper functioning of RAF Sector, Group and Command Control Rooms was what is often referred to as the colour change clock, or sometimes the Sector clock, or simply the 'Ops'

RIGHT The WAAF plotters of 'D' Watch from RAF Biggin Hill photographed during the Battle of Britain period. Cpl Elspeth Henderson WAAF (seated centre) was awarded the Military Medal for bravery during air attacks on the airfield.

Room clock. Standard twelve-hour mechanical clocks, the faces were painted with coloured segments of red, yellow and blue in each 15-minute time block, the sequence repeated around every 15-minute segment of the clock face.

The purpose of the colour segments situated around the clock face was a) to provide a rough indication of the age (in minutes) of the plots shown on the plotting tables; and b) to provide for the systematic and regular removal of out-of-date plots and tracks.

Broadly speaking, the system worked as follows:

As we have seen, each Fighter Operations Room would have a large table on which was displayed a map of the area being controlled known as the General Situation Map (GSM). Positioned around the GSM were a number of plotters (usually WAAF personnel) each of whom was connected by telephone to different sources of information, eg adjacent Group Operation Rooms, Filter Rooms and to Observer Corps centres for visual plots from Observer posts depending on the type of Operations Room.

A plotter would receive information regarding the position and direction of flight and strength (ie, number of aircraft) and the height of the aircraft or formation, together with a designation or identity number that had been allocated to that aircraft or formation.

A typical report might be: Hostile 15–20+; Height 10,000ft.

On receiving this information the plotter would place on the map an arrow symbol of the colour currently being indicated by the minute hand of the Operations Room clock – and would place beside the arrow a three-tiered plaque showing the reported designation strength and height of the 'raid'. All other plotters would be using the same colour arrows for other tracks at the same time. The sequence of colours on the clock was red, yellow, blue, so if the minute hand was pointing to red, the plotters would be using red arrows. When the hand moved on to the yellow section the plotters would start using yellow arrows. However, when the hand moved to the blue section, as well as changing to using blue arrows for current

ABOVE The standard colour change mechanical fusee movement clock used in all RAF Operations Rooms that utilised the colour-coded system for raid plotting. Map markers were tied into each of the three different five-minute coloured segments – red, yellow and blue. (Note: the clocks used in Group Operations Rooms were slightly different in that they were larger 'repeater' or 'slave' clocks and displayed the same coloured triangles, although these were positioned pointing inwards towards the centre of the clock rather than outwards.)

plots, the plotters would also remove from the board all red arrows on all tracks within their control. They would similarly remove the other colours when the next colour but one commenced. Thus, at no time could there be on the table any arrows showing plots which were more than 10 minutes old. Also, of course, the removal of the old colours cleared the way for the use of that same colour again when the clock next moved into that colour segment. In this way the table was clear of the clutter of arrows that would otherwise indicate 'stale' information and, as an immediately obvious visual indication, the colour changes were indicated on an illuminated 'traffic-light' box at the edge of the GSM.

Arrows indicated 'visual' plots obtained by

sight or by radar. There were two other types of symbols which might be used: heart-shaped symbols to indicate 'heard' pilots, ie, when, because of poor visibility or darkness, the aircraft could not be seen but only heard; and circular-shaped symbols to where an aircraft or formation was circling. These symbols would be governed by the same rules as to colour.

The raid designations shown on the three-tiered plaques were usually:

- Black H on yellow = Hostile.
- Black X on yellow background = Unidentified.
- Red F on white background = Friendly.

Additionally, other markers would be placed by plotters following the movement of RAF squadrons. These included a 'flag' marked with the squadron number, and removable numbers at the base of the marker that indicated the height of the aircraft and number of aircraft in that formation. In the case of the marker illustrated on page 72 we are looking at a formation from 65 Squadron (Spitfires) flying at 20,000ft and comprising nine aircraft. These friendly aircraft plots were also tracked on the plotting map using exactly the same system as for the hostile plots.

The colour-change system and the related clocks were in use at each type of Fighter Command Operations Room.

Other symbols might also be placed on the plotting board. For example, a white plaque bearing the inscription 'CONVOY' in red letters on a white ground so as to give the controller a visual indication of shipping convoys moving through his area of responsibility and which might need fighter cover.

The Sector controller, positioned on a balcony overlooking the table, and by watching the tracks as they moved across the table, could then use wireless to talk his fighters into position to intercept enemy aircraft.

Plotters working on the table would be told by an automatically illuminated 'traffic-light' indicator when to change the colour of the markers they placed, with the coloured lights changing as the minute hand moved into each respective five-minute segment – red, yellow, blue.

Dowding on the Dowding System

Reporting later on the system, and its success, Air Chief Marshal Dowding said:

'It appeared to me quite impossible to centralise tactical control at Command Headquarters, and even Group Commanders would be too busy during heavy fighting to concern themselves with details of interception.

'The system was that the Command should be responsible for the identification of approaching formations and for the allotment of enemy raids to Groups where any doubt existed. Group Commanders decided which Sector should meet any specified raid and the strength of the fighter force which should be employed. Sector Commanders detailed the fighter units to be employed, and operated the machinery of interception.

'The Sector Commander could see on his operations tables the positions and courses of enemy formations and of his own fighters, and was enabled so to direct the latter as to make interceptions with the former in a good percentage of occasions by day. Interception depended, of course, on the fighters being able to see the enemy, and, although the system worked adequately against enemy formations in daylight, the degree of accuracy obtainable was insufficient to effect interception against night raiders not illuminated by searchlights, or against individual aircraft using cloud cover by day.

'The system as a whole had been built up by successive steps over a period of about four years, and I was not dissatisfied with the way in which it stood the test of war.'

Direction finding (Pip-Squeak)

It was all very well, of course, for the Sector controller to know where hostile formations or 'X' plots were but this information was useless if he did not know where his own fighters were once they had left the ground. Clearly, he needed to control them on to the varying tracks of the incoming plots. To solve this problem a relatively simple system was established whereby at least two key aircraft in every formation automatically transmitted a signal for a brief period to allow Direction Finding (D/F) Fixer Stations to take a location bearing. The system was known as Pip-Squeak and was designed to operate around the TR 9D radio sets.

The TR 9D then in use by Fighter Command had a limited range of 40 to 45 miles at 15,000ft (slightly better in perfect conditions) and operated on only two crystal-controlled transmitter channels, one for normal radio telephony (R/T) and the other for Pip-Squeak. This system in the aircraft was activated by a piece of apparatus called the Master Contactor, which was a clockwork mechanism of high precision and with a thermostatically controlled heater to ensure that its temperature remained stable whatever the operating altitude. The clock was housed in a wooden box, padded with Sorbo rubber, and mounted behind the cockpit. The clock was wound up and switched to 'START' before take-off and by keying the aircraft power supply it would send a 12-volt pulse each second to the stepping motor in the Remote Contactor. This unit was mounted on the right-hand side of the cockpit and before take-off the pilot would set its indicator to the appropriate position for that aircraft. For example: Yellow Leader might be allocated 270 on the indicator dial. Once aircraft were airborne the Sector controller would call up his squadrons and instruct them to activate Pip-Squeak by saying: 'Synchronise time – 5, 4, 3, 2, 1 – Mark.' With the equipment activated, the pointer of the Remote Contactor would then rotate at 1rpm and connected to the other end of the pointer shaft was a notched cam with a make-and-break contact riding on its rim. This contact opened for 14 seconds in each minute, depending upon where the indicator had initially been set.

Pip-Squeak was normally activated by a request from the Sector controller who would ask: 'Is your cockerel crowing?' This would be the cue for pilots to operate the external switch to automatically turn the TR 9D set to transmit from its normal R/T channel to the Pip-Squeak channel for 14 seconds at the appropriate time. The transmitted signal was a shrill whistle at about 1,000 cycles. The TR 9D could then be

switched back to its normal channel by setting to 'RECEIVE'. Meanwhile, the pointer would continue to rotate on the Remote Contactor ready for Pip-Squeak to be reactivated.

The transmitted Pip-Squeak signal (if within range) would be picked up by the Sector D/F Fixer Stations, three in each Sector, and arranged in a triangle at about 30 miles distant from each other. The radio receiver at each of these stations was a Marconi DFG12 set from which the bearing could be established by WAAF personnel for each squadron's position. Comparing the timing of a particular transmission with the Fixer Station's synchronised Pip-Squeak clock, the individual squadron and its aircraft could be identified. For example, Red Leader (1–14 seconds), Yellow Leader (15–29), Blue (30–44) and Green (45–59). There was a one-second gap between each signal. As soon as the signal had been received the information would be passed to the Sector Operations Room by a dedicated GPO landline. Once these three bearings had been plotted on to the Fixer Table using simple triangulation and a piece of string the 'fixed' position was relayed to the Sector controller and placed on the General Situation Map (GSM). The controller now knew where all his aircraft were, geographically, and relative to other friendly and hostile elements. This information could now be fed back up the system to Group and Command Operations Rooms.

ABOVE The direction finding Pip-Squeak Master Contactor and clock as fitted in all RAF Fighter Command aircraft during the Battle of Britain. (Note: while this is otherwise identical in every respect to the equipment used in 1940, this is a 24-volt version, whereas the Battle of Britain equipment operated on 12 volts.)

RAF FIGHTER SQUADRON CALL SIGNS

In the air, RAF fighter squadrons were never referred to by their allocated squadron numbers, only by a radio call sign. This included commands from the Operations Rooms as well as orders from squadron commanders and between the pilots themselves. For instance, a controller directing 54 Squadron, say, would refer to the unit as Rabbit Squadron, and so on for other squadrons as per the charts here. (Note: a few squadron radio call signs remain unknown or uncertain.)

Squadrons	Fuselage code	Radio call sign	Aircraft
1	JX	ACORN	Hurricane
3	QO		Hurricane
17	YB	EDEY	Hurricane
19	QV	LUTON	Spitfire
23	YP		Blenheim
25	ZK	KUTEX	Blenheim/Beaufighter
29	RO		Blenheim
32	GZ	JACKO	Hurricane
41	EB	MITOR	Spitfire
43	FT		Hurricane
46	PO	ANGEL	Hurricane
54	KL	RABBIT	Spitfire
56	US	BAFFIN	Hurricane
64	SH	FREEMA	Spitfire
65	YT		Spitfire
66	LZ	FIBUS	Spitfire
72	RN	TENNIS	Spitfire
73	TP	HULA	Hurricane
74	ZP	DYSOE	Spitfire
79	NV	PANSY	Hurricane
85	VY	HYDRO	Hurricane
87	LK	SUNCAP	Hurricane
92	QJ	GANNIC	Spitfire
111	JU	WAGON	Hurricane
141	TW	PLATER (x)	Defiant
145	SO	PATIN	Hurricane
151	DZ		Hurricane
152	UM	MAIDA	Spitfire
213	AK	BEARSKIN	Hurricane
219	FK		Blenheim/Beaufighter
222	ZD	KOTEL	Spitfire
229	RE	KETA	Hurricane
232	EF		Hurricane
234	AZ	CRESSY	Spitfire
238	VK		Hurricane
242	LE	LORAG	Hurricane
245	DX		Hurricane
247	HP		Gladiator
249	GN	GANER	Hurricane
253	SW	VICEROY	Hurricane
257	DT	ALERT	Hurricane
263	HE	COSY*	Hurricane/Whirlwind
264	PS		Defiant
266	UO		Spitfire
Flights			
421	L-Z		Hurricane/Spitfire
422			Hurricane
Fighter Interception Unit	ZQ		Hurricane/Blenheim/Beaufighter

Squadrons	Fuselage code	Radio call sign	Aircraft
Auxiliary squadrons			
501	SD	MANDREL	Hurricane
504	TM		Hurricane
600	BQ		Blenheim/Beaufighter
601	UF	WEAPON	Hurricane
602	LO	VILLA	Spitfire
603	XT	VIKEN	Spitfire
604	NG	RUNNA	Blenheim/Beaufighter
605	UP	TURKEY	Hurricane
607	AF		Hurricane
609	PR	SORBO	Spitfire
610	DW	DOGROSE	Spitfire
611	FY	CHARLIE	Spitfire
615	KW	PANTA	Hurricane
616	QJ	RADPOE	Spitfire
Commonwealth and Allied squadrons			
1 Canadian	YO	CARIBOU	Hurricane
302 (Polish)	WX	CALEB	Hurricane
303 (Polish)	RF	APANY	Hurricane
310 (Czech)	NN	CALLA	Hurricane
312 (Czech)	DU	SILVO	Hurricane
Coastal Command			
235	QY		Blenheim
236	FA		Blenheim
248	DU		Blenheim
Fleet Air Arm			
804	Uncoded		Sea Gladiator/Martlet
808	7A		Fulmar (flown solo)

Note: Aircraft were switched between units during the battle and sometimes code letters were not changed immediately.

* Possibly only from 01/11/1940 (263 Squadron).

(x) 1941 – Possibly 1940. Possibly also used by 264 Squadron.

SECTOR CODES
In addition to the call signs used by individual squadrons, the various Fighter Command Sector Control Rooms also used their own call signs to identify themselves to the squadrons under their control. Those that have been identified are as listed below:

SECTOR	CALL SIGN
Tangmere	SHORTJACK
Kenley	SAPPER
Biggin Hill	TOPHAT
Hornchurch	LUMBA
North Weald	COWSLIP
Debden	GARTER
Middle Wallop	STARLIGHT

Wireless telephony communications

The key to communicating effectively with fighter squadrons in the air during the Battle of Britain clearly rested on a single route – radio. Or, to more accurately describe the system then in use, wireless telephony or W/T. However, the equipment being used during the summer of 1940 proved to be less than adequate for the task expected of it, with the W/T apparatus in use by RAF Fighter Command being the high frequency (HF) TR 9D set. In fact, it had been intended that by 1940 all fighter aircraft would have been converted to the very high frequency (VHF) TR 1133 sets. (TR in both cases stood for transmitter/receiver.)

In practice it was found that the range of the TR 9D set was too short and its performance too variable to give efficient air-to-ground communication for Fighter Command's interception system. Thus, experiments and arrangements were put in place as early as 1935 to develop a VHF set. At that time it was anticipated that the new VHF sets would be available 'in five years' time'. In other words, by sometime in 1940. Part of the problem with the HF sets, apart from range, was that the number of users of the high-frequency band had increased dramatically (even in wartime) from when it had been adopted 12 years earlier.

These users included civil, military and foreign stations and a real possibility existed that the sets might be jammed from stations 200 or 300 miles away and for all of these reasons it was desirable that a replacement system should work in another frequency band. However, delays in development and production of a new VHF set persisted but eventually it appeared that eight Sectors in 11 and 12 Groups, involving up to 300 fighters, could be equipped with the new sets by September 1939 and by October service trials of the new TR 1133 sets were being undertaken by Spitfires of 66 Squadron.

The results were dramatic, and exceeded all expectations with an air-to-ground range of 140 miles and an air-to-air range of 100 miles. Speech was clearer, pilots' controls simpler and quicker to operate, direction finding was sharper and in every way the TR 1133 was beyond any comparison with the TR 9D. Unfortunately, however, the first stage of the re-equipment plan did not work out as quickly as had been hoped, although it was further planned that by May 1940 an improved version of the VHF set, the TR 1143, would be coming into use even if, at that stage, only partial re-equipment with the 1133 set had been achieved and the majority of aircraft still had the old HF TR 9D sets. Production and supply of the 1133 or 1143 had failed the RAF at its very hour of greatest need. Furthermore, the operation of a force equipped partly with one type of W/T equipment and the other part of the force with the TR 9D was unworkable. It was a dire situation for RAF Fighter Command to be facing on the very eve of battle, and it led to Air Chief Marshal Dowding to signal the Air Ministry and 11, 12 and 13 Groups:

'In view of the necessity for maintaining flexibility in operation of all fighter squadrons at the present time, and limited wireless apparatus available, all VHF equipment in aircraft is to be replaced by the HF TR 9D sets forthwith.'

An angry Dowding then wrote to the Air Ministry on 1 June 1940 deploring the inadequacy of supplies which had forced him to abandon this, the most successful form of fighter communication. Only by reverting to the old HF sets could anything like a workable R/T organisation be maintained, and losing

BELOW The troublesome TR 9D wireless set, which was the standard radio equipment installed in RAF Fighter Command fighters during the Battle of Britain. It was stowed on a spring-mounted rack and retained in position by rubber bungee cords.
(Col Pope)

RIGHT The TR 9D radio tuner and controller as fitted in the cockpit of RAF fighters during the Battle of Britain. This example is fitted in a Spitfire Mk I. Pilots had to constantly tune and re-tune to stay on station or to hear orders and warnings. This could be challenging in combat situations where the left hand was also needed to alter throttle settings, etc.

the advantages of the new VHF sets was a retrograde step and a bitter disappointment. This retrograde step certainly affected the operating efficiency of RAF Fighter Command during the Battle of Britain and there are many examples of poor R/T communications recorded in the operational narratives of squadrons during the battle illustrating how unsatisfactory the high-frequency TR 9D sets were.

For example, over Chelmsford on 18 August 1940 only one section of a squadron came into action against a German formation. The other sections in the squadron failed to hear an order addressed by the squadron commander owing to loud interference by a German transmission in which conversation between enemy pilots could be plainly heard. There had also been similar experiences over Swanage on 15 August.

Sometimes, the TR 9D sets worked well, but in general too much of the pilots' time and attention was taken up in the sheer effort of passing and receiving messages, with interference a frequent distraction. As a case in point, one RAF Battle of Britain fighter pilot, Plt Off Ken McGlashan of 245 Squadron, was subsequently scathing of the ineffectual TR 9D sets. Talking of his own experience over Dunkirk in May 1940 he said: 'We still waged war with the primitive TR 9D radio as well as doing battle with the enemy. Selecting a frequency could be likened to finding a TV channel through a sea of white hash and interference. And one had to constantly keep tuning and re-tuning if one was to have any hope at all of communicating or receiving information. Of course, in the midst of combat a pilot had limited free hands with which to attend to such a job but suddenly a screech came over the ineffectual radio and filled my

BELOW The TR 9D wireless set installed in a Spitfire Mk I and viewed through the open access door. The spring-loaded mounting tray can be seen. The instruction plate on the inside of the door warns that the aircraft must not be flown without either the wireless or equivalent ballast. (Col Pope)

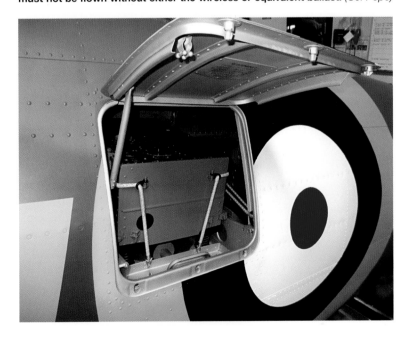

helmet with an awful deafening, squawking cacophony of static. I learned later that it was another pilot trying to warn me of five Me 109s diving on us, but I was none the wiser. On this occasion, I was shot down. Later, in June 1940, whilst on patrol over Cherbourg I spotted three enemy aircraft climbing rapidly below us. I tried to warn our leader several times, as it was obvious he hadn't yet seen them. Unfortunately, the TR 9D was true to form yet again.'

The TR 9D, however, remained the wireless set in operational use throughout the Battle of Britain but its failings were a desperate and daily worry for both fighter pilots and controllers alike. It would be impossible to say on how many occasions this ineffective piece of equipment led to the loss of pilots, the breakdown of air-to-air communications between pilots or the inability of controllers to pass intelligible information to their squadrons and the resulting failure to intercept raids.

421 Flight operations – 'Jim-Crow' sorties

As early as 26 August 1940 Air Vice-Marshal K.R. Park (AOC 11 Group) had recognised the value of getting instant feedback from squadrons as soon as they had encountered the enemy. In an instruction of that date he ordered:

'Our fighter squadrons are frequently engaging greatly superior numbers because other squadrons despatched to engage fail to intercept owing to cloud and inaccuracies of sound plotting by ground observers. To enable Group and Sector Controllers to put all squadrons in contact with the enemy, formation leaders are to report approximate strength of enemy bombers and fighters, their height, course and approximate position immediately on sighting the enemy. A specimen R/T message would be: "Tally-Ho! Thirty bombers. Forty fighters. Angels 20. Proceeding north Guildford." These reports should enable us to engage the enemy on more equal terms and are to take effect from dawn on August 27th. Acknowledge.'

Whilst this instruction took a simplistic view as to why some squadrons had failed to intercept, the reasons might well have been more to do with the dubious quality of the TR

9D wireless sets rather than any other failing. Consequently, there were almost certainly occasions when the information relayed back by the formation leader would have been neither received nor understood or, alternatively, any instruction subsequently arising would be neither received nor understood by the intended recipient squadrons! On the other hand, the transmission of a sighting report involved the possible loss of surprise in any attack, but this disadvantage was outweighed by the perceived value of the information received. Nevertheless, and despite the new reporting system, interceptions were still not numerous enough and on 6 September only 7 out of 18 squadrons despatched succeeded in engaging the enemy. On another occasion only 7 out of 17 found their quarry. It was a seemingly intractable problem that had to be solved.

From the second week in September, therefore, attempts to supplement radar warnings of high-flying raids were made in the shape of single Spitfires on dedicated reconnaissance sorties from squadrons at Biggin Hill and Hornchurch. These were despatched to patrol at maximum height on the usual routes that the enemy used to cross the English Channel and south coast. Sighting reports were transmitted via the frequently unreliable TR 9D sets back to the Biggin Hill and Hornchurch Sectors, but this valuable information usually failed to get through to the 11 Group Operations Room in time for any effective use to be made of it – or else it simply was not received by those Sectors in the first place, or was received in unintelligible or misunderstood transmissions. Consequently, and whilst the concept of these reconnaissance flights was sound, something had to be done to make them effective.

During the third week of September the Air Ministry instructed that a special reconnaissance flight be formed within RAF Fighter Command and operating under 11 Group control. Consequently, 421 Flight was established for this purpose and directions to this effect were given on 30 September. Importantly, the Spitfire aircraft allocated to the unit were equipped with the VHF TR 1143 sets and these were set up to report *directly* back to 11 Group HQ where VHF equipment had already been installed. The operations of 421 Flight became known as Jim-Crow sorties.

Whilst the essential features of the pre-established command and control system operated by Fighter Command was still very much in operation, the use of 421 Flight, for example, was a departure from the original conception but does not detract from the value of four years' careful preparation of Britain's air defence system. Rather, changes like those involving 421 Flight were tweaks and improvements gained through the experience of battle which, perhaps, echo the thoughts of the German Field Marshal Helmuth von Moltke from the 1800s, who said: 'No plan of operations extends with any certainty beyond the first contact with the main hostile force.' It is a piece of military wisdom that has resonated with commanders down the ages, and perhaps none more so than with Dowding and his senior commanders during the Battle of Britain. However, the essential features of the original plan and system were still very much in evidence; that is: radar early warning and visual tracking of the enemy made quickly available for the fighter pilot; ability to keep track of defensive fighters in the air; to position fighters where required on patrol lines and direct them as required; to enable pilots to regain their airfields in bad visibility; to facilitate the reinforcement of heavily engaged Sectors.

German assessment of the fighter control system

In the preliminary stages of the battle the Germans realised, through the interception of W/T messages, that British fighters were being directed towards their formations with great accuracy. As we have seen, they had known of the British radar system some time before the war but not of the highly developed plotting system that was linked with fighter control. Nor had they themselves experimented in the tactical employment of radar, although their technical development of it had already reached an advanced stage. Their assessment of the British fighter control system, as circulated to operational commands

THE PHONETIC ALPHABET FOR WIRELESS TRANSMISSIONS (W/T)

The phonetic alphabet in use during 1940 for wireless transmissions (W/T) between aircrew, and also between aircrew and ground stations, was wholly different to the NATO phonetic alphabet of today, which is in common use on an international basis. The 1940 phonetic alphabet is reproduced below, although this was again changed in 1942:

A – Ack	N – Nuts
B – Beer	O – Orange
C – Charlie	P – Pip
D – Don	Q – Queen
E – Edward	R – Robert
F – Freddie	S – Sugar
G – George	T – Toc
H – Harry	U – Uncle
I – Ink	V – Vic
J – Johnnie	W – William
K – King	X – X-ray
L – London	Y – Yorker
M – Monkey	Z – Zebra

on 7 August 1940, showed a very serious misconception:

'Since British fighters are controlled from the ground by W/T they are tied to their respective ground stations and thus restricted in mobility, even taking into consideration that the ground stations are partly mobile. Consequently, the assembly of strong fighter forces at determined points and at short notice is not to be expected. A massed German attack on a target area can therefore count on the same conditions of light fighter opposition as in attacks on widely scattered targets. It can, indeed, be assumed that considerable confusion in the defensive networks will be unavoidable during mass attacks, and that the effectiveness of the defences may thereby be reduced.'

The conclusion the Luftwaffe had arrived at was, in fact, the opposite of the truth. One of the advantages of the fighter control system was the ease with which threatened areas could be reinforced from other Groups.

Chapter Four

Into battle

How the battle was fought

Operational RAF fighter squadrons were held at various states of alert and were called into action as threats presented themselves to the air defence network. Both the waiting and the actual fighting was nerve-wracking and exhausting, especially as losses mounted. On the ground, wrecked aircraft had to be cleared away and damaged fighters repaired.

OPPOSITE Pilots of 19 Squadron stage a mock 'scramble' from the back of a truck at RAF Fowlmere near Duxford, September 1940. *(IWM CH1398)*

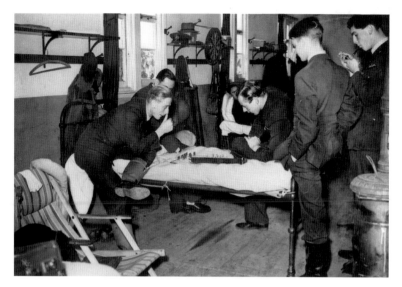

ABOVE **Pilots of 249 Squadron relax in between sorties.**

The RAF Fighter Command pilot or aircrew member during the Battle of Britain was, typically, just 21 years of age. Life on a front-line fighter squadron was demanding and exhausting, and although the levels of activity varied considerably depending upon the Group or Sector the days began early and ended just before dusk. During that time, a pilot or aircrew member could be called upon to make operational flights two or three times or more in a single day. These could be patrols or scrambles, and in between he

might be either held as available, on standby or at readiness. Each of these 'states' were nerve jangling to different degrees, the wait for a call to action being particularly stressful times for aircrew. When it came, action could be brief and frantic. Or it could involve prolonged and physically exhausting dogfighting where the mental effort, too, could be debilitating. Although pilots and squadrons were often 'rested' and moved to quieter Groups or Sectors it sometimes became impossible for them to be released from duty on rest days as Dowding had always intended. One squadron in particular, 501 Squadron, served the entirety of the battle on the front line without ever being rested. On the other hand, some squadrons saw very little action and some pilots never once saw the enemy. Overall, though, it was a tough and dangerous life with a high probability of death or serious injury. Despite public perception at the time, and since, that the fighter pilot's life was glamorous, it was very far from being so.

Readiness states

An operational RAF fighter squadron during 1940 was considered to have had four states of readiness: released, available, readiness and standby. These various states were shown, squadron by squadron, on the illuminated tote board in Group Operations Rooms.

RELEASED: In this state pilots were permitted to go wherever they chose and were not required under any circumstances* until the time that the 'released' period expired. Squadrons were always released until a definitely stated time.

AVAILABLE*: Pilots in this state were required to be able to leave the ground within 15 minutes of the time they are ordered into the air. This means they had to remain near a telephone or loudspeaker system somewhere reasonably near the dispersal areas where their aircraft were parked so that on the word to take off they could rush to their aircraft and be in the air within the required time. From this state pilots may have been required to come to the next state, which was standby. Ten minutes was allowed for the transition from available to standby.

READINESS*: Pilots in this state were to be available to take off within 5 minutes. They had to remain in the vicinity of the aircraft and be

RIGHT **Tote board in 11 Group Operations Room.**

LEFT Waiting outside the Flight hut for the call to scramble.

dressed in their flying clothing. They may be required to come to the next state, which was standby, within 3 minutes.

STANDBY: Pilots were required to be in their cockpits, engine running and aircraft pointing into wind ready for immediate take-off. Ground crews also stood at standby ready to assist in the starting and departure of the squadron. This high state of preparedness was governed by the length of time an aircraft engine could stay running without overheating. (On a Spitfire this was very limited, but a little longer on the Hurricane with airflow from the propeller across the centrally mounted radiator and oil cooler.) (*Note: Sometimes, parts of the same squadron could be at different states with, say, A Flight designated as available and with B Flight at readiness. On rare occasions, squadrons were called from released to be either at readiness or ordered to scramble if circumstances such as an imminent attack on the airfield threatened. A case in point involved 602 Squadron, scrambled from a released state on 16 August 1940 at RAF Westhampnett when the adjacent RAF Tangmere was being dive-bombed.*)

Scramble!

Once the order to scramble had been given then the squadron, or designated Flights or Sections, were expected to take off immediately. The pilots, groundcrew and aircraft were generally held at different dispersed points around the airfield and the order to scramble would be telephoned through to the respective dispersal

huts where the pilots and crews would be waiting. If held at readiness the pilots would race to their assigned aircraft. Here, the groundcrew would be waiting. The straps of the parachute would be draped ready for strapping on, and the pilot would be assisted in this process by his rigger who would already be standing on the wing waiting to help. The rigger would also assist in helping secure the Sutton seat harness as the pilot went through his brief pre-flight checks, primed the engine and thumbed the starter. Meanwhile, the fitter would be standing by with the trolley accumulator (called the 'Trolley Acc' – an electric battery trolley) plugged in ready and waiting for start-up. In cases where the order to scramble had been given whilst at standby, then this process would have been shortened by virtue of the fact that the pilot was already in the cockpit and ready to go.

The command to scramble was generally telephoned through to the pilot's dispersal hut from the Sector Operations Room, having been devolved down through the command chain as previously described. Typically, the telephone would have been answered by an airman orderly clerk who would shout out the relevant instruction to the nearby pilots, eg: 'Squadron Scramble!' or, maybe, 'B Flight Scramble!' etc. At this stage, specific instruction would be given to the pilots as to their course, height or destination. Across the years the legend of the 'Scramble Bell' has given the impression that an airman clanged a large bell, hung at

Continued on page 97

ABOVE The ensemble of a typical RAF Battle of Britain fighter pilot's kit: Irvin sheepskin flying jacket, 'B'-type flying helmet, 'D'-type oxygen mask, 1932 pattern Mae West life jacket, Mk IIIA goggles, 1936 pattern boots and 1933 pattern flying gauntlets. In practice, very few fighter pilots wore the Irvin jacket in the air as they were quite bulky in cramped cockpits, especially when worn with a parachute harness and Mae West life jacket.

WHAT THE FIGHTER PILOT WORE

There was, in fact, no universal clothing and equipment rig for the pilots and aircrew of RAF Fighter Command during 1940. Much of it was simply down to personal choice although certain pieces of equipment were a standard requirement but, even then, there were variations on a theme. There were, however, common 'styles', but what was worn, and how, depended on the individual's personal tastes and preferences. This applied equally, across the board, to both officer and NCO aircrew.

Taking a 'typical' pilot or aircrew member of the period, from head to toe, and in all cases, we might generally expect to find: flying helmet, flying goggles, oxygen mask, life jacket, flying gauntlets and parachute harness and pack. These items of kit were mandatory. However, what *was* variable to the RAF Fighter Command flier of 1940 was the other clothing, equipment and accoutrements that he wore or took into action.

Very often, pre-war pilots would wear one-piece cotton flying suits that had been privately purchased. These came in either black or white.

1 Typical headgear for a Battle of Britain RAF fighter pilot of 1940. Although there were variations on a theme, every pilot and aircrew member had to wear the standard flying helmet and oxygen mask since these incorporated a headset and microphone as well as sustaining life at altitude. Some pilots wore goggles according to preference and choice and this would not always involve service-issue equipment.

2 The 'D'-type oxygen mask was made of green woven material and incorporated a microphone with a transmit on/off switch at the front side of the mask. Oxygen was supplied via a rubber hose, which entered the black spigot seen on the left-hand side. The wiring loom, including the headset and jack-plug, are seen attached.

3 The inside of the mask was lined in a soft chamois leather. Later patterns of RAF oxygen masks, post-Battle of Britain, were manufactured from rubber.

4   Often, pilots preferred privately purchased flying goggles, with the Luxor brand illustrated here being particularly popular. In many cases, RAF fighter pilots in 1940 had been pre-war civilian pilots and had purchased their own flying clothing, including goggles.

5   Several different patterns of Air Ministry-issue goggles were used by pilots during the Battle of Britain. These were the Mk II goggles with slightly tinted lenses.

6   A fighter pilot of the period displays his complete headgear as worn operationally and including the Mk II goggles.

7   A 1932 pattern life jacket worn over a sergeant pilot's dress tunic. In practice, most pilots painted their life jackets bright yellow for added visibility in the event of landing in the sea since the colour of the life jacket as issued was very similar to the colour of the English Channel on an average day.

8   The RAF fighter pilot of the Battle of Britain routinely wore three pairs of gloves: silk inners, a chamois pair of gloves and leather gauntlets over the top. These protected against both cold and burns in the event of fire.

(All images of flying equipment courtesy of Mick Prodger)

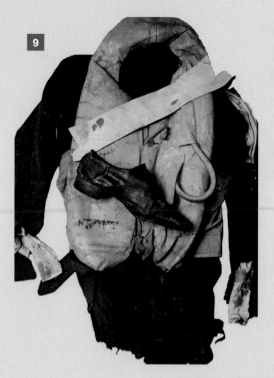

9

9 On 16 August 1940, Hurricane pilot Flt Lt James Nicolson of 249 Squadron was shot down and badly burned in an action which earned him the Victoria Cross, thus becoming the only RAF fighter pilot of the entire war to be so honoured. Shown here is the burned and tattered uniform jacket, cannon shell-damaged shoe and his yellow-painted 1932 pattern Mae West. Pilots painted the jackets yellow using aircraft dope – the same colour that would have been used for the outer ring of fuselage roundels. In this instance, Nicolson was flying simply in his uniform tunic and wearing ordinary shoes.

10 A variation on the type of boots used by the Battle of Britain fighter pilot was the 1939 pattern with their black leather bottoms and canvas uppers.

10

Invariably, the embroidered squadron badge would be sewn to the left breast pocket and with a set of RAF pilot's wings stitched above. Rank bars were worn on epaulettes, or in the case of NCOs their stripes were worn in the usual place on the sleeves. These flying overalls were very much regarded as a badge of honour by pre-war pilots and aircrew, particularly those from the Auxiliary Air Force.

Pilots and aircrew sometimes simply wore just their uniform tunic, trousers and service shoes into action and with nothing else apart from the headgear, life jacket, etc, previously referred to, although once again it all came down to personal

BELOW Flying overalls (usually in black or in white) were also commonly worn, but usually by pilots who had purchased them privately pre-war or else had been issued with them whilst at Flying Training School. Sgt H.N. Howes of 85 Squadron is seen here wearing a pair of white flying overalls. Noteworthy is his Mae West, which seems to have been painted bright red on its top half and yellow on the bottom sections.

BELOW In this instance black flying overalls have had sergeant's stripes and RAF buttons added. The pilot also wears a zipped jumper under his uniform tunic for added warmth. (This is Sgt Ken Campbell of 73 Squadron, France, May 1940. Campbell survived the Battle of France but did not fly operationally in the Battle of Britain.)

choice. Sometimes, they would wear a thick knitted woollen sweater, often roll-neck, under their uniform jackets and, mostly, aircrew would wear flying boots and occasionally with thick knitted fishermen's socks. Flying boots were generally the sheepskin-lined black leather 1936 pattern boot or the leather and canvas sheepskin-lined 1939 pattern boots. Operating at high altitude and in sub-zero temperatures, keeping warm was paramount and knitted garments, socks and scarves were commonplace. Less common, despite the popular perception, was the wearing of the Irvin sheepskin leather flying jacket. Although an issue item, these jackets were cumbersome and generally far too restrictive inside the tight confines of a fighter cockpit, especially when worn over the uniform and then having to have a life jacket and parachute over the top. Quite apart from restricted movement in the cockpit, these bulky jackets could also be an impediment when trying to escape from an aircraft in a hurry. More often than not, the jackets were worn by pilots during the cold chill of an early morning or autumnal stint at dispersal, or for wearing whilst riding their motorcycles and driving open-top cars whilst off duty. Warm and stylish they may have been, but practical for the fighter cockpit of 1940 they certainly were not. That said, there are known examples of the Irvin jacket being worn in Spitfires and Hurricanes, although they did tend to be used more in larger aircraft at this time.

Another option was the 1930 Sidcot suit. This was an issue one-piece flying overall made from a grey-green rubberised material. Comfortable and practical, the suits were fastened with zips and buttons, had stowage pockets and a detachable brown fur collar. In the event of abandoning an aircraft, these suits presented less in the way of material that might snag or catch and their 'coverall' nature protected a uniform underneath from wear, tear and oil or fuel stains. Whilst being popular with many aircrew it again came down to a matter of choice.

Typically, it was regarded as *de rigeur* for fighter pilots, both officers and NCOs, to wear the top button of their uniform tunics undone. This was never officially condoned, but a blind eye was usually turned in less formal situations. It is a practice said to have originated when pilots stuffed scarves into the tops of their

tunics, but it became a 'trademark' of the fighter pilot in 1940 and, at this time, the uniform jacket for all ranks was a brass-buttoned four-pocket belted tunic. Later, battledress blouses were introduced although there is photographic evidence that at least a few pilots in 1940 were wearing them. It is possible these were privately tailored affairs, based on army battledress tunics then in use.

The 1932 pattern life jacket in use during 1940 was issued in a drab khaki material which, as pilots noted, was very much the same colour as the English Channel on an average day. Consequently, many pilots painted theirs with yellow aircraft dope (see page 93) for greater visibility when brought down in the sea. Later patterns of life jacket (from 1941) were made of a yellow material. These jackets, orally inflated through an inflation tube, left a great deal to be desired both practically and in quality. Accordingly, captured Luftwaffe life jackets became a significant 'prize' for RAF fighter pilots and were frequently worn in favour of their discarded RAF issue ones. In a yellow rubberised material they were light and not cumbersome and included a gas inflation bottle. In terms of design and suitability, these jackets were streets ahead of the RAF issue type. Sometimes, personal emblems, names or nicknames were painted on to the life jackets.

The leather flying helmet with its headphones and attached oxygen mask combining wireless microphone was one piece of equipment that was common to all. It was not a variable or optional piece of kit and without it the pilot could neither communicate nor breathe at altitude. The headphones were incorporated into zipped ear cups with the oxygen mask, of a green fabric material and chamois lined, fixed by press studs to the helmet. An oxygen tube led from the mask to a bayonet fixing in the cockpit and leads to the microphone and headphones fed into a single cable that ended in a jack plug which, in turn, was plugged into the cockpit W/T socket. The goggles worn with the helmet, however, could vary in pattern.

Flying googles, as issued, again differed in pattern; broadly speaking, the Mk II, Mk III and Mk IV. Again, there were variations with these patterns, including flip-down sun visors on the Mk IVB for instance. Once more, personal choice came into play although the type of goggles issued to the individual was an obvious factor. Sometimes, however, the flier shunned the issued equipment and preferred privately purchased flying goggles. These would often be a set that the individual had purchased pre-war, and perhaps used at a civilian flying club. The practice of using private equipment, though, had all but ceased after the Battle of Britain.

Flying gauntlets, also issue equipment, were essential pieces of flying clothing and were worn with white silk inners and were not only a protection against cold but, also, a valuable piece of added protection against burns as, indeed, were flying goggles.

Although not essential to be carried in air operations over Britain, some RAF aircrew during 1940 chose to carry issue side-arms, usually a Webley service revolver in a webbing holster, although wearing these in the cockpit was awkward and it was not a particularly common practice.

Importantly, of course, we come to the parachute and this piece of equipment was generally stowed in the bucket seat pan of fighter aircraft with its straps left adjusted to fit and ready to be strapped on. Some pilots preferred to keep the parachute on the tail-plane and to be helped to strap it on by the aircraft fitter. In practice, this took time and the pilot also then had to make an ungainly waddle to the aircraft and struggle to enter the cramped cockpit. This was not exactly conducive to a quick get-away.

Lastly, of course, we have something worn by all service personnel the world over – the identity disc. In the case of flying personnel, they were specifically forbidden to take into the air with them papers or documents which may have been of use to the enemy in the event that such material should fall into their hands. Of course, this was a rule that was often not obeyed, although one that *was* obeyed was the wearing of service-issue identity discs. Very often, especially among other ranks, the two discs issued to British personnel were simply worn around the neck on a piece of string but, more often than not, suspended on a chain or thin leather strip.

The pair of discs with which every British serviceman, regardless of rank, was issued were made of compressed fibre, a material deemed to be more comfortable to wear in hot climates. Each disc was stamped with name and initials, rank, religion and service number and with one disc circular and red, the other eight sided and green. It is often said that one was fireproof and the other waterproof, but this is not correct. There were, though, specific purposes for each disc and particular regulations in the manner they should be worn; the green disc strung from one hole with the red disc, in turn, strung from the second hole of the green disc. In the case of the wearer's death this enabled the red disc to be quickly cut from the green disc and the green disc left with the body. In this way, another person later finding the body would know the death had been reported due to the absence of the red disc. The green disc was used for information to mark the grave. In cases where the wearer was unconscious or incapacitated they enabled a person caring for the casualty to identify them. In some cases, aircrew had their own private metal identity discs or bracelets made although the marking of these followed the same convention as the issue discs.

In all cases, identity discs were worn by RAF aircrew during the Battle of Britain.

As we have seen, flying clothing and equipment was often very much a case of mix-and-match, worn with comfort, practicality and sometimes superstition influencing the individual choice.

BELOW A pilot's identity discs. These are for Flg Off R.P. Plummer, a Hurricane pilot with 46 Squadron. In the event of death, the green disc was supposed to be left with the body. Fighter pilots were often superstitious and frequently carried lucky charms. In this case, Richard Plummer has attached a lucky horseshoe to his identity disc necklace. Contrary to regulations he wore his discs on a chain instead of being attached in the approved manner to a length of string.

ABOVE The so-called 'Scramble Bell' is something of a misnomer, but has become an iconic symbol of the Battle of Britain against the background of a common belief that a Scramble Bell was rung when the call to action came. That was not always so, but the myth (or misconception) probably owes its origins to a staged piece of period Pathé newsreel when a squadron scrambles against the clanging of a bell like this. In fact, these bells were simply station fire alarm bells, although it is true that they were sometimes purloined for use at dispersal points. This example from RAF Biggin Hill has certainly seen some action judging by the strike marks in it.
(Chris Bennett)

TERMINOLOGY

A range of code words and other pieces of official terminology, invented in 1938, was in use during the Battle of Britain to be used by aircrew and controllers during air operations and was known as 'the Fighter Code'. These code words should not be confused with slang terms (which are listed elsewhere) but were, instead, words or names for specific actions etc. They are set out in the order in which the instructions might typically be issued:

Take off and set course immediately:	SCRAMBLE
Climb to:	ANGELS
Alter course to:	VECTOR
Increase speed to normal full speed:	BUSTER
Increase speed to maximum full speed:	GATE
Reduce speed to normal cruising speed:	LINER
Circle and search:	ORBIT
Enemy:	BANDIT
Unidentified aircraft:	BOGY
Enemy sighted:	TALLY-HO!
Return and land:	PANCAKE

By this simple system, therefore, controllers were able to direct fighters on to the tracked position of the enemy. For example, on the order to scramble a squadron might be given the instruction: 'Vector 230, Angels 18.' Translated, this gave a course of 230° at an altitude of 18,000ft. However, in order to confuse the enemy who may be listening in to these transmissions a false quantity was sometimes introduced whereby Angels 18 really meant fly at 21,000ft rather than 18,000ft. After the engagement, the pilots might be ordered: 'Pancake, pancake', ie return and land.

Continued from page 91

dispersal, to sound the alert. This, however, is something of a fallacy although it does have some truth to it.

As far as the Air Ministry was concerned there was no such thing as a 'Scramble Bell'. Instead, though, some squadrons acquired a standard RAF fire bell as these could always be found hung at strategic positions around RAF stations. The intention in placing them at dispersal points was that they could usefully alert other Flights or Sections who may be dispersed further away than within earshot of the airman clerk's shouted instructions. In these cases, pilots and groundcrew who were more distant from the telephone could get the message and act accordingly. Additionally,

it would function as a better source of communicating the command to pilots who may be at standby and rather more insulated from the sounds of the outside world whilst sitting in their cockpits and, perhaps, when wearing flying helmets. It was not the case, however, that the so-called 'Scramble Bell' was always rung as the order to go. Indeed, photographic evidence would tend to suggest that these bells were not even a feature at some airfields or with some squadrons. That said, Pathé newsreel footages and the like, which feature staged scrambles, inevitably show an airman clanging the bell, although this may be more for dramatic effect than anything else!

Once started and ready to go then the aircraft would take off directly from where they were dispersed, and straight into wind. It was not a case of lining up on runways and, in any event, many of the airfields in use by Fighter Command at this time were grass only and frequently had no paved strips. Each pilot would taxy out and take off with his own section leader or flight commander in a somewhat chaotic but organised fashion and, once airborne, the entire squadron, Flight or Section would form up on the assigned leader. The leader (not always the squadron CO) would receive his orders by R/T as he got into the air. In the case of a typical squadron scramble the order might be:

'Gannic Leader, vector two two zero. Buster. Angels 20. Bandits – Brighton.'

Translated, this is telling 92 Squadron to steer a course of 220 and climb at normal full speed to 20,000ft where the squadron will encounter enemy aircraft over Brighton. The squadron, Flight or Section of 92 Squadron's Spitfires will then follow their leader to the assigned position, keeping a lookout all the time for enemy aircraft. Once the enemy are sighted, the alert 'Tally Ho!' would be called.

Throughout this whole process the indicator lights on the tote board in the Group and Sector Operations Rooms would show the controller the exact situation with each squadron – 'Ordered on Interception Patrol', 'Left Ground' and 'In Position'.

Tally-ho!

Once the enemy had been sighted the squadron, flight or section commander (depending upon the strength in which the defending forces had been deployed) would transmit 'Tally-ho!'. The pilot first spotting the enemy (not necessarily the commander of the formation) would call the alert, and add information such as 'Bandits, two o'clock above!' This would tell the other pilots the direction and attitude of the threat, and with the sky divided up into an imaginary clock face, with twelve o'clock in the dead ahead position, the other pilots would know to look ahead and slightly to the right, in the position where '2' would be on the clock dial. Once the enemy was sighted this information would have been received by the Sector Operations Room and flashed to the Group Operations Room where an illuminated signal would show: 'Enemy Sighted'. Immediately the enemy were sighted it fell to whoever was leading the formation to organise the attack. This might involve detailing one section of the formation off to deal with, say, a bomber formation, whilst the remainder tackled the fighters. The leader of the defending fighter formation would then position himself in the most advantageous position to engage and would call an order such as 'Tally-ho! Fighter attack Number One . . . Go!' This would follow a prescribed attack method as laid down by RAF Fighter Command. Alternatively, the formation would know automatically, and following pre-determined plans, how the squadron would attack and would follow their leader accordingly. On the call of 'Tally-ho!' the message would be flashed on to the same

BELOW AND OPPOSITE PAGE One of the RAF's various prescribed methods for attacking enemy bomber formations, Fighter Attack No 3.

APPROACH TACTICS APPLICABLE
TO FIGHTER ATTACKS NOS 2 AND 3

	W/T ORDER
SIGHTING	
BOMBERS	STAND BY FOR NO 3 ATTACK
No 1 SECTION	
No 2	
PHASE 1	
No 1 SECTION	
No 2	
PHASE 2	
No 1 SECTION	
No 2	
ATTACK	
ATTACK DELIVERED ON RECEIPT OF ———	No 3 ATTACK GO

FIGHTER ATTACK No 3

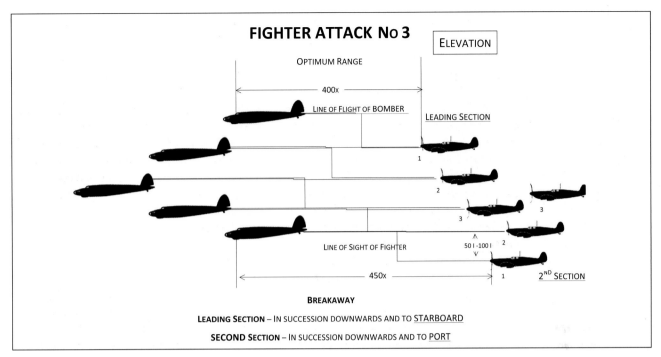

ELEVATION

OPTIMUM RANGE

400x

LINE OF FLIGHT OF BOMBER

LEADING SECTION

LINE OF SIGHT OF FIGHTER

50ı -100ı

450x

2ND SECTION

BREAKAWAY

LEADING SECTION – IN SUCCESSION DOWNWARDS AND TO <u>STARBOARD</u>

SECOND SECTION – IN SUCCESSION DOWNWARDS AND TO <u>PORT</u>

FIGHTER ATTACK No 3

PLAN

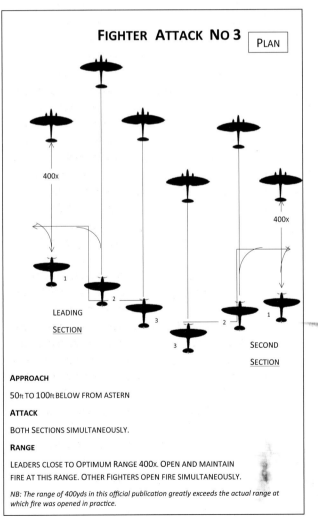

400x

400x

LEADING
<u>SECTION</u>

SECOND
<u>SECTION</u>

APPROACH

50ft TO 100ft BELOW FROM ASTERN

ATTACK

BOTH SECTIONS SIMULTANEOUSLY.

RANGE

LEADERS CLOSE TO OPTIMUM RANGE 400x. OPEN AND MAINTAIN
FIRE AT THIS RANGE. OTHER FIGHTERS OPEN FIRE SIMULTANEOUSLY.

*NB: The range of 400yds in this official publication greatly exceeds the actual range at
which fire was opened in practice.*

FIGHTER ATTACK No 3

PLAN

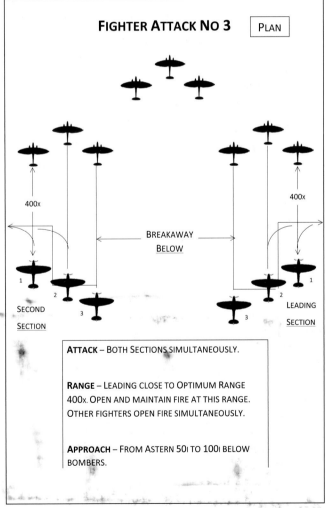

400x

400x

BREAKAWAY
<u>BELOW</u>

SECOND
<u>SECTION</u>

LEADING
<u>SECTION</u>

ATTACK – BOTH SECTIONS SIMULTANEOUSLY.

RANGE – LEADING CLOSE TO OPTIMUM RANGE
400x. OPEN AND MAINTAIN FIRE AT THIS RANGE.
OTHER FIGHTERS OPEN FIRE SIMULTANEOUSLY.

APPROACH – FROM ASTERN 50ı TO 100ı BELOW
BOMBERS.

Later in the war a famous set of air combat rules for RAF Fighter Command were drawn up by Battle of Britain 'ace' Wg Cdr A.G. 'Sailor' Malan called 'Ten of My Rules For Air Fighting'. In it, Malan set out his pointers for achieving aerial victories, and for staying alive. However, as early as July 1940 the Air Tactics Branch at the Air Ministry drew up their 'Hints and Tips for Fighter Pilots' which included the following:

AIR FIGHTING
DOGFIGHT HINTS
a) Formations quickly become broken up in a dogfight. Aircraft of sections should try, as far as possible, to keep together for mutual support.

b) If you hear the sound of firing, turn immediately. The sound almost certainly comes from an enemy fighter which is attacking you from astern.

c) Turn sharply and slightly to the right downwards. Hurricanes and Spitfires are more manoeuvrable than German fighters and they will have difficulty following your turn. The Me 109 is particularly bad at a sharp turn to the right.

d) If you are involved in a head-on attack, remember the rule of the air. When you have to break away to avoid collision, turn to the right.

e) Never waste ammunition. The golden opportunity may come when your ammunition is finished.

f) Be especially careful at the moment you break off a combat. Take evasive action immediately because you are especially liable to attack at this moment. A useful manoeuvre to break off a combat is a dive using full aileron. Regain height as soon as possible.

g) If your engine stops dive straight down to make the enemy think that he has 'got' you. Manoeuvres without engine gives the game away, and the enemy likes to concentrate on the 'lame duck'.

h) If you have to bail out, half-roll on to your back, open the lid, undo your straps and push the stick forward.

i) Never fly straight, particularly if you are alone. Keep continually turning from side to side so that you can keep a look-out behind you. If the sun is bright and is behind you it is advisable to make a 360° turn at short intervals so that you can make quite certain that the sky is clear in all directions.

j) BEWARE OF THE HUN IN THE SUN.

GENERAL HINTS AND TIPS FOR AIR FIGHTING
a) If there is a chance that enemy fighters may be about, look well before you take off, turn quickly, be especially careful while circling the aerodrome before landing and don't make a long straight approach.

b) Light AA guns from the ground are accurate and effective up to 4,000 feet. The most dangerous heights for heavy AA guns are between 4,000 and 8,000 feet.

c) Watch that your oxygen fittings do not come adrift.

d) Don't leave your transmitter on send. If you do, you make communication impossible for the whole formation and you may ruin the patrol.

e) Remember to turn on your sight and ciné-camera, if you have one.

f) If you have been in action, test your hydraulic system for possible damage before you get back to your home aerodrome.

g) If you see white or greyish smoke pouring out of an engine of the enemy aircraft, it probably means that you have damaged his cooling oil circulation. You should therefore switch your aim to the other engine. Black smoke may indicate either that the engine has been damaged or that the pilot is overboosting. There are indications that the enemy will try to produce smoke artificially so as to deceive you, so you must use your judgment as to whether you have caused sufficient damage to make it impossible for him to return to base.

h) If you are in a single-seater and have to land in the sea, bail out if possible; if you cannot, take the following action on the way down:

i. Open cockpit cover and lock in open position.

ii. Release oxygen and R/T fittings.

iii. Release parachute harness. DON'T undo Sutton harness.

iv. See that flotation waistcoat is only very lightly inflated. If it is fully inflated its buoyancy may prevent you escaping.

v. Just before you touch the water, take two or three deep breaths.

vi. As soon as the shock of touching the water has ceased, undo Sutton harness and heave yourself out of the cockpit.

vii. Blow up flotation waistcoat as soon as you reach the surface.

FINALLY
Remember that the closer the range, the more certain you are of bringing down the enemy. Remember also that everyone tends to underestimate range and that when you think you are within 200 yards of the enemy you are probably still 400 yards away.

Sector and Group indicator boards reading: 'Enemy Engaged'.

Commenting on his success in air fighting, and of his demise when being shot down and seriously injured on 1 October 1940, Plt Off 'Ben' Bennions said that the most valuable piece of advice he had been given by an old hand at air fighting was: 'If you have an enemy aircraft in front of you, always assume that you also have one behind you.' A momentary lapse of attention, or fixation on the target you were pursuing, could be fatal – and often was.

Patrols

Quite apart from a scramble, pilots were often called upon to carry out patrols in their sector when they would be engaged on looking out for the enemy or giving fighter cover to airfields or, say, protecting shipping convoys at times of heightened enemy air activity. Squadrons in the air on patrol, if they were in the right position or at a suitable altitude, might be called on by the Sector controller either to engage a hostile raid or else investigate what was referred to as an 'X' Plot. This was a plot of an unidentified aircraft or group of aircraft that had appeared in the sector. Whilst a squadron, or even a flight or section from a squadron, might be in a position to quickly get to intercept an incoming raid from their patrol line, it was not necessarily the most effective situation from which to deploy defending fighters. For one thing, the aircraft could have already been on patrol for some considerable time, and thus their ability to intercept and engage might often be limited by the fuel states of the aircraft involved. One advantage, though, was that patrolling aircraft would already be at a considerable altitude and height was often a deciding factor in determining the outcome of any engagement. Despite what is often written on the subject it was more often than not the case that RAF fighters were outnumbered, but they also failed to have the height advantage over incoming German raiders. Indeed, on less than thirty-three occasions between 8 and 18 August 1940, RAF fighters failed to have the advantage of height.* Generally, then, it was at least theoretically more effective to order fighters to engage via a scramble so long as they could be got off the ground and into position quickly enough.

FIGHTERS V. ESCORTED BOMBERS

i. It is essential that leaders should weigh up the situation as a whole before delivering attacks. Rushing blindly in to attack an enemy may have disastrous results, and will certainly be less effective.

ii. Never fly straight, either in the formation as a whole or individually. When over enemy territory alter course and height with a view to misleading AA.

iii. Keep a constant watch to the rear of the formation of aircraft.

iv. Upon hearing close gun fire, turn immediately. Hesitancy in so doing may result in effective enemy fire. Do not dive straight away.

v. Before taking off, search the sky for enemy fighters, and if they are known to be about turn as soon as possible after taking off. Enemy fighters have frequently dived on aircraft whilst taking off from their aerodrome. Similar remarks apply during landing.

vi. Conserve ammunition as much as possible. A short burst at effective range is usually decisive, and leaves further ammunition for further attacks.

vii. Exploit surprise to the utmost. The enemy has been taught to do this, and you should be prepared accordingly.

viii. Always remember that your objective is the ENEMY BOMBER.

BELOW A formation of Heinkel 111 bombers seen from port and below. Approaching from this position a fighter leader would need to determine how he and his pilots might best attack the formation by utilising one or other of the RAF Fighter Attack procedures. All the while, the fighter pilots involved would need to be aware of the likely presence of escort fighters who would inevitably be at a higher altitude and up-sun.

(*Note: *part of the reason for this was that whilst the RDF stations were detecting the approach of the enemy and were often succeeding in distinguishing between large and small formations, they frequently failed to make any estimate of height and, when they did, they usually underestimated. Additionally, the Spitfire and Hurricane took between 18 and 21 minutes to reach 25,000ft. This meant that the enemy fighters were often waiting for them and, worse, were often in a perfect position for a 'bounce'. Not only that, but a controller necessarily took into account the state of the sky and could not take the risk of sending all his squadrons so high that a German formation could slip past below the cloud ceiling.)*

Gun-sights and shooting

RAF Fighter Command's early warning and control system's chain would ultimately end at the gun-sight, gun button and machine-gun barrel of its front-line fighters. The Spitfire and Hurricane were both fitted with the Barr & Stroud GM 2 Reflector gun-sight as standard. Devised by the Barr & Stroud Company in 1935 the sight featured a lens through which a circular graticule was projected on to a glass reflector screen in front of the pilot. The graticule was bisected by a cross, with the horizontal bar broken in the centre and with the range/base setting being determined by adjusting two knurled rings around the base of the gun-sight body. The internal mechanism then set the gap in the graticule cross bar according to the required range. A central dot was added as a further aiming point. The radius of the graticule ring gave the deflection shooting allowance for hitting a target crossing at 100mph. It was illuminated by a half-silvered 12-volt light bulb held in a Bakelite quick-release holder at the base of the sight body and a clip of spare bulbs was stowed on the side of the cockpit. A Sorbo rubber pad was fitted across the front of the sight to protect the pilot from injury in the event of a crash-landing.

Writing of the sight in his 'Notes on Air Gunnery and Fighting', Battle of Britain pilot Wg Cdr E.M. Donaldson DSO, AFC, sets out its workings and operation. Although written in 1943 it remains pertinent to 1940 operations:

'The latest type of sight is the reflector sight. Instruction on this is amply covered in the manual dealing with the sight, but perhaps a few extra notes on the sight from the practical experience point of view might be appropriate.

BELOW The RAF reflector gun-sight of the Battle of Britain. Almost a predecessor to the Head Up Display (HUD) systems of modern combat aircraft, the reflector sight worked on the principle of reflecting an illuminated ring sight and graticule on to a glass screen in front of the pilot's face. *(Col Pope)*

BELOW RIGHT What the fighter pilot saw. Here, the projected ring sight is illuminated on to a reflector sight screen. Difficult to photograph, this picture shows a 'ghost' second image, which has reflected on to the inside of the armoured windscreen. *(Col Pope)*

One of the snags about the sight is that it is lighted by an electric bulb and this bulb burns in a very small compartment in the sight and consequently is inclined to get very hot. I am not trying to say that the sight is in any way unreliable because of this point, but it is of the utmost importance that before taking off on patrol duties, the pilot does switch the bulb on to see that it does light. If it does not do so, it must be changed at once. Spare bulbs must always be carried and pilots should see that the spare bulb holder is carrying the two spare bulbs it should. The other snag is the very small base anchorage and the very smallest fraction of an inch movement on this would throw the sight some feet off the target at 200 yards, and so it is of the greatest importance that the lining or harmonisation of the sight with the guns is checked frequently. For some reason or other the sight makes a very attractive article at which to clutch in order to help one get out of the cockpit; all the mechanics invariably do this and one does find oneself reaching for the sight to help one out. Of course the sight must not be touched at all once it is correctly lined. Pilots should refrain from hanging their helmets or any other articles of clothing over the sight bearing in mind that the sight was not designed as a hook for such articles. After each flight the windshield of the aircraft should be wiped off; if this is not done it seems to hinder the effectiveness of the reflection.

Operation

'The reflector sight is absolutely fool proof and all that a pilot is concerned with in the air is the switching on of the bulb and the setting of the range bar. Personally, in combat I have never used the range bar as a range finder, but in practice I find it invaluable as a check of the range that I am opening fire at and I find with this practice in combat I am able to judge the range very accurately. However, I do recommend that a range be set on the sight and I think that range should be for a 60-foot target on 300 yards, this being the size of the average bomber target. I say 300 yards because one is inclined to watch the enemy until it fills the range gap and then open fire so that in actual fact one is always very much closer when the trigger is pressed than the range one has set on the

ABOVE From the outside looking in. Here, Sgt Marian Domagala, a Polish pilot on 238 Squadron, looks out through his gun-sight and windscreen. (Note: Domagala has dispensed with flying goggles and has, instead, made his own unusual and improvised 'field modification' by fixing the sun visor from a pair of Mk IVB goggles on to the front of his flying helmet.)

sight. This means that one opens fire at the best possible range of 250 yards.

'I think also it is advisable to leave the reflector sight light switched off when not in use. It has a very intensely bright bulb and if left on for any length of time will run the battery down if the generator is not functioning correctly. I have

LEFT Spare bulbs for the reflector gun-sight were always stowed in a bracket close to the sight in both the Spitfire and Hurricane.
(Col Pope)

known generators to fail in the air and because the sight is left on the battery becomes quickly discharged and the sight is left useless.

Harmonisation

'There is no question that the careful and correct harmonisation of the sight and guns is the most important of all the points in the air fighting. It would be a pathetic state of affairs for a pilot to enter a combat and fight his

hardest, firing his guns and yet achieve nothing because his guns are not pointing where his sight is aiming. The pilot himself should make it his personal responsibility to harmonise the sights and guns on his own aircraft; under no circumstances whatever should he delegate this responsibility to anyone else.

'The procedure for the correct harmonisation of sights is laid down in the appropriate manuals and should be strictly adhered to.

'In this connection I should like to mention, not how to harmonise the guns, but at what ranges for the most effective fire one should set the harmonisation point; that is, the point at which the gun's bullets should meet. The greatest difficulty a fighter pilot has to contend with when firing wing-mounted guns is range, therefore anything which gives him more latitude in judging of range is bound to be helpful.

'I have found it most effective to harmonise the two inboard guns to say 200 yards, the

next pair at 225 yards, the next pair at 250, and so on. If one draws a plan of the path of the bullets from each gun, one will see that with a 5-foot target you have practically covered with a maximum density of bullets all ranges from 175 yards onwards.'

In order to fire the guns, the pilot had to operate a single gun button with his right thumb. The button was situated at the 11 o'clock position on the control column top and was surrounded by a knurled ring marked 'SAFE' and 'FIRE'. Before going into action the pilot had to turn the ring to 'FIRE' and all was now set to engage the enemy. Depressing the button opened a valve and allowed compressed air to flow through the system from the air reservoir and fire all of the guns simultaneously. Broadly speaking, the control column, gun button and firing mechanisms on the Spitfire and Hurricane were identical, although both control column tops had slight variations and different stores reference numbers.

Home for tea!

On returning from an operational flight it was the duty of each pilot to submit details for his individual combat report if an engagement with the enemy had taken place. These combat reports (RAF Form 'F') were required to be submitted after any engagement, whether or not an enemy aircraft had been destroyed or confirmed damaged. A large number of these individual reports are today held at the National Archives, Kew, in the document class AIR 50, and filed by squadron and in date order. The reports were often written in the pilot's own hand although others were typed up, probably by the squadron intelligence officer (IO) who would work either from notes dictated by the pilot or from a rough draft the pilot had provided. The completed reports, signed by the individual pilots, were collated by the squadron IO (generally known as 'Spy') and submitted to HQ Fighter Command. It also became the responsibility of the IO to submit to HQ Fighter Command an overall summary of his own squadron's actions on a daily basis. In turn, the duty IO at Fighter Command would compile an overall picture of the day's actions, across all Groups, for submission to the C-in-C.

Quite apart from the fact that these reports provide historians with a contemporaneous view of events in the air as they happened, they also enabled intelligence officers and senior commanders to analyse claims and losses and examine and refine air fighting tactics. They would also form the basis in determining victories that could be credited to individual pilots. The criteria for allocating a claim of destroyed, probably destroyed or damaged are set out below.

- **Destroyed** – to cover all cases in which the enemy aircraft is positively reported to

ABOVE Although posed, these Spitfire pilots of 19 Squadron are seen in what might be described as a typical post-engagement discussion, using their hands to describe the relative movement of aircraft and how they had either attacked an enemy, or perhaps had escaped from him.

BELOW One of the RAF's high-scorers was Flt Lt 'Bob' Tuck (later known as Stanford-Tuck) seen here in the cockpit of his 257 Squadron Hurricane emblazoned with no less than 23 swastikas, each one representing a victory over an enemy aircraft. The RAF did not exactly encourage such blatantly overt displays of a pilot's prowess, but imagery such as this was undoubtedly helpful for propaganda and morale purposes.

have been seen to hit the ground or sea, to break up in the air, or to descend in flames whether or not confirmation by a second source is available. This term to cover also cases in which the enemy aircraft is forced to descend and is captured.

■ **Probably destroyed** – to be applied to those cases in which the enemy aircraft is seen to break off combat in circumstances that lead to the conclusion that it must be a loss.

■ **Damaged** – to be applied to those cases in which the enemy aircraft was obviously considered damaged when under attack, such as: undercarriage dropped or engine stopped, or aircraft part shot away.

(Source: *Categories for the Assessment of Enemy Casualties*, as approved by Air Ministry Conference, 12 August 1940)

Using these criteria, a squadron IO could determine the allocation of victories to individual RAF pilots. However, it was very often the case that these were confirmed, almost arbitrarily, by the IO based solely upon what the pilot had said he had witnessed. In many cases, and in the heat and stress of battle, aircraft that were claimed as 'Destroyed', and granted as such by the IO, were not always definite 'kills'. Sometimes, too, multiple pilots claimed the same individual aircraft (and sometimes from different squadrons) such that over-claiming became

commonplace. This was always a problem in air fighting and was an issue that beset all combatant air forces. Often, too, RAF fighter pilots during the Battle of Britain claimed Messerschmitt 109s as either destroyed, probably destroyed or damaged when they were seen to dive away emitting black smoke. In fact, this was often a situation where the enemy pilot had put his aircraft into a full-power dive, a manoeuvre which resulted in a belch of black smoke from the exhausts. It was this sudden appearance of dark smoke that led some pilots to believe they had scored a victory when it was simply a case of the enemy pilot taking avoiding action, often in an entirely undamaged aircraft. Unlike some other air forces (including the Luftwaffe) claims were taken very much at face value, with no corroborating evidence from other pilots, or wreckage on the ground, being required to validate the claim. Additionally, and whilst the *Categories for the Assessment of Enemy Casualties* was intended to simplify the making of claims by pilots, it soon became apparent that it also set a problem for officers whose duty it was to assess at what rate the Luftwaffe's strength was being affected by the battle. For example, in the week following 8 August 1940, 279 enemy aircraft were claimed as destroyed, although wreckage or prisoners had only been recovered from 51. Additionally, on 15 September 1940 the figure claimed of 185 destroyed was later found to be closer to 60. The matter was also the subject of correspondence between Sir Archibald Sinclair and Air Chief Marshal Dowding during this period and exercised some thought and debate, particularly in light of questioning press coverage in foreign news media. On 16 August 1940 Dowding wrote to Sinclair, thus:

'Where the claims run into three figures it is quite impossible to arrive at anything more than an approximation of the actual numbers; not only because there is no time for detailed enquiry, but also because the pilots themselves have only a general idea of what had happened to the aircraft at which they have fired in the heat of general engagement. A pilot may be morally certain that he has destroyed an opponent at 15,000ft but before the latter has had time to do more than go into an uncontrolled spin our

RIGHT Whether enemy aircraft were actually destroyed, probably destroyed or damaged was often a contentious issue during air fighting. Some aircraft that were actually destroyed went 'unclaimed' where fighter pilots were unaware their victim had even been damaged, let alone had crashed. The stress and confusion of combat quite often made any accurate and objective assessment impossible. There can be no doubting that this Messerschmitt 109 has been fatally damaged as it dives earthwards trailing smoke.

pilot is engaged with two or three more of the enemy. Any attempt, therefore, to prove that the figures are correct can only result in proving the contrary. The main safeguard against exaggerated claims is the care with which each pilot's unofficial score is kept on the squadron and any pilot who made unsubstantiated claims would soon be 'bowled out' by others who had been in the fight with him.'

As well as these various reports and intelligence summaries, each squadron was required to submit a daily report of its activities in the Operations Record Book (ORB), the Form 540. It generally fell to the squadron adjutant to ensure this record was completed. It comprised a summary of the squadron's varied activities (including non-flying events) as well as postings to and from the squadron under a column marked 'Summary of Events'. Additionally, the ORB maintained a record of all flying, operational and non-operational, giving times of take-off and landing, the pilot's name and serial number or codes of the aircraft he was flying. This record would have been maintained by either the squadron's duty pilot (a pilot not on flying duties that day) who would monitor and record all flying movements

RIGHT Moments later and the same press photographer catches the scene as the stricken Messerschmitt slams into the Kent countryside and explodes. The plume of black smoke rising over Owens Court Farm, Selling, marks the funeral pyre of the Messerschmitt 109 E-1 of 9./JG3 after Uffz Heinrich Struwe had baled out into captivity. The likely victor in this instance was Plt Off Ronald 'Ras' Berry, a Spitfire pilot of 603 Squadron.

F/LT KENT. FORM F

COMBAT REPORT.

Sector Serial No. _____ (A) _____

Serial No. of Order detailing Flight or Squadron to
Patrol _____ (B) _____

Date _____ (C)   9/9/40

Flight, Squadron _____ (D) Flight : __A__ Sqdn. : 303 Polish

Number of Enemy Aircraft _____ (E) 40 Bombers & Numerous fighters

Type of Enemy Aircraft _____ (F) JU 88,HE 111,ME 109,ME 110's.

Time Attack was delivered _____ (G)   18,00 hours

Place Attack was delivered _____ (H)   Nr.Beachy Head

Height of Enemy _____ (J)   20,000 ft.

Enemy Casualties _____ (K) 1 ME 110 Destroyed
                                                    1 JU 88 Damaged.

Our Casualties _____ Aircraft _____ (L)   Nil

                 Personnel _____ (M)   Nil

GENERAL REPORT _____ (R)

I took off from Northolt to join up with No.1 Canadian Squadron at 2000 ft
I was leading the Squadron - 12 Hurricanes. We were vectored in a Southerly
direction, climbing all the time. When we got not far from the Coast at
11,000 ft, I saw many A/C - ME's and Spitfires probably, at 20,000 ft. We
turned N.W. I saw some aircraft cross below the Canadians.
    Suddenly out of the sun came about 40 Bombers going South. We were at
13,000 ft. I watched No.1 Canadian to see what they were going to do. They
seemed to be sending off a section or two, and I lost them in the sun. I
turned off after the Bombers, but we were too late to make good contact,
& only the leading Section did so. I caught up with one straggler, and he
started to dive into cloud, just South of the Coast. I followed and opened
fire at 500 yds. Meanwhile I was being chased up by two or three ME 109's
which were kept off my tail by Red 3 (F/O Henneberg) who was doing cross overs
behind me. After my third burst at about 400 yds - his tracer had been going
under me - the rear gunner stopped firing. I gave another short burst and I
saw a lot of pieces come off his starboard engine, and it began to pour out
dense clouds of smoke. He turned slightly to the right as he went into
cloud. I followed down into the clouds, and came out over the Channel.
It was very dark and hazy under the clouds. I could see no sight of the e/a.
As I was circling round I saw another A/C at about 1000 ft flying towards
France. I approached to investigate, and was surprised to find it was severed Coloured
with our camouflage, and had yellow mark on the side of the fuselage. At this
juncture I think the rear gunner fired. I decided to attack.

                                P.T.O.

                       Signature _J.A. Kent_ Flt.

                                { Section   Red
                     O.C. { Flight   A
                          { Squadron 303   Squadron No. Polish

---

I think it was a ME 110, but it might have been a Dornier. He
immediately dived low over the sea at about 500 ft, doing gentle
turns in order to evade me, and heading for France.
I had no difficulty in following him. His rear gunner appeared
to be firing at me until after my second burst. He did a swift turn
to the left, right across my bows, and at this angle looked very like
a DO 17. I got a very good burst in now at about 150 yds, and saw
large pieces of stuff flying off his Starboard engine, and just
a lot of smoke began to pour out of it. Immediately afterwards it
started to burn. He continued his turn and made back towards
England. I did not waste any ammunition, as he was rapidly loosing
height, so I flew along parallel, and a little above to see whether
he crashed.
At this point a ME 109 came out of the cloud and started a quarter attack
on me, so I turned to meet him, where upon he made off very fast towards
France. I was unable to catch him, so I turned back to follow my
victim. I caught up with him just as he hit the water about ten miles
South of Beachy Head. Immediately there was a large flash of flame.
I saw the tail sticking out of the water and as I watched it
disappeared, leaving only a large smear of oil, and I think I saw a
rubber boat. I decided not to attack it as I wanted to conserve my
remaining ammunition in case I had need of it.
I flew around Newhaven, and rocked my wings, but I saw no boats going
out, so as I was getting short of petrol I returned to base.

    In general I would say that we were too low and too late for a
successful interception, and we did not see the enemy bombers soon
enough, as they were in the sun. They must have been coming from a
higher altitude as they were going at great speed when I saw them, and
it was very difficult to catch up with them.

LEFT Ultimately, the post-engagement discussions had to be translated into individual combat reports compiled by each pilot and submitted to the squadron intelligence officer (IO). This example was completed by Flt Lt J.A. 'Johnny' Kent of 303 (Polish) Squadron after a successful battle on 9 September 1940 near Beachy Head.

or else it would simply have been completed by an airman clerk.

Reproduced opposite is a typical example of an individual combat report.

Shot down

Quite apart from the combat reports of successful pilots and aircrew there were, of course, those who found themselves in the most unenviable position of being shot down during the Battle of Britain. Whilst they, too, were obliged to complete a combat report of the engagement which ended in their demise, the details were necessarily brief. However, quite apart from the 535 men who died on operational flights during the Battle of Britain,, those who survived such frightening and harrowing experiences as being shot down often had an engaging story to tell. One who survived such an incident, and left his story for posterity, was 20-year-old Spitfire pilot, Sgt David Cox of 19 Squadron. On 27 September the Duxford Wing, comprising 242, 312 and 310 (Hurricane) Squadrons and 19 (Spitfire) Squadron, was ordered to patrol the area of Manston and Dover:

'19 Squadron was the top squadron at about 28,000ft, and after about five minutes on the patrol line a large number of Me 109s attacked from out of the sun. Although it was not long after noon the sun was at an angle, it being the end of September, and to the advantage of the Luftwaffe.

'19 Squadron was flying four Vics of three – a useless formation, as apart from the Squadron Commander everyone else was concentrating on keeping in formation and not looking out for the enemy.

'The first I knew was a shout of "109s" over the radio and we made a "split-ass" turn to port as the 109s burst in amongst us. Immediately the No 3 of my own vic on the left went down with smoke coming from the Spitfire. Later I learnt he was killed – it was Pilot Officer Burgoyne who joined 19 Squadron on the same day in May 1940 as myself.

'After a few hectic moments spent avoiding the 109s I found myself alone. I was a few miles inland over Dover and a lone Hurricane was being attacked by seven Me 109s. I started to go to his assistance, but before I could give him any effective help he went down in flames. I believe it was Pilot Officer Homer of 242 Squadron.

'The seven 109s then turned their attention to me. They were obviously top class. All of them were yellow-nosed aircraft, and they formed into a circle around me, with some above to cut off any escape.

'After many hectic moments turning into their attacks as soon as I saw one behind me, and then taking pot shots at them – more to boost my morale than in any hope of hitting one – so the end inevitably came.

'I had got near to the one below me and momentarily concentrated too long on firing at him. There was a flash and a loud bang in the cockpit and at the same time I felt as if I had been kicked in the side.

'For a second or two I was stunned and let go of the control column. I remembered dazedly thinking "This is it", and wondering how long it would be before I hit the ground.

'Then suddenly I decided it was not "it". I grabbed the control column and yanked it back.

ABOVE **When Sgt Pilot Cyril Babbage, a Spitfire pilot with 602 Squadron, was shot down into the sea off Bognor Regis on 26 August 1940 he was rescued by a rowing boat and brought ashore. Armed soldiers have accompanied the oarsmen – just in case the parachutist should have turned out to be German. The paucity of any organised air-sea rescue service undoubtedly resulted in the deaths of many RAF pilots and aircrew brought down over the sea during the Battle of Britain.**

My Spitfire went into a vertical climb, and as it lost speed I levelled out, tore off my helmet, undid the hood, undid my straps, rolled the aircraft over on its back and thrust the control column sharply forward.

'The negative "G" had the effect of shooting me out like a pea from a pod. I quickly pulled the rip cord on my parachute and was promptly jerked about in all directions as it opened. This

LEFT **Some pilots were shot down or crashed multiple times during the Battle of Britain. Once again, Sgt Babbage's Spitfire was hit and damaged over the English Channel on 12 October 1940 but on this occasion he was able to limp back to land. His Spitfire overturned in a forced-landing near Lewes although Babbage was unharmed and later posed for the camera, sitting on his upturned Spitfire.**

RIGHT **Many pilots, though, were not so lucky as Cyril Babbage. Nineteen-year-old Plt Off Peter King of 66 Squadron died when his parachute failed after being shot down over the Medway area on 5 September 1940. His Spitfire crashed into the mud at Hoo Marina, Kent, where a naval officer inspects the shattered wreckage.**

was because in the panic take-off from Duxford I had not used my own aircraft but one used by a giant of 6ft 4in; I am only 5ft 7in. I was lucky not to fall out of the harness!

'As I slowly floated down I felt a lot of pain in my right leg. I looked down and I saw the flying boot on my right leg had many holes in it, out of which blood was now appearing.

'I landed in the corner of a field and I was picked up by two farm labourers, who took me into a farm house and laid me on a settee. I was feeling pretty grim by then and must have looked it as the farmer got out a bottle of Whisky which he gave to me, with the comment

that he was keeping it for Victory Day (and this was in 1940!) but I looked as if I could do with it, although Whisky is the worst thing to give anyone with open wounds.

'I arrived at an emergency hospital near Ashford in rather a high state. I did not require much to put me under in order for the surgeon to take several large fragments (some as large as 10p pieces) of an explosive cannon shell out of my leg.'

Aside from those killed on operations during the Battle of Britain, RAF pilots who were shot down but either made forced landings or else baled out, were in the favourable position of

RIGHT Sometimes it was mechanical failure rather than the Luftwaffe who were the enemy. Here, Sgt Pilot Herbert 'Jim' Hallowes of 43 Squadron has successfully forced-landed his Hurricane (P3784) at Amberley in West Sussex after his engine seized during an operational flight. Hallowes was unharmed, but it later transpired that the engine failure had resulted from an omission by his groundcrew to refill the Hurricane's oil tank.

Notwithstanding the almost complete absence of any effective RAF air-sea rescue cover during the summer of 1940, the Germans, not long arrived on the Channel coast, quickly had an effective rescue system in place involving high-speed launches and Heinkel 59 seaplanes.

On 9 July one such He 59 was intercepted by Spitfires of 54 Squadron over the English Channel and forced down on to the Goodwin Sands, its crew captured. The RAF Air Intelligence report into the downing of the He 59 was comprehensive and seemed to leave little doubt as to its apparently humanitarian intent:

'The aircraft, which was unarmed, landed as soon as it was attacked by Spitfires. It suffered no damage apart from a broken petrol feed or tank. It has since been brought ashore near Walmer Lifeboat Station.

'The men were unarmed and whatever else they may or may not have been doing they seem to be genuine sea-rescue Red Cross workers. This crew previously saved a Sqn Ldr Doran and his observer from the sea off Stavanger.

'The aircraft was equipped with stretchers, a rubber dinghy, oxygen apparatus and other medical stores.

'They had ordinary two-way radio equipment which was, they stated, used solely for navigation and receiving messages in connection with their job. The crew stated that they had definite instructions not to report any points of operational significance. They stated that their names were registered with the International Red Cross authorities and they were glad to have an opportunity of explaining their organisation. The crew said that there were between 12 and 15 of these He 59s and these were moved about fairly considerably. This particular crew have in recent months been to Bergen, Stavanger, Amsterdam, Cherbourg and Boulogne.'

However, RAF Fighter Command were uncomfortable about the presence of these rescue aircraft in the battle area and on 14 July 1940 Air Ministry Order 1254 was issued:

'It has come to the notice of His Majesty's Government in the United Kingdom that enemy aircraft bearing civil markings and marked with the Red Cross have recently flown over British ships at sea and in the vicinity of the British coast, and that they are being employed for purposes which HM Government cannot regard as being consistent with the privileges generally accorded to the Red Cross.

'HM Government desires to accord ambulance aircraft reasonable facilities for the transportation of the sick and wounded, in accordance with the Red Cross convention, and aircraft engaged in the direct evacuation of sick and wounded will be respected, provided that they comply with the relevant provisions of the Convention.

'HM Government is unable, however, to grant immunity to such aircraft flying over areas in which operations are in progress on land or at sea, or approaching British or Allied territory, or territory in British occupation, or British or Allied ships.

'Ambulance aircraft which do not comply with the above requirements will do so at their own risk and peril.'

As a consequence of that order, pilots of RAF Fighter Command were ordered to engage and shoot down any He 59 rescue seaplanes that were encountered around the British coastline.

BELOW Unlike the RAF, the Luftwaffe had a fully organised air-sea rescue service on the English Channel coast during the summer of 1940. This utilised high-speed launches and rescue seaplanes including the Heinkel 59 B-2 seen here. These Heinkel seaplanes were painted white and marked prominently with the Red Cross, although the Air Ministry decreed that these aircraft were not immune from attack and ordered they be shot down.

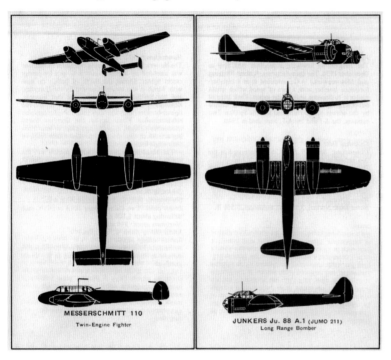

BELOW Recognition cards were also produced of both enemy and Allied aircraft types and gave silhouette views of aircraft from various angles.

being over home territory. This meant that medical assistance (if it was required) could be got to them relatively quickly and unwounded pilots could be swiftly returned to their units. However, a few RAF Fighter Command pilots during the Battle of Britain were unlucky enough to be taken prisoner of war (POW). These situations arose when combats and engagements took place far out over the

English Channel or over the French coast, although these events were relatively rare. On some occasions, RAF pilots who had been shot down in the Channel were picked up by the highly efficient German air-sea rescue service, and although their lives were saved they were, nevertheless, POWs. In total, ten RAF pilots were taken prisoner during the Battle of Britain.

Intelligence

Aircraft recognition

One of the responsibilities of the squadron IO was to ensure instruction for pilots and aircrew in the art of aircraft recognition. It was clearly essential for personal survival, as well as for success in air fighting, that pilots and aircrew were entirely *au fait* with air-to-air identification of all enemy aircraft and from all angles. Equally, it was important that they could identify friendly aircraft from all angles, too.

Regular lectures and instruction sessions were held, posters and models adorned the walls of dispersal huts and pilots and aircrew were expected to spend time studying the subject in detail. After all, their lives depended on it. However, in the stress and tension of combat situations mistakes were not uncommon and there are known occasions when tired or confused RAF fighter pilots mistakenly joined up with formations of Me 109s, for example. There were also frequent cases of 'friendly fire', often with fatal consequences. Mostly, these were heat-of-the-moment events and where the pilot or aircrew concerned had split seconds to make a decision. In those moments it could well be a matter of kill or be killed. The wrong decision could be fatal, either way. Thus, it was not a case of some pilots or aircrew being trigger-happy but, rather, that they had to make difficult decisions in situations of great stress. Additionally, those pilots or aircrew could be feeling unwell through motion sickness or disorientation, and perhaps trying to squint against a bright sky in order to establish if the aircraft was friend or foe. Even in successful engagements against enemy aircraft it was not uncommon for RAF fighter pilots to misidentify their victims. A common but understandable error was to muddle the

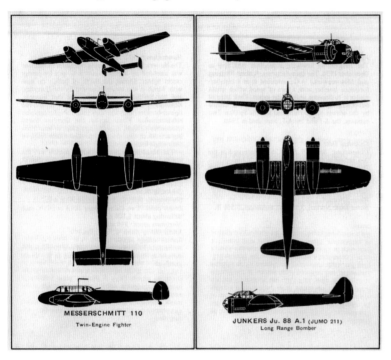

MESSERSCHMITT 110
Twin-Engine Fighter

JUNKERS Ju. 88 A.1 (JUMO 211)
Long Range Bomber

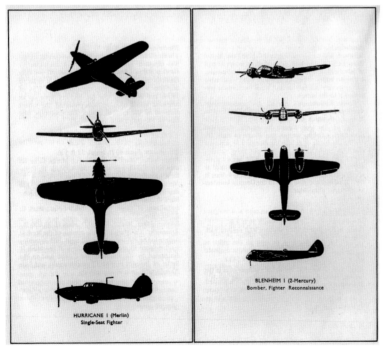

HURRICANE I (Merlin)
Single-Seat Fighter

BLENHEIM I (2-Mercury)
Bomber, Fighter Reconnaissance

identities of the Messerschmitt 110 and Dornier 17; understandable because of their roughly comparable size, twin engines and twin-fin configurations.

A mistake that was frequently made by pilots and aircrew in 1940 was to identify the Messerschmitt 109 as a Heinkel 113. The latter aircraft did not technically exist but was, instead, the He 100 D-1. The type was built in very small numbers, mostly pre-production models, and never went into full-scale production or Luftwaffe service. However, German propaganda in 1940 showed the few aircraft that had been built assembled together and with different spurious unit markings in different settings, calling it the 'He 113'. The intention was that the Allies would believe that a new type was both in production and in service, and the ruse worked. Often, RAF combat reports are filled with accounts of engagements with 'He 113 fighters'. In truth, none were ever in service and, for the most part, the RAF airmen involved were engaging Me 109s. Unfortunately, there is also evidence pointing to Hurricanes being shot down in error by other RAF pilots who claimed their hapless victim to be a 'He 113'.

Camera-gun footage
A limited number of RAF fighters during the Battle of Britain were fitted with wing-mounted

ABOVE Aircraft recognition was a skill that was vital for a fighter pilot's success and his survival. Pilots were not only encouraged to constantly 'gen up' on aircraft types but they also had to attend compulsory aircraft recognition lectures by the squadron IO. Here, pilots learn the view of enemy aircraft from every conceivable angle using recognition models, while the hut walls are plastered with recognition posters.

BELOW One enemy aircraft type features quite often in RAF pilots' combat reports during the Battle of Britain period – the Heinkel 113. Although pilots often reported engaging with them in combat, and frequently claimed them as destroyed, none were ever shot down. The simple reason for this was the fact that the He 113 in Luftwaffe service was a complete myth. Only a handful were ever produced, and those were used for the home defence of factory airfields in Germany.

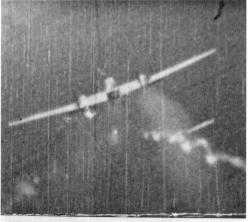

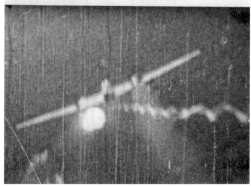

ABOVE The camera never lies. Although the results were often very indistinct, some aircraft were fitted with the G.42 camera gun. The cameras were synchronised to run when the gun button was operated and were intended for the recording and assessment of combat successes. This example is fitted in the wing root of a Hurricane and has its side door hanging open, revealing the film cassette marked '501', indicating 501 Squadron.

RIGHT Four successive frames from the gun camera footage shot by Flt Lt Wilfred 'Paddy' Treacy, a flight commander on 74 Squadron during early 1940. This footage was shot during an engagement with a Messerschmitt 110 near Dunkirk on 24 May 1940 and shows white streaks of bullets heading for the Me 110 with the final frame showing a flash of flame behind the port engine. Treacy was later killed leading a fighter sweep over France on 20 April 1941.

camera guns. These were ciné cameras aligned with the guns and set into the wing root of Hurricanes and Spitfires to record the success, or otherwise, of the pilot's shooting. The cameras were triggered automatically to run when the gun button was operated and the exposed film could be used to assess both the pilot's shooting ability and combat results.

Crash recovery

The salvage and recovery of wrecked aircraft lost during the Battle of Britain became an important element in the overall operation of the RAF in 1940 and whilst not coming directly under the aegis of RAF Fighter Command it was an operation that involved the recovery of both Fighter Command's own aircraft and those

RIGHT Such were the numbers of wrecked German and British aircraft littering the countryside in 1940 that the RAF found it hard to cope with the clearance of wrecks. The difficulty was exacerbated by vehicle and personnel losses of the main unit involved (49 Maintenance Unit) sustained during the Junkers 87 Stuka attack on RAF Tangmere on 16 August 1940. The scale of the problem faced by the RAF is summed up in this cartoon of 4 September 1940.

"Eglantine Cottage? Go down the lane past the Messerschmitt, bear left and keep on past the two Dorniers, then turn sharp right and it's just past the first Junkers."

it had shot down. Thus, it became an important and highly visible element of RAF operations during the battle period.

When an RAF aircraft did not return from a training or operational flight its parent unit had a duty to notify the Air Ministry, who in turn informed HQ 43 Maintenance Group, Cowley, Oxford. It was the responsibility of this unit to notify the RAF Maintenance Unit (MU) which covered the area in which the aircraft had been lost. The process then was that the aircraft would be inspected by the MU's crash inspector and arrangements made for collection and disposal. The procedure for enemy aircraft was that they were first inspected by an RAF technical IO from the AI 1(g) Department who had to 'release' the aircraft before they could be dealt with by an MU.

Strict procedures for dealing with crashed

BELOW LEFT Sqn Ldr John Ellis DFC, the CO of the Spitfire-equipped 610 Squadron, visits the crash site of a Messerschmitt 109 downed on 30 August 1940 with one of his pilots in order to scavenge for souvenirs.

BELOW Sometimes wrecks were so badly smashed up they revealed little in the way of useful intelligence. Such was the case with this Heinkel 111, which exploded into the ground on 30 August 1940.

aircraft were laid down and, generally speaking, were rigidly adhered to. Responsibility for guarding downed aircraft rested with the Army until taken over by the RAF or salvage organisations. POWs were required to be handed over at once to the nearest military units for eventual interrogation by the RAF's Air Intelligence Department, working from Cockfosters in London, and designated AI 1(k).

The brunt of responsibility for clearance of aircraft wrecks in the main battle areas of Kent, Sussex, Surrey and Hampshire during 1940, however, fell to 49 MU based at RAF Faygate near Horsham in West Sussex. Situated beside the main London to Chichester railway line the site grew into a collection of wooden huts, dominated by a timber and canvas portable Bessonneau hangar and a sprawling dump of wrecked aircraft. Very few domestic facilities were provided at the site and thus all of the

RIGHT This relatively intact Messerschmitt 109 E-4 of Stab.III/ JG54 crash-landed at Hengrove, Kent, on 12 August 1940 with Oblt Albrecht Drehs taken POW. The men of 49 MU load the bullet-holed aircraft on to an RAF flatbed lorry.

personnel were billeted out with families, mostly in nearby Horsham.

Apart from the few men who remained permanently on site at Faygate under the command of the unit's CO, Sqn Ldr Goodman, most of the men were divided into a number of crash parties of 8 to 10 men each who were mostly from the MU section working on actual salvage operations, each party being under the command of a senior NCO. In addition the unit had a number of crash inspectors, mostly of pilot officer rank, who visited each aircraft that was to be recovered and assessed any particular problems and decided on equipment and manpower required for the salvage operation.

Not to be confused with the crash inspectors of the MU were the IOs of Air Intelligence 1(g) – AI 1(g) – who visited each shot-down German aircraft to compile a report. One AI 1(g) officer was attached to each MU, including Faygate, in order that each part of the country could easily be covered rather than rely on officers working from the unit's HQ in Harrow Weald. However, and with the unprecedented level of aerial activity over the UK in the summer months of 1940, it soon became obvious that the existing chain of MU bases around the country could

not cope with the large numbers of wrecked aircraft littering the countryside. Particularly hard pressed was 49 MU. It was, perhaps, the loss of a number of vehicles including a Ford V8 staff car and a Commer low-loader during the attack on RAF Hawkinge on 12 August 1940, followed by the death of two drivers and the loss of three Commer low-loaders, a Coles crane and a Bedford 3-tonner during the 16 August raid on Tangmere, which persuaded the Air Ministry that existing facilities provided by 49 MU were no longer able to cope with the ever increasing workload. Thus, prior to the formation of a further MU (86 MU, based at Sundridge, Kent, from early 1941), the Air Ministry engaged a number of firms of civilian contractors from the road haulage industry. Among these civilian companies were Coast Transport Ltd, Portsmouth Carriers and Messrs A.V. Nicholls and Co, the latter operating from Brighton under direct control of 49 MU.

Unlike the RAF recovery parties those of Messrs A.V. Nicholls and other civilian firms consisted of untrained men working with little equipment and often under conditions of extreme difficulty. Usually, only two men were despatched on a recovery job and were expected to

BELOW To cope with the workload civilian haulage firms were contracted by the Air Ministry to help clear away the wrecks once they had been examined and released by the technical inspectors of AI (1)g. Here, Messrs A.V. Nicholls of Brighton are pictured with another load of aircraft scrap to transport to 49 MU's base at RAF Faygate near Horsham, Sussex. The load includes the float of a Heinkel 59 B-2 brought down by the RAF.

RIGHT Sometimes, it was just a case of hauling or digging shattered wrecks from fields, woods, beaches, streets or marshes.

RIGHT The final destination of wrecked German aircraft would be the MU depots followed by scrap processing plants, where they were 'reduced to produce' before going into the alloy smelters. This yard includes the fuselage of Uffz August Klick's Messerschmitt 109 E-7 of 3./LG2, shot down on the Isle of Sheppey on Sunday 15 September 1940, the day universally marked as Battle of Britain Day. Note the chalked graffiti: 'All good Germans are Dead. Or will be.' The comment doubtless reflects the mood of the time.

dismantle, cut up or dig out a buried wreck depending on the circumstances of the crash.

One difficulty encountered by the military and civilian gangs alike was the wholesale removal of souvenirs from crashed aircraft. Such was the level of the problem that the Minister of Aircraft Production issued a statement on 6 October 1940, urging the public not to remove material or equipment from crashed aircraft. This was later followed by the issue of Standing Orders for the Guarding and Salvage of Crashed Aircraft, in which the subject of souvenirs was covered.

Apparently it was the intention to supply souvenirs from enemy machines to the personnel who had guarded them, or to any other individual with a claim to a souvenir. However, souvenirs could only be released upon application to the RAF AI 1(g) IO.

With the daily arrival of wrecked aircraft at Faygate from RAF and civilian gangs, a vast graveyard of jumbled aeroplanes soon formed there. Eventually, and after useful spares had been stripped out of RAF aircraft, all were consigned to scrap and for reprocessing by

the Northern Aluminium Co at their vast depot near Adderbury, Oxfordshire. It was to here that the wrecked aircraft were finally taken, along with thousands of aluminium pots, pans, hot-water bottles, tennis racquets, car badges and other items that had been collected from the British public following an appeal for aluminium. In fact, and contrary to popular belief, the aluminium sourced in this manner was of little value to the aircraft industry since it was soft 'commercial' aluminium and not the hardened Duralumin material used in aircraft construction. Before arrival at the Adderbury plant, however, these domestic items had all been laboriously pick-axed by RAF MU personnel to prevent further use in the purpose for which they had originally been intended! The final product of alloy ingots was then re-issued from Adderbury to the aircraft industry by the Ministry of Aircraft Production.

The Civilian Repair Organisation

The Civilian Repair Organisation (CRO) was a branch of the Air Ministry and, later, of the Ministry of Aircraft Production. It was an organisation formed in 1939 to coordinate maintenance and repairs of military aircraft by civilian firms since, as with crash recovery, it became clear that arrangements involving the RAF (or even the main aircraft manufacturers themselves) would not be able to cope with wartime demands.

As early as 11 September 1939, 1 Civilian Repair Unit (CRU) was established at the Cowley works of Morris Motors, to be staffed by civilians but under the management of the Air Ministry. On 6 October 1939, Sir Kingsley Wood (Secretary of State for Air) officially appointed William Morris (Lord Nuffield) as Director General (Maintenance) to organise and manage the Civilian Repair Organisation (CRO) and to control the CRUs and all participating civilian firms. The CRO administration was established at Magdalen College, Oxford, but on 14 May 1940 the overall supervision and responsibility for the CRO was transferred from the Air Ministry to the Ministry of Aircraft Production, under Lord Beaverbrook. No 1 CRU was supplemented by 1 Metal and

Produce Recovery Depot (1 MPRD), which was established adjacent to the existing Cowley works. At Cowley, a support unit was established by the RAF in the form of 50 MU in order to transport damaged aircraft and parts to the CRU and to firms participating in the CRO, as well as for the collection of non-repairable parts and scrap for materials reclamation at MPRD. Other RAF MUs and civilian contractors from around Britain also assisted in this process.

The civilian firms under individual contracts from the CRO were mostly existing companies engaged in the production, maintenance, repair and operation of aircraft in Britain. These were supplemented by additional companies in the engineering and woodworking industrial sectors who were deemed appropriate in terms of their established fields of expertise. Repairs to whole aircraft, or to parts of aircraft, were often carried out in dispersed industrial factories and then transported back to airfields for reassembly and test flying before redelivery to RAF units. For cases of minor repairs that could be achieved quickly, aircraft could be flown to a CRO firm based at an airfield, repaired, and flown out the following day by the same pilot, these becoming known as 'fly-in' repairs. There are recorded instances of RAF Fighter Command aircraft being landed at the manufacturer's airfields by the same pilots who had flown the aircraft in an action which had resulted in the damage for which repairs were required.

BELOW Hurricane L1936 pictured at the workshops of a Civilian Repair Organisation unit.

Chapter Five

The participants

*The men and women of
the Battle of Britain*

Some 2,900 pilots and aircrew took part in the Battle of Britain, supported by a huge team on the ground – fitters, armourers, riggers, engineers, drivers, medics, administrators and WAAF personnel. More than 540 fliers were killed as well as a number of ground personnel, and an unfortunate duty for the RAF was burying both their own dead as well as those of the enemy.

OPPOSITE This photograph of 249 Squadron at RAF North Weald, Essex, shows the officer pilots of the squadron walking away from a Hurricane in what became a famous photograph of the period. It was first used as the frontispiece in the 1941 HMSO publication on the Battle of Britain.

ABOVE The pilots and aircrew of RAF Fighter Command hailed from all parts of the British Commonwealth, occupied Europe and the free world, including volunteers from a then neutral America. This is Plt Off Phillip Leckrone from Salem, Illinois, who flew with 616 Squadron during the Battle of Britain. He was killed in a flying accident on 5 January 1941.

BELOW Desperately short of pilots during the Battle of Britain, RAF Fighter Command drew in pilots from other RAF Commands as well as 56 Royal Navy pilots from the Fleet Air Arm. This is Sub Lt Arthur Blake who flew Spitfires with 19 Squadron. He was shot down and killed at Chelmsford on 29 October 1940.

Whilst the vast organisation of the Air Ministry and Royal Air Force required an army of administrators, clerks, accountants, cooks, drivers, medics, technicians, meteorologists, wireless specialists and a hundred-and-one other trades to support the various Commands and units, it is the 'sharp end' of RAF Fighter Command with which this manual concerns itself. Essentially, these were the combat fliers (pilots and aircrew) and the groundcrew (fitters, riggers and armourers) who served with the various operational squadrons.

Pilots and aircrew

It is generally accepted that something in the order of 2,945 pilots and aircrew participated in the Battle of Britain. That is to say that these men served on an accredited Battle of Britain squadron or unit and flew the requisite minimum of one *operational* flight during the period 10 July to 31 October 1940. Serving as an operational pilot on an accredited squadron was not sufficient qualification alone to be considered Battle of Britain aircrew and there were, on establishment, considerably more than 2,945 pilots and aircrew serving with RAF Fighter Command during that period. However, unless those pilots or aircrew flew on an operational flight during that period they were not deemed Battle of Britain participants. As such, they did not qualify for the Battle of Britain clasp to the 1939–1945 Star campaign medal and, if survivors, they did not qualify for post-war membership of the Battle of Britain Fighter Association. Equally, if they became casualties during the 10 July to 31 October period but had not flown on an operational flight they would not be included on any official Roll of Honour. A case in point is that of Sgt Sydney Ireland, a Spitfire pilot with 610 Squadron, who was killed in a flying accident whilst carrying out dogfighting practice from Biggin Hill on 12 July 1940. Although his death came within the qualifying period, and he was serving on an accredited squadron, he had not yet flown the required single operational flight when he was killed. Consequently, he is not regarded as a Battle of Britain participant or casualty.

Surprisingly, no formal official list of Battle of Britain combatants is maintained by either the RAF or MOD and the accepted roll of participants is based largely on investigations carried out across many years by researchers, enthusiasts, family members, and the Battle of Britain Fighter Association. As a result, that list has varied up and down in its total across the decades as previously unrecognised participants have either come forward to claim their Battle of Britain clasps or family members have discovered previously overlooked evidence which make it clear that their relative took part. In many cases, the original squadron Operations Record Book has been unclear about whether personnel qualified and, in some cases, those record books have failed to properly identify exactly who that airman was. For example, it can be difficult to be sure who an individual is when, in some cases, they are referred to as just, say, Sgt Smith. With no identifying initials or service number there can be no clarity. However, if the individual or family can present evidence in the form of log books or some other official record, then they will be awarded the clasp and added to the roll of participants.

In total, some 535 of those accredited pilots and aircrew became casualties during the qualifying period.

Some 15 national groups were involved as participants in the Battle of Britain, made up as follows:

Great Britain – 2,345	Jamaica – 1
Australia – 32	Newfoundland – 1
Barbados – 1	New Zealand – 127
Belgium – 28	Poland – 145
Canada – 112	Rhodesia – 3
Czechoslovakia – 88	South Africa – 25
France – 13	United States – 9
Ireland – 10	Stateless – 1

Flying training

Before recruits selected for aircrew training got anywhere near an aircraft they first had to endure the rigours of an Initial Training Wing (ITW). For many Battle of Britain aircrew this began with either 4 ITW (Bexhill on Sea) or 5 ITW (Hastings). Here, the hapless recruits were put through the paces of basic training: drill, PE, rifle practice, learning about service life generally . . . and then more drill! Both ITWs were accommodated in a series of seafront

hotels, flats and large houses that had all been vacated and commandeered for the duration. Drill, PE and route marches were frequently conducted up and down the deserted and often windswept promenades, and along a coastline over which many of them would very shortly be doing battle. Appropriately, perhaps, the motto of RAF Training Command was *Terra Caeloque Docemus:* We Teach on Land and in the Air.

From their ITWs, with their 'square-bashing' done, the recruits would be posted out to

LEFT The veritable backbone of RAF Fighter Command pilots during 1940 was made up from sergeant pilots, many of them pre-war RAFVR pilots. One such was 21-year-old Sgt J.H.M. Ellis who served as a Hurricane pilot on 85 Squadron. He was shot down and killed on 1 September 1940 but his body was not found until 1992 when his aircraft was recovered at Chelsfield, Kent. John Ellis was buried with full military honours at Brookwood Military Cemetery, Surrey, in 1993 with family members present.

LEFT Poles and Czechs also swelled the ranks of RAF Fighter Command. This is Sgt Vojtěch Smolik of 312 (Czech) Squadron and although he became operational just after the Battle of Britain he is typical of those from occupied countries who escaped to England to carry on the fight against Germany. In this photograph he wears a service-issue one-piece Sidcot flying suit, which was popular with some pilots. The Hurricane is P3888, DU–O.

LEFT Initial flying training for pilots was typically carried out on the Tiger Moth. Inevitably, there were accidents and mishaps and this is Tiger Moth N6625 of 30 Elementary & Reserve Flying Training School, which was written off in a forced-landing at Selston, Nottinghamshire, on 22 May 1939.

Spitfires or Hurricanes. There were, of course, dual-control Spitfires or Hurricanes and it was thus expected that the novice pilot would first simply read the pilot's notes, be shown around the cockpit controls and then make his first tentative solo flight on the fighter. The attrition rate for trainee and novice pilots killed whilst undergoing flying training (at all stages) was significant during the period that RAF Training Command worked at an increasing pace to keep up a supply of replacement pilots. There was undoubtedly a diminution in the performance of newly trained pilots as corners were cut in order to get them on to the front line quickly so as to replace operational losses (as well as the toll of casualties arising from the Battle of France), which were having an impact on the operational capabilities of squadrons.

On posting to a squadron the pilot would generally first be sent out on 'Sector reconnaissance sorties' in order to familiarise himself with the airfield, the area of operations and with the squadron aircraft. When the squadron leader was satisfied that a pilot was combat ready, he would be placed on the roster for duty and would thereafter be expected to take his place on any scrambles or patrols. Sometimes, this would follow a period of dual flying with the CO in the squadron's Miles Magister communications aircraft in order to assess the new pilot's abilities.

Once the pilot had been committed to his first operational sortie it was, quite literally, a baptism of fire. Many new pilots came to their first squadrons with very few hours and little flying experience, especially on type. A case in point was that of Plt Off John Ramsay of 151 Squadron. Just one month separated his first Hurricane flight at 7 OTU, RAF Hawarden, and his death in action on 18 August 1940. He flew very few operational sorties between posting to the squadron on 30 July and his death, and

BELOW Pilots later progressed to the North American Harvard and these student pilots of 6 Flying Training School pose perhaps rather apprehensively in front of an aeroplane that could be quite a handful to fly. The pilot second from right is Flg Off Basil Fisher who was killed in action with 111 Squadron over Selsey on 15 August 1940.

various Elementary Flying Training Schools (EFTS). Here, theory of flight as well as flying instruction was undertaken, usually on the Tiger Moth or the Blackburn B-2. At the EFTS the trainee pilot would make his first solo flight and this was typically at around seven or eight hours. From here he would move to a Flying Training School (FTS) and, at this stage, he would progress to the Miles Master and North American Harvard, aircraft with performances a little closer to the Spitfires or Hurricanes they might expect to fly operationally in the event that they were posted to Fighter Command.

Should he complete his stint at FTS satisfactorily, the trainee would at last be awarded his coveted 'wings', officially called the Flying Brevet, and be posted to an Operational Training Unit (OTU) for final training on either

with a little over 24 hours on the Hurricane to his credit in total. That, though, was more than many and his survival time on the squadron was far longer than it was for some. Take, for instance, the case of Flg Off Arthur Rose-Price who, although a flying instructor, had no combat experience and arrived on his posting to 501 Squadron and immediately was ordered off on a patrol. Later that afternoon he failed to return from another sortie. His car remained unpacked outside the mess. His fellow pilots did not even get to learn his name before he was gone.

In the case of aircrew selected for non-pilot flying duties, these would all follow the ITW route before 'streaming' into Bombing and Air Gunnery Schools or Air Navigation Schools as appropriate.

A number of pilots were seconded from different Commands (Coastal, Bomber and Training) to make up the shortages in RAF Fighter Command at the height of the Battle of Britain. Additionally, a number of Fleet Air Arm pilots also found themselves posted to RAF Fighter Command squadrons. In these instances, a brief course at an OTU to familiarise 'on type' preceded postings to operational fighter squadrons. However, and despite the overall attrition rate, there was never a shortage of volunteers for aircrew duties.

Groundcrew

The relatively small number of active aircrew in each squadron unit at RAF Fighter Command rather belies the true number of personnel who made up the establishment of those operational squadrons. Additionally, the support staff at the home airfield (who were attached to the station HQ rather than to resident squadrons) could make up many hundreds when considering the trades and duties covered. On the squadrons themselves it might be expected that one would find fitters, riggers and armourers as the 'key' ground personnel and with one of each category usually assigned to an individual aircraft and pilot. The fitter would have been responsible for issues relating to the engine and its maintenance, as well as looking after ancillary equipment, refuelling, re-oiling etc. Meanwhile, the rigger would have responsibility

ABOVE A portrait photograph, flying log book, pilot's brevet (wings) and medals of Plt Off John Ramsay, Hurricane pilot on 151 Squadron, shot down and killed on 18 August 1940. This was the hardest-fought day of the battle and only one month separated John's first flight in a Hurricane to his death in combat. The 1939–45 Star in the medal group carries the Battle of Britain clasp on its ribbon, awarded to all pilots and aircrew who flew at least one operational sortie with an accredited Battle of Britain squadron between 10 July and 31 October 1940.

LEFT Flg Off Arthur Rose-Price, from Concepcion in Chile, did not even have time to unpack his car after being posted as a Hurricane pilot to 501 Squadron at RAF Kenley on 2 September 1940 and being shot down later that same day. No trace of him has ever been found.

(colloquially called 'Chiefy') would make the decision to pull the aircraft from the flight line, but with any major decisions regarding repairs and rectification resting with the squadron engineering officer.

During the Battle of Britain a total of 312 RAF ground personnel were killed and another 451 wounded in air attacks against airfields and installations. This total includes three WAAF personnel and one NAAFI lady killed along with several aircrew who also died or were wounded on the ground. Despite perceptions to the contrary, which was possibly engendered by the post-bombing scene from the film *Battle of Britain* (1969), the number of WAAFs killed in air attacks was low. However, the scriptwriter for the film might be forgiven in view of the fact that in a 1942 HMSO publication a WAAF officer, talking of an air raid on a fighter station, is quoted thus:

'All was now deathly silent. I climbed through debris and round craters back towards the WAAF guardroom. As I drew nearer, there was a smell of escaping gas. The mains had been hit. Another bomb had fallen on the airwomen's trench, burying the women who were sheltering inside.'

Almost certainly, this refers to an attack on RAF Biggin Hill during August 1940, although no WAAF personnel were actually killed in that air raid.

Overall, though, the total figure of ground personnel casualties is a sobering one, especially when compared against combatant aircrew who suffered 535 casualties from among their number. Those serving on the ground with the RAF were equally combatants in the Battle of Britain, their role a key one in ensuring the overall operation of the air defence system.

ABOVE Although taken well before the Battle of Britain this image of a 79 Squadron fitter, rigger and armourer taking breakfast at dispersal on the tail of one of the squadron's Hurricanes would have been typical of the battle period. This three-man team were the key players in keeping the fighters in tip-top order, maintained and, crucially, turned around again rapidly after each sortie.

BELOW RIGHT Part of the turn-around included the replenishment of used oxygen cylinders. In this photograph the TR 9D radio installation in the Hurricane can also just be seen.

FAR RIGHT The oxygen cylinder as fitted in the Spitfire Mk I. The white stencilled instructions warn that water or grease coming into contact with the valve may cause explosions. *(Col Pope)*

for the airframe, including basic running repairs, replacing oxygen cylinders etc, instrumentation, keeping the canopy and windscreen spotlessly clean, patching the doped canvas patches over the gun ports and helping the pilot strap in. As might be expected, the armourer would be responsible for both the maintenance of the aircraft's weapons and for rearming between sorties. He would also be accountable for the gun camera (if fitted) and the removal and replacement of exposed film cassettes. Issues relating to the wireless equipment would be dealt with by a specialist electrical tradesman, or 'sparks', although there would not be a dedicated wireless specialist per aircraft. On return from a sortie the groundcrew would enquire of their pilot if there had been any snags and would then seek to rectify them during the turnaround. If an aircraft were to be declared unserviceable due to a fault, or because of damage, the flight sergeant in charge

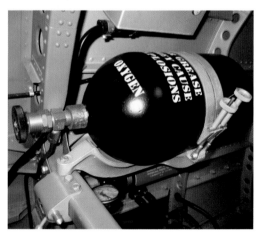

ABOVE Fitters work in the open, at dispersal, on the Merlin engine of a 501 Squadron Hurricane. The jacked-up tail might indicate that some gun alignment work is also under way.

ABOVE Refuelling two Hurricanes of 111 Squadron from a petrol bowser. The fact that the pilots are seated in the cockpit and the armourers sit ready to see to the guns might indicate that the aircraft have just returned from a sortie.

ABOVE LEFT 'Everything OK, Sir?' This 73 Squadron fitter sees off his pilot on a sortie. The pilot is Plt Off R.A. Marchand, who was killed in action on 15 September 1940, Battle of Britain Day.

ABOVE Scramble! Two 501 Squadron Hurricanes make a rapid getaway during August 1940. Both of these aircraft were shot down over Kent on 18 August 1940, the hardest-fought day of the Battle of Britain.

LEFT Battle damage repair in the field. Here, AC E.S. Mulholland, a fitter on 615 Squadron at RAF Kenley, admires his handiwork of hastily applied canvas repair patches on the bullet-holed fuselage of 'his' Hurricane. The aircraft involved, P2801, KW–T, eventually carried Sgt D.W. Halton to his death on 15 August 1940.

Whilst this book covers the specific operations of RAF Fighter Command and its directly associated organisations during the Battle of Britain, this account would be incomplete without mention of the part played during that period by RAF Bomber Command. That is especially so given the fact that Bomber Command suffered heavier casualties than any other RAF Command during the Battle of Britain, with a total of 718 personnel lost. Additionally, it is important to consider in this context the famous 'Never in the field of human conflict' speech by Prime Minister Winston Churchill in which he referred to 'the few'.

A popular misconception has always been that this was a specific and particular reference to the pilots and aircrew of RAF Fighter Command. However, examination of the full text of his speech shows that this was most certainly not the case and Churchill went on to single out the bomber crews for special praise in his speech to the House of Commons on 20 August 1940, although it has been suggested that the content of this speech, and reference to 'the few', arose from a visit the Prime Minister made to the 11 Group HQ at Uxbridge after which he told his Chief of Staff, General Ismay: 'Don't speak to me. I have never been so moved.' Then, later, he leaned across to Ismay and said: 'Never in the field of human conflict has so much been owed by so many to so few.' This being the case there

can be little doubt that Churchill's *inspiration* for his momentous speech must have been from witnessing, first hand, the work of RAF Fighter Command, even if his speech ultimately reserved the greatest *specific* praise for the work of Bomber Command. However, the post-war context of this speech has certainly been generally regarded as marking the memory of the heroic defence of Britain by pilots of RAF Fighter Command during 1940.

However, RAF Bomber Command, although poorly equipped with medium bombers and lacking sufficient technology to bomb accurately, continually assaulted German military and industrial targets. This included Luftwaffe airfields and bases in occupied Europe. Nevertheless, the appearance of taking the fight to the enemy during the Battle of Britain was just as important in raising the morale of the British population as was the actual damage inflicted on the enemy. Whilst it is questionable as to how effective the bombing attacks against German industrial targets actually were at this time, the relentless campaign waged by RAF bombers against German forward airfields, invasion ports, barges and vessels in France, Belgium and Holland certainly placed a check on German invasion plans.

The part played by RAF Bomber Command in the actions of 1940, then, should not be overlooked. Its Order of Battle showed an average of around 40 operational squadrons during the Battle of Britain.

RIGHT Bomber Command Bristol Blenheim crew.

Women's Auxiliary Air Force (WAAF)

The part played by women of the Women's Auxiliary Air Force (WAAF) during the Battle of Britain was an extremely important one in the overall organisation of RAF Fighter Command. Whilst WAAFs were posted as part of the establishment of a fighter squadron, they performed other vital roles within the Command and also with Signals Command. In particular, this included Operations Room plotters and telephonists and operators at radar and signals stations. Additionally, the station establishment at fighter airfields would have its own complement of WAAF personnel acting as clerks, telephonists, drivers, cooks etc.

During the early years of its mobilisation the WAAF found itself in a rather invidious situation. It was not a separate entity, as was the case with the ATS and its 'parent' Army, but was virtually welded into the skeletal framework of RAF organisation and administration. Yet its members served under a different code of discipline than that firmly established for the RAF. In day-to-day routine matters, for example, WAAF officers and NCOs had greatly restricted powers of command over any RAF male of whatever rank, yet RAF officers and NCOs had almost full powers over airwomen in work and disciplinary matters. Another, if minor, example of this difference was the fact that exchanges of salutes between WAAF and RAF, at all levels, depended entirely on an individual's code of courtesy, and was not 'enforceable', this latter aspect remaining so until the close of the war.

A further complication during those years of the war concerned routine disciplinary powers over WAAF personnel held by either WAAF or RAF officers. Though subject to the Air Force Act (like all airmen) in many routine matters, including civil offences, members of the WAAF in 1939–41 could not be charged with the offence of desertion or absence without leave, due to a legal ruling then by the Judge Advocate General. Nor could any disciplinary charge be dealt with summarily, ie within the individual's particular unit, but could only be proceeded with by the way of a full court martial, however trivial the offence might have been. Even then, no WAAF officer was

LEFT WAAF recruiting poster.

BELOW The WAAF contingent at RAF Kenley are inspected by HM King George VI during the early summer of 1940. On 18 August these young women would be in the front line and under fire.

LEFT Typifying the courage displayed by WAAFs under fire, Sgt Elizabeth Mortimer was awarded the Military Medal (MM) for helping to render safe a number of unexploded bombs at RAF Biggin Hill on 18 August 1940.

The Royal Air Force was no different to any other military service in being inextricably bound up in the red tape of officialdom. Chits, forms, dockets, logs and records all had to be completed – and often in the proverbial duplicate or triplicate, of course. And it made no difference that the Battle of Britain was in full swing; the serviceman's battle with paperwork could take no respite. Here, however, we take a look at just a few of the primary records kept in 1940 by the RAF, the Air Ministry or those actually participating in the Battle of Britain, quite apart from the obligatory combat reports referred to previously. Of those records that survive, or are accessible, these are a few of the documents that help us today to understand and interpret the detail and minutiae of the Battle of Britain.

Pilot's flying log book – RAF Form 414

Each pilot or aircrew member had a duty to complete a daily record of their flying hours in a flying log book; in the case of pilots this was the RAF Form 414.

In a tabulated form, pilots were required to enter date, aircraft type, aircraft number, pilot's name, duty and cumulative totals. At the end of each month an ink-stamped box had to be completed giving the cumulative totals and was signed off by the squadron CO.

Log books could be endorsed in the event of any flying indiscretion resulting in official censure.

Prior to the Second World War flying log books of deceased officers and airmen were forwarded to next of kin when no longer required for official purposes. However, on the outbreak of war this practice was discontinued for the duration of hostilities. Log books of missing or deceased aircrew completed during this period were forwarded to the RAF Central Repository at Colnbrook, Slough, Bucks, where they were recorded and kept in safe custody. A similar practice was observed for the log books of personnel who were declared POW.

BELOW A typical RAF pilot's flying log book of the Battle of Britain period, in this case for Hurricane-equipped 151 Squadron.

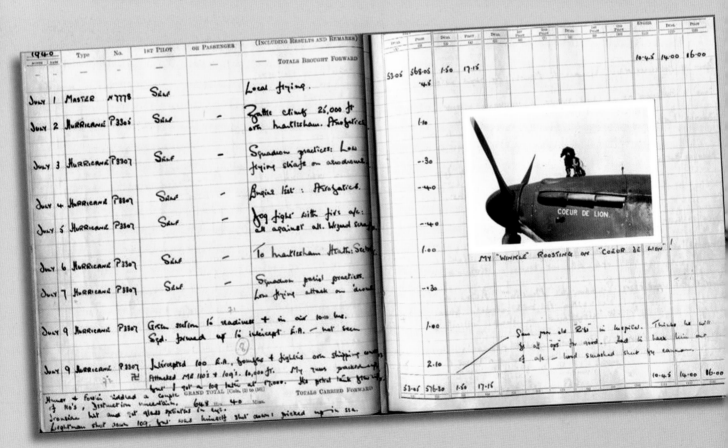

In January 1946 authority was given by the Air Ministry for the release of the log books of members of RAF aircrew whose service ended in one of the following ways:

(i)   By discharge or release from the service.
(ii) By death.
(iii) Subject to approval by permanent withdrawal from aircrew duties.

The decision was widely publicised both in newspapers and on the radio and the next of kin of deceased aircrew were encouraged to request the flying log book of their late relative. Those flying log books that still remained at the repository were retained after the war until 1960. At this point it was again widely advertised to the public that the flying log books still held could be claimed by airmen or their next of kin. Of those left unclaimed a small number were preserved as examples, and these are now held at the National Archives in the Air 4 series. The remainder were destroyed in late 1960.

A large number of log books are also held by the RAF Museum, Hendon, having been donated by the original owner or by family members. Those held at Hendon include several examples from the Battle of Britain.

Log books form an important record of an individual's participation in the Battle of Britain and a most useful study tool for researchers.

Aircraft Movements Card – Air Ministry Form 78

Form AM 78 was described as the Aircraft Movements Card and was, in effect, the official record of the history of every individual RAF aircraft, tracing its life from factory to its operational units and eventually to it being struck off charge.

Recorded on the form were the type and serial number plus details of the contract under which the aircraft had been built, its delivery date to the RAF, units to which it was allotted, engine number and details of any write-off or strike-off details (ie, reason for loss) along with total flying hours that the airframe had accrued.

Aircraft accidents – Air Ministry Form 1180

A great many losses of RAF aircraft during the Battle of Britain were the result of flying accidents rather than through combat. In these cases, a record was kept on an Aircraft Accident Record Card, the AM Form 1180, in order to record details of aircraft accidents so that the causes could be analysed and the resulting data used in accident prevention. A relatively common cause of loss during the Battle of Britain was through supposed hypoxia (oxygen starvation) where aircrew suffered an interruption or failure of their oxygen supply when operating at high altitudes. The cause of death for some aircrew operating during the Battle of Britain was not always directly through enemy action.

Aeroplane maintenance – Form 700

The Form 700, or Aeroplane Maintenance Form, was the record of all servicing and maintenance carried out on the airframe and recorded such essential details as engine changes, daily inspections, etc. It was signed off by the pilot in charge of the aircraft when he took over responsibility for the aircraft from the ground personnel and it was also signed off by the responsible member of the groundcrew, and often by the flight sergeant in charge, and kept at the home airfield. A second form duplicated all of the information contained in Form 700 and was designated the Form 700 (Travelling Copy) and was completed in exactly the same manner. It was stowed in the aircraft before flight, usually in the map box, for reference if the aircraft landed away from its home airfield. The Form 700 was routinely destroyed once an aircraft was lost or otherwise struck off charge.

Personnel record – Air Ministry Form 1406

A detailed personal record was kept in relation to every individual who served in the RAF. This included promotions, appointments and other service details along with personal information such as date of birth, address of next of kin, etc.

permitted to sit as a member of any court martial since a WAAF officer was not regarded an officer within the meaning of the Air Force Act. In simple practice this extraordinary ruling meant that any airwoman placed on a disciplinary charge could not be forcibly 'punished' in the normal service manner, but had to agree to be 'punished' appropriately. If the airwoman declined to accept punishment she could simply leave the service without notice, with no possibility of any charge being preferred against her. Such were the peculiarities insofar as they were applicable to WAAFs serving during the Battle of Britain.

The psychological effect upon long-serving airmen and officers of the RAF during 1939–40 of meeting young girls in the WAAF within what for decades had been an all-male enclave varied considerably. Fortunately, perhaps, the average reaction from the bulk of airmen and male officers was initially one of surprise, amusement and good humour which, by the close of 1940, changed to unfettered admiration and support from those who had witnessed at first hand the superb bearing of WAAFs who had served at front-line airfields and radar stations through Luftwaffe assaults during the Battle of Britain. A significant number of WAAF personnel during this period were decorated for gallantry in the face of the enemy. These girls (many were still less than 21 years of age) remained at their posts despite strafing, bombing, and scenes of carnage and horror. Their refusal to quit is all the more praiseworthy when it is remembered that each girl technically had it within her own decision to desert or to remain among such terrifying conditions.

The original principle for formation of the WAAF had been one of substitution, whereby airwomen could eventually take the place of airmen in certain non-combat duties and trades in order to release able-bodied men for more active zones and duties. In the beginning trades open to WAAFs were few. WAAF officers, in 1939, were appointed solely for administration duties while non-commissioned airwomen could only be employed in administration as clerks, or become cooks or kitchen orderlies, equipment assistants, balloon fabric workers or drivers of RAF mechanical transport. By the end of 1940, however, a total of 18 trades were open for WAAF 'substitution', including several technical or mechanical trades.

Contrary to the somewhat glamorous image of life in the WAAF portrayed in recruiting outlets, it was a fact that, in practice, the WAAF rank and file often faced the same dismal wartime accommodation and lack of facilities and amenities suffered by a majority of male non-commissioned ranks, especially on operational stations or wartime airfields. In deference to traditional custom and contemporary codes of morality, WAAF personnel were, whenever practicable, accommodated and fed separately from equivalent male personnel. In terms of actual pay, the WAAF suffered inequality with their male counterparts throughout the war, being paid at virtually all levels of rank roughly two-thirds of the daily rates enjoyed by equivalent airmen, NCO or officer ranks. This inequality also applied to the bureaucratic scale of ration allowance, whereby an airwoman was accounted for as 'four-fifths of an airman's allowance'. The official reasoning for this was that: '. . . It is well known that women need and actually consume less food than do men.'

What became clear throughout the Battle of Britain was that no inequality in terms of bravery existed between the WAAF contingent and their male counterparts when under attack on the ground at various RAF establishments.

The casualties

In total, and during the official period of the Battle of Britain, around 535 aircrew of RAF Fighter Command lost their lives and it became the responsibility of the casualty's parent unit to contact next of kin and notify them. For speed, this distressing news was conveyed by Post Office telegram and bore just the bare details and almost standard content couched in the following stark terms:

'Regret to inform you that Sgt A. Smith has been killed in action today. Letter follows.'

The dread of seeing a telegram boy arrive on his bicycle was common to many service families and the grief at the bad news that often ensued is painful even to imagine.

ABOVE AND RIGHT The delivery of formal telegrams were dreaded by all wartime families having members serving in the armed forces. This was the awful news that Flg Off Richard Plummer, a Hurricane pilot with 46 Squadron, had been shot down and injured on 4 September. Terribly burned, he died ten days later.

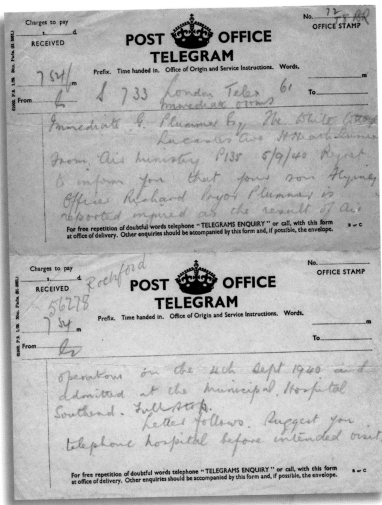

The promised letter came almost inevitably from the commanding officer of the casualty just a day or so later, and was generally followed up by another letter from the squadron adjutant giving details of effects that were to be sent home as well as enquiring as to the next of kin's wishes regarding a funeral.

Such funerals were conducted at the

BELOW LEFT AND BELOW Perhaps unusually, the full military funeral of Flg Off John Hardacre was recorded photographically when it was held at All Saints Church, Fawley, Hampshire. John Hardacre of 504 Squadron was shot down over the sea on 30 September 1940 and his body washed ashore on 10 October.

RIGHT **Post-war, service graves were marked with standard pattern Commonwealth War Graves Commission headstones (officially grave markers) like this to Plt Off Richard Hutley, a Hurricane pilot of 213 Squadron, who died on 29 October 1940. His grave is at St Andrew's Church, Tangmere.**

BELOW Some families chose to erect private monuments, such as this elaborate example to Plt Off Roy Marchand at Bromley Hill Cemetery. This memorial has now been removed and placed at the spot where he was killed near Teynham, Kent, and the grave marked by the Commonwealth War Graves Commission. In this photograph the original white wooden War Graves Commission marker (then the Imperial War Graves Commission, or IWGC) can be seen to the right of the new memorial. This was the standard pattern temporary marker originally placed on British war graves.

expense of the Air Ministry and, generally, were burials with military honours. In respect of casualties with next of kin living in the British Isles then the body of the casualty could be sent home for interment (usually being despatched by rail to their home town) in a burial ground of the family's choosing and with the nearest RAF station providing the funeral escort party, honour guard, etc. In some cases, though, families would choose for the casualty to be buried alongside fallen comrades at a designated burial ground near to the casualty's home airfield. Many churches or cemeteries local to RAF airfields consequently began to collect significant numbers of RAF graves.

Soon after burial the graves were marked with simple white wooden grave markers by the Imperial War Graves Commission (IWGC, later the Commonwealth War Graves Commission, CWGC) and bearing just the casualty's name, rank and date of death.

Of the 535 casualties suffered by RAF Fighter Command a total of 179 were ultimately reported as missing in action, almost one-third of them. In other words, no trace of them could be found and, ultimately, their deaths were presumed. In these instances, the next of kin would be notified by the same process: a telegram followed by a letter. However, if news was forthcoming as to the whereabouts or fate of the airman involved then the matter would be handed from the parent unit to the RAF's Casualty Branch at the Air Ministry in London. The Casualty Branch would keep the family apprised as to any news. Distressingly, this was often not forthcoming. In some cases, however, a body was washed ashore either in this country or perhaps on the north European shoreline. Occasionally, although only a few times during the Battle of Britain, news would come via the International Red Cross that the individual was a POW in Germany. In cases where no news was forthcoming then death was presumed after a period of six months had elapsed.

In cases where the next of kin were either from overseas and from one of Britain's dominions, or from other occupied European countries, there could be no question of repatriating the bodies of those casualties.

RIGHT The letter sent to the wife of Sgt Reg Johnson after he was shot down and wounded on 15 September 1940.

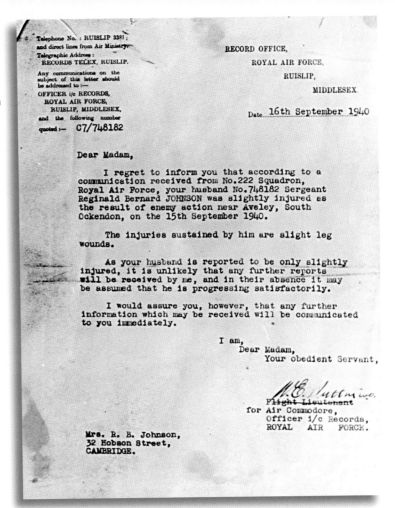

Thye Indeed, it had always been a matter of policy to bury or commemorate British or Commonwealth war dead in the theatre where they died and this policy was only relaxed at the time of the Falklands Conflict in 1982. In the case of casualties from occupied European countries it was often the case that news of their deaths could only be filtered through to families via underground sources.

As to commemoration of these casualties many families chose to erect their own private headstones. Sometimes these were quite elaborate affairs. Often they were touchingly simple, although a common theme would be a pair of RAF wings adorning the headstone. In the majority of cases, however, families chose to await the end of hostilities and erection of a War Graves Commission standard pattern headstone. Again, these were simply marked with rank, name, initials, service number and date of death. Additionally, families were invited to submit their own private inscription, which could be added at the foot of the headstone. Non-Commonwealth burials (eg, Poles, Czechs, Belgians, French) were either marked post-war with their own national pattern headstones or, particularly in the case of the Belgians and French, exhumed for reburial in their home country.

Of the 179 Battle of Britain aircrew of RAF Fighter Command who remained missing, these men were commemorated by name on the Commonwealth Air Forces Memorial at Runnymede in Berkshire. This memorial carries the names of some 20,331 casualties of RAF and Commonwealth air forces from the war of 1939–1945 and who have no known grave. It was unveiled by Her Majesty the Queen in 1959.

(Note: subsequent to the erection of this memorial sixteen RAF Fighter Command casualties of the Battle of Britain have been found and buried, or else their current resting place has been identified.)

In cases where pilots or aircrew were injured, then families and next of kin were often notified in a letter sent from the RAF Records

BELOW Officially, aircrew were forbidden to take with them into the air anything other than identity discs and identity card. In practice, the rule was often flouted and when the body of Plt Off David Harrison of 238 Squadron was washed ashore at Brighton on 9 October, after being shot down over the sea on 28 September, his wallet was found in his tunic pocket and returned to the family. Its contents presented a sad record of a young life cut short.

THE IMPACT OF LOSS

From the diary of Pilot Officer Arthur Hughes DFC*
Thursday 12 September 1940

Today I had the fateful telephone call from Air Ministry. Dave is missing from a sortie yesterday, when the squadron went up to meet a force of Ju 88s. I had a gut feeling that something was wrong, and now I am certain that my dear brother is dead. How can one go missing in 24 hours? I suppose there is a faint chance that he will be picked up in the Channel, but with the numerous vessels on the lookout for aircraft shot down there, it seems unlikely . . . and I just have a feeling. I asked the Air Ministry bloke to withhold this news from Mother and Dad until after the wedding on Saturday, but he said they had already been told. So that will throw a damper on the whole affair. Poor Kathleen, poor parents, poor little Joan. For their sakes I shall have to keep up pretence of hope, but my heart is heavy. He would have been 23 in another two weeks. This is the end of my youth, and who knows what the future will bring?

In 1941 my brother was awarded a posthumous DFC. His commanding officer wrote in the Squadron War Diary:

'In Flight Lieutenant D.P. Hughes the squadron and the country has sustained a severe loss. Tall and fair, of a very quiet and sincere temperament, his performance showed him excellently suited to be a fighter leader. A son of the Manse he has proved yet again the sure foundation of a Puritan home. Long before his last flight he had earned the DFC, which it is hoped may yet be awarded.'

*Refers to the loss of Flt. Lt. David Hughes, 238 Squadron, shot down on 11 September 1940.

Office at Ruislip setting out the circumstances, nature of injury and, usually, the hospital or medical facility where the casualty was being cared for. The injuries sustained by Sgt Pilot Reg Johnson of 222 Squadron, shot down and injured on 15 September 1940, were a case in point, with his wife receiving a matter-of-fact letter advising her of the circumstances of her husband being wounded in what had, after all, been a life-or-death engagement.

Enemy casualties

In accord with the articles of the Geneva Convention it fell to the RAF (or nearest military unit) to bury Luftwaffe casualties whose bodies were recovered in the British Isles. These airmen were buried with military honours, usually including an RAF escort and firing party. Additionally, they were buried in coffins draped with their national flag. Notification of their deaths was communicated to their families via the International Red Cross and they were sent a card including a photograph of the IWGC grave marker (an identical marker to that provided for RAF burials) along with details of the burial location. Very often these casualties were buried adjacent to RAF graves, although sometimes they were isolated graves in remote locations close to the place of death. Post-war those German graves in burial grounds that did not include a plot already maintained by the CWGC were exhumed and reburied in the German Military Cemetery, Cannock, Staffordshire. Here, the vast majority of Luftwaffe casualties from the Battle of Britain are interred. A few families elected to have the bodies of next of kin returned to Germany or Austria for reburial, although this had to be at the expense of the individual family.

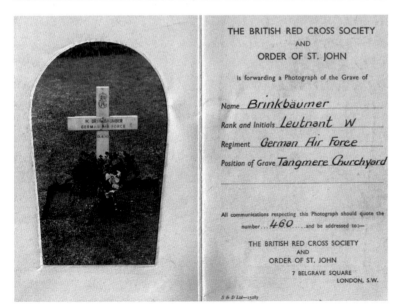

LEFT RAF Fighter Command also regularly buried the dead of its enemy, the Luftwaffe. When German casualties were found, identified and buried within the British Isles a photograph of the grave and its location was sent to the next of kin via the International Red Cross. This was the photo card send to the family of Junkers 88 crew member, Leutnant Karl-Wilhelm Brinkbäumer, shot down on 13 August 1940.

In terms of injured (non-fatal) casualties these were very often first dealt with at either the nearest civilian hospital (both RAF and Luftwaffe cases) or at Casualty Clearing Stations run by the Royal Army Medical Corps. From here, RAF cases might be transferred to specialist hospitals such as the Queen Victoria Hospital, East Grinstead, where serious burns patients were treated by pioneering plastic surgeon Sir Archibald McIndoe. Other RAF casualties were sometimes transferred to the RAF Hospital, Halton. Seriously injured Luftwaffe cases were transferred to the Royal Herbert Military Hospital, Woolwich, for treatment. On recovery, these aircrew were transferred to POW camps or, in the case of very badly injured airmen, some were repatriated on compassionate grounds (from 1943 onwards) and under reciprocal arrangements organised by the International Red Cross.

LEFT German grave marker to Lt Brinkbäumer.

Summary

Dealing with battlefield casualties has always been an unfortunate consequence for combatant nations to attend to. During the Battle of Britain it became an essential duty for RAF Fighter Command, both in dealing with its own losses as well as in the burial of those of its enemy. In terms of purely British casualties, though, it was the first war where a battle's fatalities died at home and could be buried at home in any numbers.

BELOW Luftwaffe crew members were also buried with full military honours, including firing parties, and with coffins draped in the swastika flag.

Chapter Six

The other defences

Guns, balloons and searchlights

Britain's air defences in 1940 comprised more than simply its front-line fighter force. Coming under the overall control of RAF Fighter Command's 'Dowding System' was a network of anti-aircraft guns and barrage balloon defences backed up by searchlights, sound locators and, later, gun-laying radar equipment. This comprehensive command and control system proved crucial to the nation's survival in 1940.

OPPOSITE The Gun Operations Room (GOR) for the 1st Anti-Aircraft Division situated in the lift shaft of Brompton Road Tube station in London. All information plotted on the RAF Group Operations Room table was copied to Brompton Road. Guns could not engage until permission had been granted by RAF Fighter Command. The AA HQ was in direct telephone contact with all gun sites via an open multi-phone system. Although functionally part of the Army, anti-aircraft control came under the operational jurisdiction of Fighter Command. *(WW2 Images)*

Whilst the principal 'weapon' of Britain's air defence in 1940 was the fighter, supplementary defensive measures in the form of anti-aircraft gun batteries and balloon barrages were established to protect key targets. Some of these were at fixed installations (eg, the 4.5in gun, or fixed balloon sites) but most anti-aircraft guns and balloons were relatively mobile and could be quickly deployed to meet changing threats. Overall, the anti-aircraft guns and balloons fell under control by RAF Fighter Command.

Anti-Aircraft Command

As we have seen, Anti-Aircraft Command was unusual in that it was an Army command that effectively fell under the control of the RAF. In this case, RAF Fighter Command. Its role during the Battle of Britain was certainly both an important and a significant one, albeit that its defensive effectiveness is open to some question. However, its role was firmly established inside the overall 'Dowding System'.

ABOVE General Sir Frederick A. Pile Bt, DSO, MC, GOC Anti-Aircraft Command.

GENERAL SIR FREDERICK A. PILE, BT, DSO, MC

General Officer Commanding-in-Chief, Anti-Aircraft Command

Born in 1884, Frederick Alfred Pile (2nd Baronet) was commissioned into the Royal Artillery in 1904 and initially served in India before the First World War when he was involved in the retreat from Mons as a staff captain with the 1st Division. He became a brigade major with the 40th Division in 1916 and in the closing stages of the war he became a general staff officer with 22nd Corps in France. After the war he was appointed brigade major with the Brighton and Shoreham District, before a transfer to the Royal Tank Corps in 1923. In 1928 he became commander of the 1st Experimental Mechanised Force, and then Assistant Director of Mechanisation at the War Office. He went to Egypt in 1932 as commander of the Canal Brigade Mechanised Force before becoming General Officer Commanding 1st Anti-Aircraft Division in 1937 and, in 1939, being made General Officer Commanding-in-Chief of Anti-Aircraft Command, a position he held until 1945. He thus became the only British general to retain his same command throughout the entire war. He died in 1976.

BELOW A 4.5in HAA battery fires a nocturnal salvo. Many thousands of rounds were fired during the Battle of Britain and Blitz by such batteries, although actual success rates in terms of hits were exceedingly low.

In September 1939, Britain's anti-aircraft defences were organised in a Command HQ, seven divisional headquarters, and with a varying number of brigades in each division and a number of gun and searchlight units in each brigade. The Command HQ was established at Stanmore, Middlesex, conveniently adjacent to the HQ of RAF Fighter Command. It was jointly responsible for the air defence of Great Britain, although the AOC-in-C RAF Fighter Command was in overall operational command.

The areas allotted to each of the seven divisions during the Battle of Britain were as follows:

1st – The Metropolitan area of London.
2nd – Northern East Anglia, the East Midlands and Humber.
3rd – Scotland and Northern Ireland.
4th – North West England, the West Midlands and North Wales.
5th – South Wales, South West and Southern England.
6th – South East England and Southern East Anglia.
7th – North East England.

(Note: *an additional organisation, directly controlled from Command HQ, was responsible for the anti-aircraft defence of the Orkneys and Shetlands.*)

It is essential to emphasise that these AA divisions were in no way comparable to ordinary divisions of the Field Army, being of no fixed size and at times being up to four times as large as a normal division whilst covering many thousands of square miles of country.

The failure of the campaign in Norway convinced General Pile of the paramount importance of anti-aircraft defences and he thus pressed for and secured a large expansion of the Command and its weaponry during 1940. At the outbreak of war the total number of heavy anti-aircraft guns in the Command totalled 695, many of which were of old and obsolescent types and a number of which were only on loan from the Royal Navy. The approved and recommended total at this time stood at 2,232 guns. The position, then, with light anti-aircraft guns was even worse, there being only 253 out of an approved total of 1,200, some of which had again been borrowed from the Royal Navy. Of the best light anti-aircraft gun, the 40mm Bofors, there were only 76 extant. Searchlights, however, were in a somewhat better position, there being 2,700 out of an approved total of 4,128 and a recommended total of 4,700.

The increase in equipment levels, which largely came about through General Pile pressuring for adequate defensive resources, was still way below the establishment minimum requirements once the Battle of Britain had got under way, though. However, at the end of 1939 there were 850 heavy guns, 510 light guns and 3,361 searchlights and at the beginning of July 1940, when the Battle of Britain began, there were 1,200 heavy guns, 549 light guns and 3,932 searchlights. As for manpower, and as a result of the introduction of conscription in 1939, it was intended to allot 20,000 troops every three months to help man these defences and by July 1940, the total manpower in Anti-Aircraft Command stood at 157,319.

DISPOSITION AND NUMBERS OF ANTI-AIRCRAFT GUNS

21 August and 11 September 1940

	21 August	11 September
1st AA Division (London District)	HAA – 128	HAA – 235
	LAA – 38	LAA – 44
	LMG – 167	LMG – 161
2nd AA Division (North East Anglia, the East Midlands and Humber)	HAA – 179	HAA – 131
	LAA – 78	LAA – 82
	LMG – 765	LMG - 835
3rd AA Division (Scotland and Northern Ireland)	HAA – 158	HAA – 169
	LAA – 122	LAA – 132
	LMG – 378	LMG – 367
4th AA Division (North West England, the West Midlands and North Wales)	HAA – 199	HAA – 186
	LAA – 80	LAA – 84
	LMG – 389	LMG – 397
5th AA Division (South Wales, South West and Southern England)	HAA – 309	HAA – 291
	LAA – 181	LAA – 190
	LMG – 547	LMG – 553
6th AA Division (South East England and Southern East Anglia)	HAA – 188	HAA – 185
	LAA – 185	LAA – 141
	LMG – 415	LMG – 397
7th AA Division (North East England)	HAA – 118	HAA – 114
	LAA – 62	LAA – 55
	LMG – 270	LMG – 277

(Note: HAA – heavy anti-aircraft guns; LAA – light anti-aircraft guns; LMG – light machine guns (anti-aircraft).

Anti-aircraft weaponry

Whilst the effectiveness or otherwise of anti-aircraft guns is open to some debate they were, nevertheless, a significant part of Britain's air defence system. The numbers of enemy aircraft destroyed or damaged by anti-aircraft guns was, proportionately, somewhat low given the scale of effort employed and the number of rounds fired. However, it is difficult to assess the actual effect that anti-aircraft fire had upon German bomber formations, although it is undoubtedly the case that it played a part in distracting or disrupting such attacks and often greatly affected the morale of bomber crews. On the negative side, and from a defensive point of view, gunfire could be equally dangerous to RAF fighters who would often be engaging enemy formations, which were simultaneously being fired upon by anti-aircraft guns as the German aircraft entered

artillery zones. A number of British aircraft were hit, damaged or destroyed due to such 'friendly fire' episodes during the Battle of Britain. Additionally, shell splinters (and sometimes unexploded shells) would fall to earth and this frequently resulted in damage, death or injury.

During the Battle of Britain, Anti-Aircraft Command used five main types of anti-aircraft weapon:

40mm Bofors gun

One of the best-known light anti-aircraft guns, the 40mm Bofors gun was a truly versatile and effective weapon in its primary role to counter the threat of dive-bombers and low-flying aircraft, but it could also be effective against ground targets. It operated in every theatre of war and played an important role in the air defence of Great Britain during the Battle of Britain. Its adoption came about to meet the requirement for a high-performance, mobile anti-aircraft gun suitable for air defence in the field. The choice of gun selected for this role was the Swedish design built by Bofors AB. Negotiations began in December 1936 and in 1937 a batch of guns and ammunition was ordered from Bofors. The manufacturing rights were also obtained, thus allowing the gun to be

BELOW The Bofors 40 mm light anti-aircraft gun.

BOTTOM A Bofors gun and gun crew in their revetment and engaged on airfield defence at an RAF Fighter Command station.

BOTTOM RIGHT 40mm high-explosive round

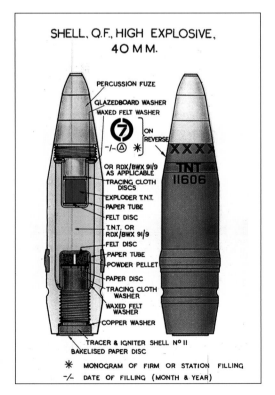

SHELL, Q.F., HIGH EXPLOSIVE, 40 M M.

PERCUSSION FUZE
GLAZEDBOARD WASHER
WAXED FELT WASHER
ON REVERSE
OR RDX/BWX 91/9 AS APPLICABLE
TRACING CLOTH DISCS
EXPLODER T.N.T.
PAPER TUBE
FELT DISC
T.N.T. OR RDX/BWX 91/9
FELT DISC
PAPER TUBE
POWDER PELLET
PAPER DISC
TRACING CLOTH WASHER
WAXED FELT WASHER
COPPER WASHER

XXXX
TNT
11606

TRACER & IGNITER SHELL Nº II
BAKELISED PAPER DISC
✱ MONOGRAM OF FIRM OR STATION FILLING
-/- DATE OF FILLING (MONTH & YEAR)

built in Great Britain and the Commonwealth.

The Bofors gun fired a 2lb (40mm) high-explosive shell fitted with a 250 impact fuse. The shell was also fitted with the 11 Tracer and Igniter. This provided a self-destroying tracer capability that allowed the fall of shot to be observed and corrected as required, as well as a self-destruct capability, which prevented the fused shell from falling to the ground, exploding on impact and causing unnecessary damage or injury. On firing, the tracer element fitted in the base of the shell was ignited. This burned for 7 seconds after which a self-destruct initiator detonated the shell. The 40mm shell had a muzzle velocity of 2.790ft/sec. The gun could be fired in either single shot or bursts at a rate of 120 rounds/min. When fitted with open sights it could be used for direct fire deflection shooting. It could also be fitted with speed corrector equipment, which was of a Polish design. This allowed the target's course to be applied to a mechanical corrector, which then transmitted deflection data to the sighting mechanism. The speed could be adjusted after opening fire using observation to obtain a hit. The Polish-designed corrector was not manufactured in Great Britain because another device (the British-designed Kerrison or LAA 3 Predictor, an electro-hydraulic system) was chosen to be used with the British-manufactured Bofors gun. This system required three additional operators and provided a remote automatic gun-laying capability by tracking the target via a telescope. The system computed corrections using vertical and lateral height information as well as ranging information. It required highly trained and experienced gun detachments as well as a remote power source to operate the predictor equipment. There were few guns with this equipment at the outbreak of war, with only a few regular LAA batteries being equipped.

The gun was fired by means of a pedal operated by the loader who fed clips of rounds into an autoloader located on the top of the gun. The empty cases were ejected to the front of the gun. The gun was manned normally by a crew of seven men. It could be traversed through 360 degrees, depressed to 60 degrees and elevated to 90 degrees. The Bofors proved to be versatile, reliable and robust in service and was responsible for shooting down a number of

low-flying enemy aircraft during its service with Anti-Aircraft Command.

Vickers 2pdr

Classified as a light anti-aircraft (LAA) gun the Vickers 2pdr (often referred to as the 'Pom Pom') was accepted for land service as an anti-aircraft gun in 1936.

During the early thirties there had been much

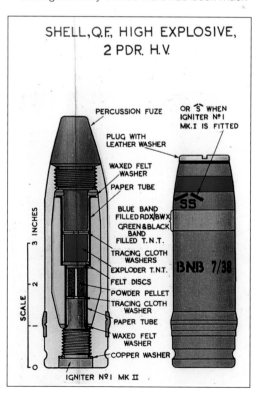

ABOVE The Vickers 2pdr 'Pom-Pom' gun. A small number of these guns remained in service during 1940.

LEFT 2pdr high-explosive round

indecision in the Air Ministry regarding the calibre of gun required to counter the threat of low-level air attack. Additionally, the Chief of the Imperial General Staff had specifically refused to sanction the development of any LAA weapon above a 0.5in calibre. The Army, however, had differing and strong views about this. Trials carried out had shown that to inflict immediate destructive damage to an aircraft, the least requirement was for a 2lb impact-fused high-explosive round. As a result, they had been looking for appropriate guns that offered a high rate of fire, mobility, and the ability to fire the appropriate weight of projectile required. The only suitable British contender then available was the Vickers 2pdr Mk VIII anti-aircraft gun, which had been employed by the Royal Navy as an LAA gun on ships for some years. During trials this was found to be heavy and unsatisfactory for service on land without drastic modification, and its performance was less than impressive. Recognising that some form of defence for vulnerable points liable to low-level and dive-bombing attack as a stop-gap measure was needed, the Vickers 2pdr was adopted in 1936 for this role. As a result, 60 twin-barrel Mk VIII guns on static Mk II mountings suitable for adaptation to land mounting were eventually ordered.

At the time of its service introduction the 2pdr Mk VIII had been an advanced weapon,

but by the outbreak of war in 1939 the rapid improvements in aircraft design had rendered it obsolete. It had a low muzzle velocity (2,300ft/sec), lacked a satisfactory design of explosive shell and was not provided with tracer ammunition, which is important in a LAA gun to allow the flight of the projectile to be observed, thus allowing fire to be corrected to hit the target.

Employed as a stop-gap design only, the 2pdr filled the role of LAA gun until the far more suitable 40mm Bofors gun was adopted, although a number were still in service during 1940.

3.7in gun

The need for a high-performance, purpose-designed heavy anti-aircraft gun to replace the 3in 20cwt gun was identified during the 1920s. It was not until 1932, however, that the specification for a new AA gun was issued. During the 1920s and early 1930s, improvements in gun technology and ballistic science directly benefited the design of the new AA gun. The requirement issued was for a gun with a muzzle velocity of 3,000ft/sec, firing a shell with a weight of 28lb, with an effective ceiling of 35,000ft, to be road transportable at a speed of 25mph and weighing in total no more than eight tons. It was the great British armament firm Vickers that came up with a design to meet these requirements and by 1934 had produced a mock-up version. With some modifications, which included the addition of a loading tray, a mechanical rammer for manual operation and the provision of a manually operated fuse setting machine, the Vickers design was approved by the Master-General of Ordnance (MGO) and would become the 3.7in HAA gun. The first guns were built in 1936. The new gun incorporated semi-automatic breech mechanism functionality (where on firing the gun's recoil was used to open the breech, eject the empty cartridge case and re-cock the firing mechanism) as used in its predecessor the 3in 20cwt. The muzzle velocity delivered was 2,670ft/sec. The gun could be traversed through 360 degrees and could elevate to 80 degrees. The mobile mounting consisted of a limber and carriage mounted on two wheeled trailers.

When brought into action the towing limber and rear two-wheeled carriage was removed,

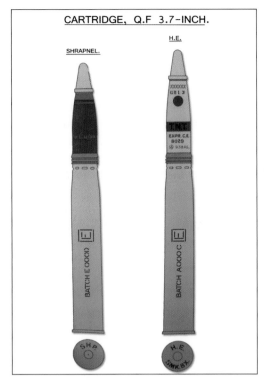

CARTRIDGE, Q.F 3.7-INCH.

SHRAPNEL.

H.E.

four folded legs extended and the gun with the front two-wheeled carriage still attached raised into the firing position. The new gun exceeded the original weight specification, weighing in at either 9 tons 12cwt or 10 tons 6cwt depending on the weight of barrel fitted. The ammunition fired comprised a fixed round (both shell and cartridge joined together), which weighed 49lb. The gun was loaded by placing the round with its time fuse already set on a loading tray. This was then positioned behind the breech and the round then rammed into the breech using a wire rope rammer. The breech was closed and the gun fired. A trained crew could fire at a rate of 15 rounds/min, but prolonged firing at this rate could lead to barrel overheating.

The high-explosive shell weighed just over 28lb and was fitted with a 199 powder-filled time fuse, which was pre-set to detonate the shell after a given time to match the time of flight to the target. The time setting required to ignite the fuse was achieved by inserting the fuse into a setting machine before loading into the gun.

Vickers began production of the gun in 1937, but with the gathering storm of war in Europe seemingly imminent and the growing pace of rearmament in Great Britain, an increased production was soon recognised as being

required. To meet this demand a simpler, static design was introduced where the running gear, legs and raising equipment were eliminated and the gun simply placed on a static mounting which could be bolted on to a hold-fast.

This weapon became one of the mainstays of Britain's anti-aircraft defence during the Battle of Britain period.

QF 3in 20cwt

The 3in heavy anti-aircraft (HAA) gun was originally adopted during the First World War, where it had become the principal and most effective AA gun then in service. Its design originated from a naval weapon, but to employ it in the anti-aircraft role several improvements to the original design were incorporated to make it more suitable for that purpose. These included adding a semi-automatic breech, where on firing the gun's recoil was used to open the breech, eject the empty cartridge case and re-cock the firing mechanism. When the next round was loaded the breech automatically closed and the gun was ready to fire again. The gun was originally designed to fire a 12lb shrapnel shell with a muzzle velocity of 2,500ft/sec. This shell was found to cause excessive barrel wear, suffered from poor accuracy and was unstable in flight. As a result, an improved larger streamlined shell was introduced in 1916 weighing 16lb with a muzzle velocity of 2,000ft/sec. Its effective range was 16,000ft with a maximum ceiling of 22,000ft.

The 3in guns were employed as part of HAA batteries, on the basis of eight guns per

ABOVE A Heinkel 111 over the East End of London during September 1940. AA gunners would look to target individual bombers or formations in either continuously pointed fire, predicted concentration, or box barrage engagements. Apart from actually destroying the bombers, disrupting their ability to accurately target their objectives was also the intention.

BELOW When the bombers evaded the fighter, AA or balloon defences and got through to their targets, then the consequences could be both dramatic and catastrophic. Here, a fuel storage depot at Thameshaven burns during September 1940.

When engaging aircraft, heavy anti-aircraft batteries usually employed one of three methods: Continuously pointed fire, predicted concentration fire or a box barrage.

Continuously pointed fire

This was the most dangerous type of AA fire. Each gun unit tracked the target aircraft, usually the formation leader, at a predicted distance in the sky in front of it. The guns fired at maximum rate and for as long as the target aircraft remained in range or crossed the bomb release point. For this type of fire the predictors and height finders needed to have the aircraft continuously in view to allow visual aiming, either by day or illuminated at night by searchlights.

Predicted concentration fire

This type of fire was less effective than continuously pointed fire. It was used when darkness or cloud prevented visual fire control. The gunners fired short barrages at points in the sky through which it was predicted the target aircraft would pass.

Box barrage

This was the least effective and most wasteful type of barrage. It was used when darkness or cloud prevented the use of other fire control methods and good information was not available on the location of targets. The gunners fired into a 'box' of sky just ahead of the supposed bomb release line in front of the bomber's expected target. The so-called 'London Barrage' involved this type of fire. During September 1940, AA gunners fired a quarter of a million shells at night, most of them into thin air. Their efforts accounted for under a dozen enemy aircraft.

General Sir Frederick Pile: 'The volume of fire which resulted, and which was publicised as a "barrage", was in fact largely wild and uncontrolled shooting. There were, however, two valuable results from it: the volume of fire had a deterrent effect upon at least some of the aircrews and there was a marked improvement in civilian morale.'

The weapons outlined in this chapter were the principal anti-aircraft guns in use at the time of the Battle of Britain by Anti-Aircraft Command. The effectiveness or otherwise of these weapons has always been the subject of some doubt. However, there were certainly a number of enemy aircraft which could be definitely confirmed as having fallen to anti-aircraft guns during the period.

As to statistics, claims made by the 6th Anti-Aircraft Division, which covered a significant portion of south-east England (including the Debden, North Weald, Hornchurch, Biggin Hill and Kenley Sectors) during the period July to October, were of 203 enemy aircraft destroyed by day and 18 at night. There can be no doubting that this daylight figure is over-inflated, with the high number by day probably being due to the fact that gunners were often shooting aircraft that they could see, that were also being attacked by fighters and where they could also witness the destruction of aircraft they knew they were shooting at. The reality, for the most part, was that these aircraft were being destroyed by fighters. Other statistics for this division, though, highlight the astonishing volume of ammunition expended. In the first 14 months of the war Bofors guns had fired 200 rounds for each aircraft claimed as destroyed, and HAA guns engaging seen targets used 298 rounds for each aircraft claimed as destroyed and 2,444 rounds per aircraft destroyed when firing at unseen targets. Across Anti-Aircraft Command as a whole the numbers of rounds fired by guns of all classes for each aircraft claimed as destroyed were 334 in July, 232 in August and 1,798 in September. Almost certainly, the September 'spike' may be attributed to the Luftwaffe launching its day-and-night assault on London and other cities from 7 September.

(Note: *preparations were made by all AA defences to assume a secondary ground defence role: Bofors were provided with anti-tank ammunition and sited to cover approaches to aerodromes, vulnerable points etc. Certain 3.7in guns suitably sited were given an anti-shipping role, and preparations were made for barrages to be laid down on certain beaches. Under the immediate threat of invasion in May 1940, mobile columns of AA troops were formed for ground defence, but these troops reverted to their AA role before the Battle of Britain began.*)

ABOVE The burned-out tailplane of a He 111.

BELOW Often, too, non-military and industrial targets suffered. This is the result when fighter-bombers got through on 15 September and dropped bombs close to Woolston railway station near Southampton.

battery. They continued to serve on long after the First World War as the main HAA gun, both in the static and mobile roles, although the new 3.7in HAA gun would eventually supersede it. In 1939, however, many were still in service although the gun was rapidly becoming obsolete. When the British Expeditionary Force (BEF) deployed to France in 1939, 48 3in guns were sent over to France. It had been suggested that the BEF should be equipped with the newer 3.7in HAA gun, but those responsible for making such decisions in the BEF stated that they preferred to keep the 3in guns. So, it was only by chance that many of the HAA guns left in France after Dunkirk were the older 3in 20cwt guns rather than the more modern 3.7in HAA guns that would be important in the air defence of Great Britain during the Battle of Britain. However, a few of the surviving 3in guns remained in use, briefly, for home defence during 1940.

4.5in heavy anti-aircraft gun

At a corresponding time with the development of the 3.7in HAA gun, came the recognition that an even more powerful high-angle heavy anti-aircraft gun for land service was also required. The gun chosen to fulfil this role was not to be a completely new design, but derived from an existing naval quick-firing gun originally designed to arm the new carriers being built in the 1930s and fitted in twin mountings. Although designated as a 4.5in gun, the actual bore diameter of the naval gun was actually 4.45in, which was replicated in the land service design.

As the original naval gun had been designed for mounting in twin turrets onboard ships, and the land service version required only a single and static mounting, the design needed significant change and simplification. Emplaced in static positions, mounted on holdfasts set in

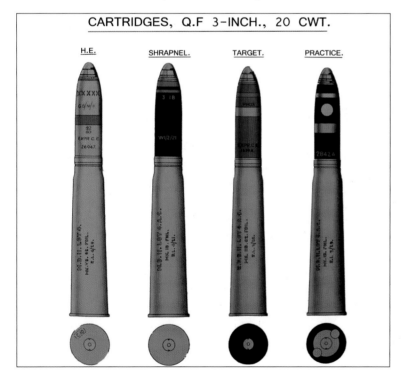

CARTRIDGES, Q.F 3-INCH., 20 CWT.

H.E.   SHRAPNEL.   TARGET.   PRACTICE.

BELOW The 4.5in heavy anti-aircraft gun in its armoured gun shield 'turret'.

concrete, the guns were mounted behind large steel gun shields giving them the resemblance of a ship's gun turret. The total weight of the gun was 16.5 tons and it could traverse through 360 degrees and elevate up to 80 degrees. A 55lb high-explosive shell was fired at a muzzle velocity of 2,470ft/sec. The maximum ceiling attainable was 42,000ft but its normal operating ceiling was between 22,000ft and 28,000ft. The 4.5in gun in terms of operation was very similar to the 3.7in gun and fired a fixed round weighing 86lb and featured the same loading tray, ramming and fuse setting mechanisms. The rate of fire was 8 rounds/min. The first 4.5in guns were in place and ready for operation in February 1939.

Searchlights

Searchlights were an essential part of night-time defences. Up to 1939 the responsibility for the manning of searchlight units had largely rested with Territorial Army (TA) Royal Engineer units, supported by a smaller number of Royal Artillery (TA) units. This changed in 1939, however, when the responsibility for searchlights was fully handed over to the Royal Artillery, with the Royal Engineer TA searchlight units changing cap badges and becoming TA Royal Artillery units. With a few exceptions this transition was largely completed by 1 August 1940. A modernisation programme for searchlight equipment had

been instituted in 1935. Up to that time, the main equipment of the TA units was the 120cm SL projector with the units being equipped with First World War vintage lorries. The replacement searchlight adopted was the 90cm projector, which was lighter, smaller and powered by a high-density arc lamp. The beam could be manually guided using visual observation or directed in conjunction with sound-ranging equipment. The new searchlight was mounted on a small tracked chassis and could be easily transported by lorry. To power these searchlights, commercial lorry-mounted Tilling Stevens and Thornycroft generators were employed along with Lister diesel 15kva generators mounted on a towed two-wheel

ABOVE The standard 120cm SL projector in use by the Royal Artillery during the Battle of Britain.

Under the command of the Royal Artillery, a searchlight regiment was commanded by a lieutenant colonel and consisted of three or four batteries, each led by a major, with a strength of 11 officers and 365 other ranks. A battery consisted of four troops each with six searchlights and was usually commanded by a captain. Both the 120cm and 150cm searchlights had ten-man detachments on static sites.

Whilst searchlights obviously played no active role in the day fighting of the Battle of Britain, per se, they certainly played their part in the limited night-fighting and anti-aircraft operations of the period. Additionally, searchlight posts seem to have been tasked with the meticulous logging of daytime events in their own operational areas with the war diaries of such units held at the National Archives, Kew, being filled with the minutiae of incidents and events that help researchers assemble the detail of air fighting on individual days. These records list aircraft shot down, parachutes seen, times, map references, etc. Additionally, several Luftwaffe aircrew were taken into captivity by men from searchlight posts during the Battle of Britain. As Air Chief Marshal Dowding reported:

'Owing to the close spacing of searchlight sites they formed a valuable source of intelligence and rapid reports were able to be made upwards of casualties to friendly and

chassis. Just prior to the outbreak of war a new 150cm searchlight was introduced. Mounted on a four-wheel trailer, it produced an intensely bright narrow beam, produced by a high-density carbon arc lamp used with a large reflector. It was capable of penetrating mist and low cloud and could illuminate targets up to 20,000ft. Searchlights were designated in centimetres as opposed to inches due to the concave reflector being classed as an optical instrument (optical instruments, which were sourced from Europe, were all measured in centimetres and millimetres).

RIGHT As Air Chief Marshal Dowding reported, the searchlight units also played a valuable part during the daytime by recording the fall of enemy aircraft and noting other 'incidents of importance'. Here, men of a searchlight unit in Kent examine six German parachutes on 11 September 1940.

enemy aircraft, pilots descending by parachute and other incidents of importance. In addition, they have been able to provide valuable reports of isolated enemy aircraft, trace of which had been lost by the Observer Corps.'

The searchlight units were a component part of Anti-Aircraft Command and, as such, fell under the direct control of RAF Fighter Command as an integral part of the 'Dowding System'.

RAF Balloon Command

The role played by the barrage balloon during the Battle of Britain was also significant and one which was performed by a relatively 'new' Command within the RAF, albeit that it also fell under the overall control of RAF Fighter Command during 1940.

Air Vice-Marshal Owen Tudor Boyd CB, OBE, MC, AFC
Air Officer Commanding, RAF Balloon Command

Boyd was born in 1889 and served as an Army officer in India from 1909 and during the First World War he was a pilot in the Royal Flying Corps on the Western Front. By 1918, however, he was commanding 72 Squadron in Mesopotamia. During the interwar years he served mostly in RAF staff officer posts, although in 1922 he was given command of 24 Squadron. In 1936, Boyd was promoted to air commodore and went to 1 Group RAF. He was then appointed to a staff post at the Air Ministry in December 1936.

In 1938, as an air vice-marshal, Boyd became Commander-in-Chief, RAF Balloon Command, which he led throughout the Battle of Britain and through part of the Blitz. On 1 December 1940 he was replaced, promoted to air marshal and appointed deputy to the Air Officer Commanding-in-Chief (AOC-in-C) Middle East. On his way to Egypt to take up his appointment his aircraft was forced down in Sicily and he was taken POW by the Italians. He was freed from captivity in 1943 when Italy capitulated and died in England in 1944.

The background
Prior to the establishment of RAF Balloon Command it was recognised by the Air Ministry

that thought needed to be given to an effective barrage balloon defence of Britain. Thus, a balloon group was brought into being in 1937. Known as 30 (Balloon Barrage) Group it was primarily responsible for the establishment of a curtain of balloons protecting the approaches to London. RAF Balloon Command itself was formed on 1 November 1938 at RAF Stanmore Park, Middlesex, comprising a HQ and several balloon groups.

As the war progressed, and as an influx of WAAF personnel joined the air force, more and more women were trained in the

ABOVE The standard KB barrage balloon in use during the Battle of Britain. Each balloon cost £500 and required some 20,000cu ft of hydrogen gas to inflate at a cost of £50 per balloon.

LEFT Air Vice-Marshal Owen T. Boyd, AOC, RAF Balloon Command.

specific role of barrage balloon personnel. This became the norm, but for the most part, though, barrage balloon squadrons during the Battle of Britain were made up with an establishment of RAF airmen.

The balloon barrage would consist merely of the cables by which the balloons were held captive. Later on, extra hanging cables were added and some of these had explosive devices

BELOW The RAF also operated maritime barrage balloon squadrons, which sailed to protect convoys. This is a balloon of 952 Squadron flying from HMS *Borealis*. In practice, the balloons proved unsuccessful when used to protect convoys because German fighters would merely sweep ahead of any incoming bombers and shoot down the balloons. Such was the case on 8 August 1940 in the English Channel when Convoy CW9 PEEWIT was attacked. In that instance, not only were the balloons shot from the sky but HMS *Borealis* was also bombed and sunk. The maritime balloon experiment during the Battle of Britain was a failure.

attached. At first sight, such a defence might appear rather haphazard or ineffectual, but if a few simple calculations are made it will be found that it is far more effective than might at first be imagined. Assuming an aircraft of a 70ft wingspan passed through a line of balloons tethered at 100yd intervals there would be something just less than a one chance in four of it hitting a cable – a pretty formidable risk which no attacker could afford to take. Even though contemporary bombers of the period were able to reach altitudes above 20,000ft, a balloon barrage at only 10,000ft, if it were of sufficient density, would theoretically reduce the fighters' task of finding the bombers by a depth of 10,000ft out of perhaps 20,000ft. That lower 10,000ft was also in the murkiest part of the atmosphere that needed to be searched. At that time, low-flying aircraft were the least vulnerable to AA fire and defending fighters. This was due to the fact that there was insufficient time for the gun or searchlight to be trained on the aircraft before it had disappeared again, and intercepting fighters also found the raiders difficult to spot against the background of an intricate countryside or urban sprawl. So, the balloons also served to potentially drive the attackers up to an altitude where they could be more easily engaged by searchlights, guns and aircraft.

Obviously, balloons flown at any altitude in daylight made good targets in fine weather but such conditions were those in which guns and fighters could also operate most effectively. Night and bad visibility were the times when a balloon barrage was most needed by the defence, and it was in such conditions that the balloons would be fairly immune from attack. The first method of siting balloons was to moor them approximately on the perimeter of the area to be defended. If, however, they were sited equidistantly over a circular area then the probability of impact was from two to three times as great as it was when the same number of balloons were sited equidistantly, but only round the circumference. These methods were known respectively as 'field siting' and 'perimeter siting'.

Dive-bombing, however, was a mode of attack which no defence system could afford to ignore and it would be met to a certain extent at least by field-sited balloons, whereas the perimeter method would be of little or no value. Lastly, by using field siting, a barrage of very high impact value could be achieved without the necessity of handling balloons in dangerously close proximity to one another. However, in the case of dive-bombing attacks it was not unusual for German fighters to 'sweep' the target area prior to the raid and shoot down any balloons.

Losses due to unexpected weather changes far exceeded expectations and squadrons were forced to conserve stocks by keeping about two-thirds of the balloons deflated. There was also a growing demand for balloons to be flown from waterborne moorings in estuaries as a deterrent to mine-laying aircraft, or towed behind tugs as protection for coastal convoys. On land, the balloons were often flown from winch-equipped lorries for ease of mobility whilst permanent sites used combinations of screw pickets, buried railway sleepers and sandbags to hold them down. One of the most important factories making balloons was at Kelvin Hall, Glasgow, where many thousands were produced. However, the balloons proved to be popular targets for German fighters in the hours of daylight along Britain's south coast during the Battle of Britain, with many of them being shot up and set ablaze by Me 109s.

One of the first Luftwaffe aircraft to fall to a balloon was a He 111 of KG27 on 13 September 1940. Returning from a raid on Merseyside, the bomber struck a cable over Newport, Monmouthshire, and plunged into a residential area. Two children were killed on the ground as well as three of the crew, only the pilot baling out in time. Earlier, over Plymouth on 22 July 1940, a Ju 88 tried to avoid a balloon but stalled and landed on top of it. Luckily, the propellers did not penetrate the hydrogen-filled envelope and the aircraft slid off with no forward speed. The crew prepared to bail out, but then their pilot regained control and was able to drop his load of mines and make good his escape.

Quite apart from the hazard presented to Luftwaffe aircraft by the balloon barrage, a number of RAF aircraft were also lost throughout the war following collisions with balloon cables, including some lost during the Battle of Britain. One such casualty was Flg Off Ralph Hope of 605 Squadron, killed when his

Hurricane struck a barrage balloon cable over South Norwood, London, on 14 October 1940.

ABOVE No 961 Squadron's balloons at Dover were also badly mauled by the Luftwaffe during the Battle of Britain. Here, a Messerschmitt 109 strafes one of the balloons.

LEFT Moments later and the highly flammable hydrogen is ignited and the balloon falls earthwards, wreathed in flame and smoke.

The organisation

When the new RAF Balloon Command came into being on 1 November 1938 under the command of Air Vice-Marshal O.T. Boyd CB, OBE, the Auxiliary Air Force had formed balloon squadrons which, by August 1940, had reached a total of 49. These were numbered in the 900 series, up to five squadrons being administered by a Balloon Centre. Several of these centres in a particular geographical area then came under the control of a barrage balloon group with all training in balloon handling being given at RAF Cardington, Bedfordshire, where 1 Balloon Training Unit was based. Unfortunately, balloon production was unable to keep pace with demand so that on the first day of war less than half the planned Balloon Command establishment could be deployed – 444 in London and 180 elsewhere in the country.

Barrage balloon – the technical details

Each barrage balloon was made up of a series of panels, totalling 24 in number from the bow to the stern. However, from the top to the bottom of the balloon each panel was called a 'Gore' and these were named 'A-F' inclusive. Every panel was of an exact size and fabric workers had to sew and glue the seams together to construct the balloon, the material being a silver-grey rubberised fabric. The construction process meant inhaling considerable fumes from benzene-based solvents of the period, and on medical advice the workers were given an extra pint of milk a day to help protect the digestive system from adverse chemical effects caused by the materials in use.

The lower one-third of the balloon, called a ballonet, was not filled with hydrogen but was filled with air from a scoop on the underside and near to the bow. Between the upper compartment and the lower compartment was a sheet of balloon fabric and the principle was that as the balloon rose into the air the hydrogen gas would expand and in order

to prevent bursting the balloon the lower diaphragm would be forced down into the ballonet, which was vented to the air. In this way the balloon did not appear to change shape as the balloon expanded down into the air-filled ballonet. The wind forced into the forward scoop enabled the ballonet to remain open and capable of taking the extra volume from the expanding top part of the balloon.

At the rear of the balloon were three 'fins' and these were filled with air from the scoops and, when inflated, they maintained the balloon head into wind. This gave stability to the balloon.

At the joint of Gores 'B' and 'C' were five rigging patches used to attach the picketing lines and these were in turn fixed to handling guy lines to enable the balloon to be handled on the ground. When bedded down the picketing lines were securely fastened to large concrete blocks set out in a diamond shape. Alternatively, the picketing lines would be attached to screw pickets like huge metal corkscrews twisted into the ground.

Between Gores 'D' and 'E' were six similar patches used for the rigging legs. Known as 'ton patches', they were supposed to withstand a weight pull on them of one ton.

Each of these patches was positioned at a precise point along the length of the balloon and each of the rigging legs that came with these was of a precise length. This enabled the six cables to meet at an exact point under the balloon and meant that the force of the balloon upward was distributed in a specific way along the cables as they met at one specific point known as the crossover. In practice this meant that the balloon flew at a slight incline to the ground nose down. After the crossover the flying cable was connected and this led to the winch.

If the air pressure in the ballonet exceeded a specific level, for instance in a high wind, there was a pressure relief valve in the ballonet that helped keep the pressure within set limits.

Partly on Gore 'A', but mostly at Gore 'B', at panel 10, was a special panel called the rip panel. This was designed as a strip securely glued down on to the fabric and, underneath, a hole in the body of the balloon. Between the balloon and the rip panel was a strand of very sharp cheese wire. In turn, this was attached to a cord coloured red and pulling on this cord

BELOW The Mk VII Series 1 KB balloon.

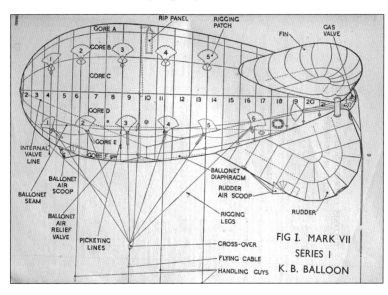

caused the wire to slice through the rip panel, thus exposing the hole in the balloon and venting the hydrogen to the atmosphere. So, in an emergency the rip panel could be activated and the balloon deflated in order to prevent it from running amok in bad weather. Crews were reluctant to use this unless absolutely essential, as refilling it with hydrogen and repairing the panel was costly. However, balloons not infrequently broke their moorings and RAF fighter pilots were sent off in pursuit in order to shoot them down because the trailing cables had potential to cause havoc to both power and telephone lines.

Sound ranging

Although sound ranging was very much being superseded by gun-laying radar at the time of the Battle of Britain, it remained a system that was still in use to a limited extent during the battle period. Sound-ranging units were part of Anti-Aircraft Command.

Sound ranging is a method used to determine the distance between a given point and the position of a sound source by measuring the time lapse between the origin of the sound and its arrival at the listening location. Its use in air defence had been developed during the First World War on land to locate enemy artillery batteries and for air defence purposes to counter the threat of German heavy bombers. Between the wars, much development work had been done to further develop sound ranging as a method of locating enemy aircraft. Large static sound-locating walls and dishes had been built, together with mobile sound-ranging equipment which was being developed. During 1938, and as a result of this development work, new sound locators were being introduced into service with the Royal Artillery. The locators comprised smaller mobile units as well as bigger units fitted with large parabolic receivers and sensitive microphone detectors which, due to their size, were mounted on four-wheel trailers. A further development soon followed with the invention of Visual Indicating Equipment (VIE). This utilised a cathode-ray tube enabling the operators to see sound readings converted to a visual display, which greatly improved accuracy in relation to locating the source of the sound target.

Sound-ranging equipment was utilised for directing searchlight beams as well as for assisting in the plotting of night-time raids. When working in pairs it could also be used to select points to fire heavy anti-aircraft concentrations. As a technology, sound ranging was becoming outmoded in 1940 and was eventually entirely superseded by the development of radar*. However, this fairly basic audible system still played its part in the Battle of Britain.

(*Note: *whilst the gun laying Mk I radar had gone into service by 1940, the part it played in assisting anti-aircraft guns during the Battle of Britain was minimal. Although the system gave accurate ranges on enemy aircraft the azimuth indications were imprecise and it could not measure elevation and was thus incapable of directing fire even with a low degree of accuracy. General Pile later said of the equipment: 'The teething troubles with the radar were enormous. By the beginning of October 1940 we had not succeeded [with gun laying radar] in firing a single round at night.' Later modifications and improvements eventually provided effective equipment, although this did not see service until after 1940.*)

ABOVE Although outmoded technology, there was a certain reliance on sound ranging against German bomber formations to assist with AA gun direction at night-time. Gun-laying radar was still in its infancy and did not really come into effective operation until the Blitz had got under way. This is one of the relatively primitive sound locators still in use during 1940.

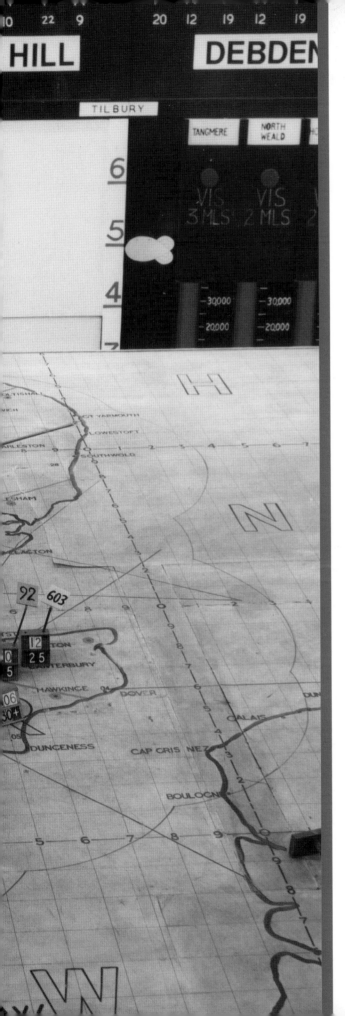

Epilogue

Did it all work?

━━━━━(●)━━━━━

The failure of an effective air defence system in France had contributed massively to the defeat of that country earlier in 1940. That said, the eventual conquest of France and the Low Countries was an inevitability in the face of German military might, although that hastened demise was watched across the English Channel by Dowding who knew, very soon, that the test of his 'Dowding System' must come.

OPPOSITE Britain's integrated early warning command and control system was a key to the successful outcome of the Battle of Britain.

Although possibly apocryphal, a scene from the 1969 film *Battle of Britain* is surely germane. In it, Dowding is in conversation with a Cabinet minister who tells him that Churchill puts great faith in radar. Dowding responds: 'It's vital, but it won't shoot down aircraft.' The minister goes on to chide Dowding for not exactly exuding a spirit of optimism, to which the C-in-C of Fighter Command responds: 'God willing, we will hold out minister.' In response, the minister asks if he is to tell Cabinet that Dowding is trusting in radar and praying to God. This question elicits a chuckled response: 'More accurately the other way around. Trusting in God and praying for radar. But the essential arithmetic is that our young men will have to shoot down their young men at a rate of four to one, if we're to keep pace at all.'

In essence, this exchange typifies not only the reality of the situation facing Britain and RAF Fighter Command in the late spring and early summer of 1940, but also the uncertainty as to how the Dowding System would perform under the stress of attack. Of course, Dowding was right to have been apprehensive as to how his system would stand the test but, in the event, the system worked almost exactly as intended. Of course, anxiety on the part of Dowding would have surely been exacerbated by the fighter aircraft and pilot losses so recently sustained in France. Altogether, 396 Hurricanes and 67 Spitfires had been lost in the French campaign and just over 280 fighter pilots were either killed or made POW in that period. It would be well into July before all the Command's squadrons were fit for operations and, even then, there was still a deficiency of pilots amounting to 20% of the establishment. Notwithstanding this grave situation, Dowding had earlier fought and won a battle to stop any further fighter aircraft being sent to France. Quite rightly, on 16 May he stated in a letter to the Under Secretary of State for Air: 'If the home defence force is drained away in desperate attempts to remedy the situation in France, defeat in France will also involve the final, complete and irremediable defeat of this country.'

There can be no doubt at all that without Dowding's brainchild of an integrated early warning and command and control system, and without his obstinate stand against sending more fighters to France in the spring of 1940, the outcome of the Battle of Britain would have been very different.

Insofar as any 'victory' was achieved during that battle, however, then this could not have been the result without the Dowding System. Yet, this wording might seem to imply revisionism and infer that victory was not, after all, achieved. That is not the case. What *is* the case, though, is that no *outright* decisive victory over the Luftwaffe was gained by way of its complete defeat. Instead, and as the result of the Dowding System, the Luftwaffe was prevented from realising the air superiority it required in order for Hitler even to consider mounting any invasion attempt of the British Isles in 1940.

During the course of 1940, and as set out in the main body of this book, it became necessary to refine, fine-tune and modify the system in the light of operational experience. Broadly speaking, though, the system remained unchanged and unbroken. That said, one 'failing' might be regarded as the pre-war decision to site Sector Operations Rooms directly on the Sector airfields. As experience showed, this rendered them vulnerable to air attack and a decision was quickly taken to relocate these vital operations rooms at remote sites away from airfields which might be subject to bombing. If Sector Operations Rooms were knocked out and neutralised in the chain of command from Fighter Command HQ and Group HQ then it would remove a vital link in the system and leave no means by which to control the fighters, which would be left impotent.

As we have seen, difficulties with wireless transmissions and issues with accurately reading radar plots often caused problems in intercepting raids, although the wireless situation was dealt with later by VHF sets and the estimating of raid strengths was gradually resolved. However, the weakness of radar being unable to 'see' inland was not always helpful, especially with visual plotting by the Observer Corps being dependent upon weather and light conditions. Thus, raids could be 'lost' to the plotting and control system once the coast had been crossed and it was not always possible to control fighters on to incoming raids before the enemy had reached the coast.

In terms of issues relating to the actual fighting by RAF squadrons, much was learned about tactics through the experience of battle. For instance, rigid and inflexible 'air display'-type formations were potentially disastrous since they required all of the pilots to concentrate on keeping formation and with only the CO being able to look around him. The lessons learned included the adoption of the highly successful German 'finger-four' formation with the aircraft flown in a formation resembling the position of four finger-tips on an outstretched hand, thus giving greater visibility and ability to mutually cover and protect each other. Additionally, the lack of any proper air-sea rescue service during the Battle of Britain resulted in the lives of a great many RAF fighter pilots being lost over water. However, that deficiency was being plugged even as the battle was being fought and a full RAF air-sea rescue service was in place by the next year involving rescue vessels and search aircraft.

All things told, the entire system worked when it was most needed. Perhaps a testimony to its success was the fact that the same system remained in operation, virtually unaltered, until the end of the war. Tweaks and improvements were certainly made, and this included the later change from the 'five-minute change segment' on plotting boards to a two-and-a-half minute system in order to take into account the increasing relative speeds of newer types of aircraft. But little else of the system was materially revised.

When Churchill said 'Never in the field of human conflict was so much owed by so many to so few. . .' he was, of course, making reference to the pilots involved. However, in terms of success during the Battle of Britain, none of this could have been achieved without the Dowding System.

Appendix 1

Glossary of slang terms

A range of slang and colloquial terminology came into common usage during the period of the Battle of Britain, and specifically by the RAF. Not all of it can be attributed directly to the 1940 period, with much of it evolving across the history of the RAF since 1918. However, some of it has continued in use up until the present day and is no longer exclusive to the service. Below are listed some of the more commonly used examples that have a particular connection to the Battle of Britain period:

Ace A term normally used to denote a fighter pilot who has achieved five or more victories over enemy aircraft.

Bind Someone or something that is boring or depressing.

Black Error of judgement (as in 'Putting up a black').

Blood wagon Ambulance.

Bought it Killed or missing.

Bounce To inflict a surprise attack.

Brolly Parachute.

Bumph All paperwork.

Burton Killed or missing (as in 'Gone for a Burton').

Chief (or Chiefy) Flight sergeant.

Chit A document or note.

Dicey A close shave or difficult situation (as in a 'Dicey-do').

Ditch To land on water (from 'Down in the ditch', ie, English Channel).

Dogfight An expression meaning a melée of fighter aircraft in combat, although this became an official expression in terms of its usage by the Air Ministry and RAF.

Drink Slang term for the sea (as in 'Down in the drink').

Erk Any airman below rank of corporal, and used generically for all ground tradesmen.

Flamer An aircraft which had gone down in flames.

Gong Medal.

Kite Aircraft.

Mae West A colloquial name for life jackets as worn by aircrew during the Battle of Britain. Named after the well-endowed American Hollywood actress. Fighter pilots wearing life jackets took on the appearance of having her ample assets!

Pancake To make a belly-landing (also used as official terminology to denote an instruction to return to base).

Prang To crash.

Scrambled egg Gold trim on peaked caps of group captain and above.

Scraper Thin centre ring of squadron leader's rank badge (as in 'He's got his scraper', ie, he has been promoted from flight lieutenant to squadron leader).

Shooting a line To tell a tall story or exaggerate one's exploits.

Sparks Wireless tradesmen. Derived from cloth trade badge worn on sleeve of qualified personnel.

Victory roll An aerobatic manoeuvre carried out as an expression of exuberance after destroying an enemy aircraft.

Wad Cake or bun.

Wizard Very good, excellent or first class.

Appendix 2

Sources

Primary

The National Archives (UK)
The following document classifications of document groups were consulted during the preparation of this book:

AIR 10 – Air Publications
AIR 13 – Balloon Command
AIR 16 – Fighter Command
AIR 17 – Maintenance Command
AIR 22 – Periodical returns, summaries and bulletins
AIR 27 – Operations Record Books, RAF Squadrons
AIR 29 – Operations Record Books, RAF Stations and miscellaneous units
AIR 32 – Training Command
AIR 40 – Directorate of Intelligence
AIR 50 – RAF combat reports

Secondary

Anon, *The Air Force List August 1940* (HMSO, 1940)
Anon, *The Battle of Britain: RAF Narrative* (MLRS Books, c.2000)
Anon, *Winged Words – Our Airmen Speak For Themselves* (William Heinemann, 1941)
Bowyer, Chaz, *Royal Air Force Handbook 1939–1956* (Ian Allan, 1984)
Bowyer, Michael J.F., *Aircraft for the Few* (PSL, 1991)
Brooks, Robin J., *Aerodromes of Fighter Command Then & Now* (After the Battle, 2014)
Collier, Basil, *Leader of the Few* (Jarrolds, 1957)
Collier, Basil, *Defence of the United Kingdom* (HMSO, 1957)
Delve, Ken, *Source Book of the RAF* (Airlife, 1994)
Goulding, James, *Camouflage & Markings* (Ducimus, 1970)
Grehan, John and Mace Martin, *Defending Britain's Skies 1940–1945* (Pen & Sword, 2014)
Halley, James J., *Squadrons of the Royal Air Force 1918–1988* (Air Britain, 1988)
James, T.C.G., *The Growth of Fighter Command 1936–1940* (Whitehall History Publishing, 2002)
Lake, Alan, *Flying Units of the RAF* (Airlife, 1999)
Lucas, Paul, *Camouflage & Markings: The Battle for Britain* (SAM, 2000)
Mason, Francis K., *Battle over Britain* (McWhirter Twins, 1969)
Mason, Francis K., *The Hawker Hurricane* (Aston, 1987)
Morgan, Eric B. and Shacklady, Edward, *Spitfire: The History* (Key Publishing Ltd, 1987)
Ogley, Bob, *Biggin on the Bump* (Froglets, 1990)
Price, Dr Alfred, *Blitz on Britain, 1939–45* (Ian Allan, 1977)
Price, Dr Alfred, *Britain's Air Defences* (Osprey, 2004)
Prodger, Mick J., *Luftwaffe vs. RAF* (Schiffer, 1998)
Ramsey, Winston G., *The Battle of Britain Then and Now* (After the Battle, 1980)
Rawlings, John D.R., *Fighter Squadrons of the RAF* (MacDonald, 1969)
Simpson, Geoff, *A Dictionary of the Battle of Britain* (Halsgrove, 2009)
Tanner, John, *Fighting in the Air* (Arms and Armour Press, 1978)
Thetford, Owen, *Aircraft of the Royal Air Force* (Putnam, 1976)
Wallace, G.F., *The Guns of the Royal Air Force 1939–1945* (William Kimber, 1972)
Ward, Arthur, *A Nation Alone: The Battle of Britain – 1940* (Osprey, 1989)
Winslow, T.E., *Forewarned is Forearmed* (William Hodge, 1948)
Wood, Derek and Dempster, Derek, *The Narrow Margin* (Hutchinson & Company, 1961)
Wood, Derek, *Attack Warning Red* (Macdonald and Jane's, 1976)
Wynn, Kenneth, *Men of the Battle of Britain* (Frontline, 2015)
Zimmermann, David, *Britain's Shield: Radar and the Defeat of the Luftwaffe* (Sutton, 2001)

Websites

Battle of Britain Memorial Trust
http://www.battleofbritainmemorial.org/the-memorial/
Battle of Britain London Monument
http://www.bbm.org.uk/
Battle of Britain Museum, RAF Museum Hendon
http://www.rafmuseum.org.uk/london
Bentley Priory Museum
http://bentleypriorymuseum.org.uk/
Battle of Britain Bunker
http://www.raf.mod.uk/battleofbritainbunker/
Battle of Britain Memorial Flight
http://www.raf.mod.uk/bbmf/
Battle of Britain Historical Society
http://www.battleofbritain1940.net/

Index